Touring the
Antebellum South
with an
English Opera Company

THE HILL COLLECTION
Holdings of the LSU Libraries

Anton Reiff Jr. in 1862.
The engraving was made during his tenure as
director of the opera in Australia.

Touring the Antebellum South with an English Opera Company

Anton Reiff's Riverboat Travel Journal

Edited, with an Introduction, by
MICHAEL BURDEN

LOUISIANA STATE UNIVERSITY PRESS

BATON ROUGE

Published by Louisiana State University Press
www.lsupress.org

Designer: Laura Roubique Gleason
Typeface: Minion Pro

COVER IMAGE: *Scene on the Upper Mississippi* (*Am Ober-Mississippi*), courtesy Library of Congress.

LIBRARY OF CONGRESS CATALOGING-IN-PUBLICATION DATA

Names: Reiff, Anthony, Jr., 1830?-1916, author. | Burden, Michael, 1960- editor, writer of introduction.
Title: Touring the antebellum South with an English opera company : Anton Reiff's riverboat travel journal / edited, with an introduction, by Michael Burden.
Other titles: Hill collection.
Description: Baton Rouge : Louisiana State University Press, [2020] | Series: The Hill collection : holdings of the LSU Libraries | Includes bibliographical references and index.
Identifiers: LCCN 2020009421 (print) | LCCN 2020009422 (ebook) | ISBN 978-0-8071-7395-4 (cloth) | ISBN 978-0-8071-7445-6 (pdf) | ISBN 978-0-8071-7446-3 (epub)
Subjects: LCSH: Reiff, Anthony, Jr., 1830?-1916—Diaries. | Reiff, Anthony, Jr., 1830?-1916—Travel—Southern States. | Pyne and Harrison English Opera Company—Travel—Southern States. | Opera companies—Southern States—History—19th century. | Opera companies—England—History—19th century. | River boats—Mississippi River—History—19th century. | LCGFT: Diaries.
Classification: LCC ML1711.4 .R45 2020 (print) | LCC ML1711.4 (ebook) | DDC 792.50975—dc23
LC record available at https://lccn.loc.gov/2020009421
LC ebook record available at https://lccn.loc.gov/2020009422

For Juliana and Ralph

Contents

Illustrations and Credits

Figures

14. MOUNT VERNON   158

Mount Vernon in the 1850s. Anonymous photographer, stereoscope, from an unknown collection, albumen print, 1850s. The Miriam and Ira D. Wallach Division of Art, Prints and Photographs: Photography Collection, The New York Public Library.

Map

THE ROUTE TAKEN BY THE PYNE AND HARRISON TROUPE ON TOUR FROM JANUARY UNTIL MAY 1856   Opposite page 1

Map by Mary Lee Eggart.

Acknowledgments

As usual with a project such as this, there are many organizations and individuals who provided assistance toward its completion. My first thanks go to the Hill Memorial Library of Louisiana State University at Baton Rouge, where the original manuscript of Anton Reiff's diary is housed, and whose staff gave their support to this edition. The Huntington Library, San Marino, California, awarded me the Mayers Fellowship, during which the bulk of the editing was done and the commentary shaped, while the Bodleian Library at Oxford, the British Library, the New York Public Library, the State Library of Louisiana, the State Library of Victoria, and the Barr-Smith Library at the University of Adelaide all provided workspace at different times during the project. The staffs of all these institutions, plus George Washington's Mount Vernon Estate, Museum, and Gardens; the Historic New Orleans Collection; the Indiana Historical Society; the Kentucky Historical Society; the McCracken County Public Library; the Mobile Public Library Local History & Genealogy Department; and in particular, Readers' Services at the Huntington were all generous with their time and their resources.

Research funds provided by the Faculty of Music at the University of Oxford and the Warden and Scholars of New College, Oxford, supported the project. My research assistant at the time I began work on the diary, Kevin Skelton, undertook the initial transcription, and unraveled some of the more fantastic possibilities offered by Reiff's text. My personal thanks are due to Judy Bolton, Colin Coleman, Gina Costello, Betsy Cupp, Mary Lou Eichhorn, Valerie Ellis, Judy Fleming, Wendy Heller, Henry Hope, Matt Jaeger, Hermione Lee, Nathan Lynn, Jonathan Morton, Corrine Nordin, Robert C. Ritchie, Roger Savage, Laura B. Simo, Judy Smith, Rebecca Smith, Elaine Smyth, Robert Ticknor, Rowan Tomlinson, and Peter Tregear. Discussions with Barbara Haws, whom I met at a very late stage of this edition, caused me to rethink some of my own assumptions about the text, and brought her expertise to bear on the history of the Reiff family. I would also like to make specific acknowledgment of Katherine K. Preston's 1993 volume *Opera on the Road: Traveling Opera Troupes in the United States, 1825–1860,* which tells the story of the intrepid singers who crisscrossed the country. It provides a detailed picture of the work of all of the opera companies, a picture that provides a context for understanding the journey of the Pyne and Harrison Troupe.

My overriding memory of working on the diary is of an incident that occurred during a visit to New Orleans to see the sites that Reiff himself had visited. I emerged from the St. Louis Cemetery No. 1, and at the next block, outside Our Lady of Guadalupe at 411 North Rampart Street, I was confronted with a man made up as Jesus Christ and carrying a cross; I had encountered the end of the Good Friday Nine Churches pilgrimage, which echoed the tableau vivant that Reiff saw at the Gaiety Theatre on Wednesday, 22 January 1856.

A Note on the Edition

Editorial Method

The source for this edition is the Anton Reiff Journal, Mss. 3274, Louisiana and Lower Mississippi Valley Collections, Louisiana State University Libraries, Baton Rouge. Consisting of 142 numbered pages, it is entitled "Scenes in the Back Woods." The manuscript was purchased from the dealer, Joseph Rubinfine, in 1978. It has two sections missing, pages covering the dates 1 to 28 March, pages 56 to 74; and a fold of pages—probably two, possibly four—from around page 121. Numbers of the original journal pages appear in brackets at the appropriate points in the running text.

In general, Reiff's text is fluent and, to illustrate his points, he frequently inserted small drawings and maps. When he wanted to add supplementary comments, Reiff marked them with the music sign for *dal segno*. The *dal segno* sign—a cut "S" with two dots—marks the point in music to which the player should return; in the edition, it has been taken to mean "insert the supplementary text at the point of the sign." On one or two occasions, Reiff wrote the date, followed by a single sentence, and then abandoned the entry. The spaces he left on some of the pages suggest that he intended to expand on some of those entries at a later date. Occasionally, he adds a drawing to elucidate his text, but all but a few are basic line drawings. The general appearance of the diary can be seen in figure 1, and a few particularly detailed illustrations are included at the appropriate place in the diary.

The most difficult thing to interpret is Reiff's punctuation. The period scarcely makes an appearance, the comma almost never. His one sign is the dash, which functions as modern-day commas, semicolons, colons, periods, and indeed, in other contexts: examples include opening some sets of brackets with the usual curved bracket but closing it with a dash. He also uses it to separate thoughts: "Nothing specially occurred until we passed Mount Vernon—we did not pass on that side of the river—the tomb seems of a brown colour—and very near the house—the place is on a small hill—and is quite

Scenes in the Back Woods

The Ice getting very thick — Last night
Men were engaged repairing our wheel which had
been broken badly — also the Paddle Box.
To day two Steamers passed going up the "F. G. Wickell" and
the "Tecumseh" it is quite an event for a
vessel to pass the passengers rush out to see it
as eagerly as if it was at Sea — when
After shoving through the Ice till about
twelve Oclock we stop'd — again tied the vessel
to a Tree — in the Forest and on the
rivers bank — about twenty two miles
below "Evansville" at a place called
"Diamond Island Bend" Henderson County
Kentucky —

American Exploring Com^n

After dinner (as the scheme of the A. E. C.) I
suggested we should explore the wilderness to which
we had arrived — We started ashore — the ground was
covered with Snow about an inch in depth — the
Bank is about twenty feet high and precipitous
Nothing but a magnificent Forest to be seen
The Trees very large — saw the trunk of one
lying just on the shore which seems upon a
rough guess (they call me Yankee here, so I am
privileged to Guess) to be about forty feet in
circumferance — Two immense Sycamores looked
not only astonishing large but exceeding picturesque.

The first page of Anton Reiff's "Scenes in the Back Woods,"
Mss. 3274, LSU Libraries, Baton Rouge, LA.

surrounded with trees." This is not unusual for Reiff's time. In the edition, only a small amount of the original punctuation has been retained, with a minimum of modern punctuation added.

In the source, the heading for each entry—day, date, place, page number—is provided erratically, incompletely, and in a variable form by Reiff; in the edition, these details and the headings have been silently standardized, and should be regarded as editorial. As a general rule, missing words have been inserted as sparely as possible and obvious errors silently corrected. The following have been silently substituted throughout: "of" for "off," "off" for "of," "were" for "where," "where" for "were," "there" for "their." Words such as "every where" and "a head" have been rendered in their modern form.

The Commentary

The aim of the commentary is to illuminate Reiff's text, a text that emphasizes people, places, and present events. He has almost nothing to say about the work of the opera company, giving the merest of hints of the rehearsals that must have taken place and the performances that we know were given. As it happens, the story of the Pyne and Harrison tour has been largely told by Katherine Preston in *Opera on the Road,* and so the commentary here is limited to the identification of the performances given and venues used, with the cast list provided for the first performance of each opera, but not thereafter. Newspaper commentaries on performances, which only provide a mixture of puffs and flattering post-performance write-ups, have largely been omitted. The names of people for which no information has been found beyond their mention in the diary are noted as "not further identified."

Bibliographical Note

Definitions are taken from the *Oxford English Dictionary,* 2nd edition (1989), cited as *OED,* followed by the volume number and page number. Biographical details are taken from the *Oxford Dictionary of National Biography* (2004), cited as *ODNB,* and from the *American National Biography* (1999), cited as *ANB.*

In the case of well-known figures whom Reiff only encounters at a distance—such those whose names appear in the list of senators he sees in action at the Capitol in Washington—the figure is identified with a biographical note relevant to the context in which Reiff encounters him. Unless otherwise referenced, users of the commentary are referred to the *American National Biography* (1999) for further information.

Unless stated otherwise, general musical details are taken from *The New Grove Dictionary of Music and Musicians,* 2nd edition (2001); *The Grove Dictionary of Musical Instruments,* 2nd edition (2015); *The New Grove Dictionary of Opera* (1992), abbreviated *GDO*; and *The Grove Dictionary of American Music,* 2nd edition (2013).

Unless stated otherwise, all essential information on the boats on which Reiff traveled has been taken from Lytle and Holdcamper, *Merchant Steam Vessels of the United States, 1790–1868* (1975); its supplement by Mitchell (1978); and from *Lloyd's Steamboat Directory and Disasters on the Western Water* (1856).

Touring the Antebellum South with an English Opera Company

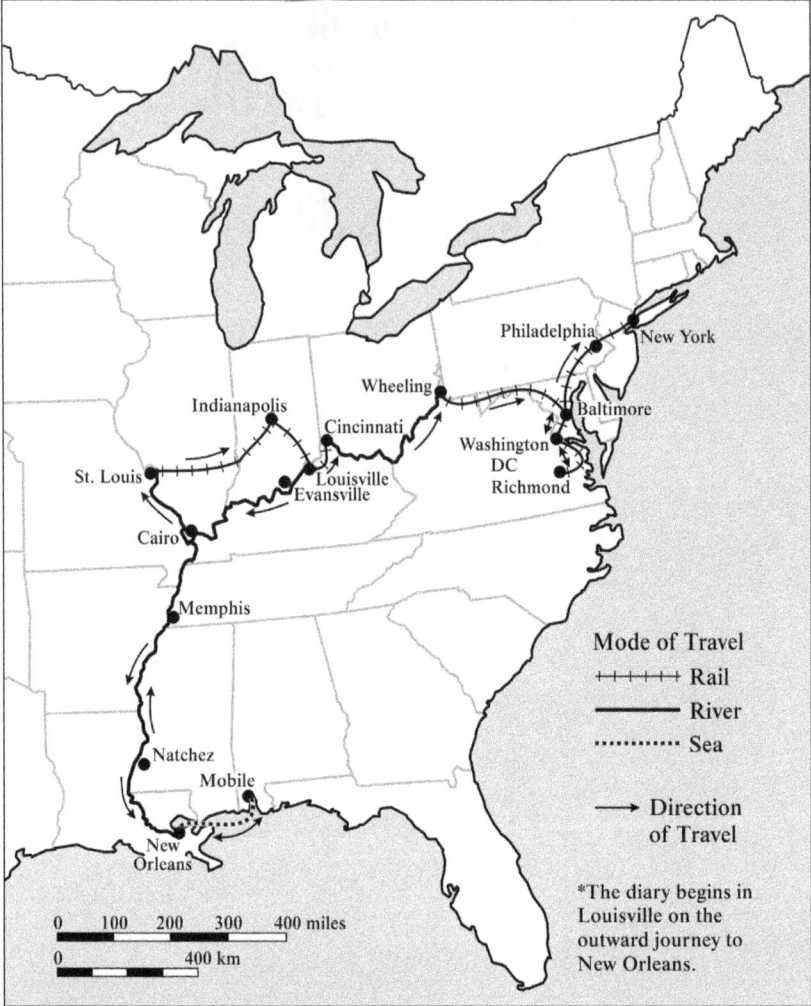

The route taken by the Pyne and Harrison Troupe on tour from January until May 1856. Reiff's diary opens on 8 January 1856 on the Ohio River, downstream from Louisville, Kentucky, where the company had finished an engagement with a performance of Bellini's *La Sonnambula* on 5 January. It closes as some members of the company arrive back in New York on 24 May, having given their final performance of the tour, Donizetti's *The Daughter of the Regiment,* on the previous evening at Washington's National Theatre.

INTRODUCTION

When sometime after 5 January 1856 the paddle steamer *Thomas Swann* finally broke through the ice in Louisville, Kentucky, and moved off down the Ohio River toward New Orleans, the conductor Anton Reiff must have been delighted. Reiff was traveling as musical director with the Pyne-Harrison English Opera Troupe, which had been playing at the Louisville Theatre since 31 December 1855, and which had been on tour, starting in Boston, since the second week in November. The delay to the boat's departure during what was one of the coldest winters of the nineteenth century—it was later referred to as "The Winter of the Big Freeze"[1]—may well have been the reason that Reiff began his diary, "Scenes in the Back Woods." As recorded in his own text, he was a slightly restless tourist, and the enforced deferral of the start of the journey would have given him the opportunity to go ashore, purchase an exercise book, and begin his narrative.

The Pyne-Harrison Troupe was the joint venture of the English singers Louisa Pyne and William Harrison. While it was an ensemble company, there is no question that its star was Louisa Pyne. The nineteenth-century edition of the *Grove Dictionary of Music and Musicians* recounts that her "voice was a soprano of beautiful quality and great compass and flexibility; she sang with great taste and judgement, and excelled in the florid style, of which she was perfect mistress."[2] Her New York debut on 9 October 1854 was at the Broadway Theatre in Bellini's *La Sonnambula,* a work that showed off what was, by all accounts, a lyrical and elegant voice, one which in the United States earned her the nickname "The Skylark." William Harrison, Louisa Pyne's business partner, was a tenor who had made his debut at Covent Garden on 2 May 1839 in the premiere of William Rooke's *Henrique.* Under the great promoter of English opera, Alfred Bunn, Harrison created

1. Hereford, *Old Man River,* 244.
2. *Grove Dictionary of Music and Musicians,* ed. Fuller-Maitland (1904–10), IV, 323.

roles in Michael Balfe's *The Bohemian Girl*, William Vincent Wallace's *Maritana*, and Julius Benedict's *Brides of Venice*. Pyne and Harrison had long been artistic associates and involved in company management, and while the core of the company was small—it consisted of Pyne, Harrison, Pyne's sister Susan, Conrad Borrani, and Henry Horncastle—it was a consistent group to which other performers were added along the way as required. And it was more evenly focused than previous touring companies, who were grouped around star singers. They left for New York in 1854, and after a short season there began touring, first to Philadelphia and then back to New York, then Boston, New York, and Philadelphia. In New York, the company's repertory included *Maritana*, *The Bohemian Girl*, and Daniel Auber's *The Crown Diamonds*, and their touring during this first season took them from New York to Boston, for which they added Auber's *Fra Diavolo* and a version of John Gay's *The Beggar's Opera* to their repertory; to Philadelphia, which included *Cinderella* and Henry Bishop's *Guy Mannering*; and to Providence, Rhode Island. This was to set the general pattern of the troupe's routine, a punishing schedule that included towns north (Boston, Providence, and up to Montreal) and towns south (Philadelphia, Washington, and down to New Orleans).

Back in New York in time for the opening of the 1855–56 season, their successes there included premiere stagings of J. Howard Wainwright and George Bristow's *Rip van Winkle* at Niblo's Garden, which opened on 27 September, a work which then played almost nightly until 18 October. Their season closed with a string of single performances—*The Bohemian Girl*, *Maritana*, *Cinderella*, *Daughter of the Regiment*, and *The Crown Diamonds*—followed by benefit performances of *Rip Van Winkle* for Bristow and stage manager William Moore, *The Barber of Seville* for Harrison, and *The Love Spell*—a version of Donizetti's *L'elisir d'amore*—for Pyne. Both Harrison's and Pyne's performances were billed as "farewell benefits," and indeed, their last performance was on 3 November; by the 6th, they were in Providence. The cast for the company's core production of *Rip Van Winkle*—Louisa Pyne (Alice), Susan Pyne (Dame Van Winkle), Harrison (Edward Gardenier), Horncastle (Edward Vileoeur), and Joseph Stretton "late of Covent Garden" (Rip Van Winkle)[3]—was also the basis of the company that went on

3. *Spirit of the Times*, 5 October 1855, allocates no roles to Louisa Pyne, Horncastle, and Stretton.

tour. There was also the bass Franklin Boudinot, the tenor C. H. Warre, the tenor George T. Atherton (who the diary suggests was a particular friend of Reiff's), Frank R. Swan, and a Mr. Ghor. William F. Brough was the troupe's manager and agent. But added to this lineup was Anton (or Anthony) Reiff, a violinist and keyboardist. Born in about 1830,[4] he was the product of a German father, also Anton, who is recorded as coming to the United States from Germany in 1827 and is noted elsewhere as having family in Mainz. Anton Sr. was a bassoonist with the New York Philharmonic, and is also recorded playing the oboe and the French horn and singing for many years as a tenor in the St. Patrick's Cathedral Choir. He was also the first vice president of the New York Philharmonic Society. His wife—Anton Jr.'s mother, Sarah née Dobbs[5]—was American born and bred: the clue lies in this diary, for Reiff makes reference to his "grandfather's place in Jersey." This was a claim that would explain his otherwise unaccountable familiarity with the state which stood him in such good stead when flirting with the wealthy Miss Price of Mobile.[6] His early career was, according to his *New York Times* obituary, spent in Jenny Lind's orchestra at Castle Gardens, and he appears to have been freelancing in New York at the time he was hired by Pyne and Harrison.[7]

At the end of the tour, the company dispersed, Pyne and Harrison returning home on a Cunarder, the *Persia*, the first steamship belonging to the line. Reiff, however, was now employed by the buccaneering impresario William Lyster (1827–1880), through his taking over the management of his brother Frederick's New Orleans–based opera company. It toured to San Francisco, and then went by ship to Melbourne, where it (and Reiff) would

4. Reiff's birth date is usually given as 1830, making him 26 years old during the trip. This tallies with the 1855 census for the 16th Ward, New York City, which gives the family as Anthony Reiff Sr., 52 years; Anne Reiff (presumably née Dobbs), 43 years; Anthony Reiff Jr., 25 years; and Ambrose Reiff, 9 years. My thanks to Barbara Haws for her assistance with this note.

5. "The elder Reiff married a Miss Dobbs of the family connected with Dobb's Ferry. The Dobbs were descendants of the Hardenbroecks, a New York Dutch family related to the Roosevelts." See "Descendants of the Philharmonic Founders," *Philharmonic Symphony League Bulletin*, IV (1 October 1941–3 April 1942), 3.

6. When Anton Sr. died in 1880, Anton Jr.'s brother Phillip is recorded living in New Jersey also.

7. *New York Times*, 7 October 1916. See Reiff's April 1913 account of working with Jenny Lind in "Recollections of a Musician, Orchestral Players & Conductor: Jenny Lind," New York Philharmonic Archives.

play a major role in the development of opera in Australia, both in the repertory that was staged there and in the performance standards he demanded.[8]
He was, subsequently, also musical director for the Louise Kellogg and the
Parepa Rosa opera companies. Reiff returned to New York in 1864 and died
there on 6 October 1916, by then a stalwart of the musical scene, a former
president of the Musical Mutual Protective Union, the father of two daughters,[9] the oldest living member of the American Institute, and, untruthfully,
a founding member of the New York Philharmonic Society.[10]

But in 1856, Reiff was a much younger man, with a slightly bumptious,
rather forward, personality. Not only are these traits clear from the diary's
entries, but Reiff himself acknowledged them as characteristic of his own be-
havior: "Darkie perceived we were 'Gemmen' immediately. Stretton's dignified moustache, Horncastle's portly form, and my impudent manner—combined with the fact that we are more fastidious and give more trouble than
any one else—established the *fact* that we *were the people!*"[11] Impertinent all
that may have seemed, but for the modern audience, these passages of wry
self-assessment provide welcome less-than-earnest insights into the diarist's
character, which emerges as charming and unaffected, and which engages
those he meets. On one walk with Atherton and Boudinot, Reiff recounts
that they were invited into a cabin "where was his sister a young lady named
Mary and her husband. Their names was Mr and Mrs Rankins, Mary's name
being the same. She was really very glad to see three Single Gentlemen. She
asked us almost immediately if we were married! We arrived here at twelve,
and at three we know the Rankins familiarly enough for them to call us by
our christian names."[12]

The arrival of strangers was an event, one that, of necessity, saw the quick
establishment of acquaintance, and with the possibility of at least a few days
of good company and flirtation, and perhaps raised hopes for something
more. But it was a social exchange played out against a background of tacit
acknowledgment that such acquaintance would be transitory. This scene en-

8. See Love, *The Golden Age of Australian Opera.*

9. They benefited from his estate, valued at some $6,000; see "Anthony Reiff," in the *Bill
Board* 29 (30 June 1917), 4.

10. He had been in fact the youngest member of the society (*New York Times,* 7 October
1916).

11. Page 111 herein. All quotations from the diary are taken from the present edition.

12. Page 21.

capsulates the inherent isolation of those living in the river towns, or even of those residing in a settlement the size of Mobile, Alabama; the county had by the 1850 US Census a population of around twenty-seven thousand. It was an isolation which swept class, and caution, aside: had Reiff been in New York, it seems unlikely that a jobbing musician would have been received so warmly into the bosom of many of the families—including the Prices of Mobile—that they met.

Reiff was not only bumptious, but generally excitable, a character trait that almost led him into disaster. In one of the great set pieces of the diary, he is challenged to a duel by a Colonel Young of California, while the boat was somewhere below Cairo, Illinois. The point of dispute was the seat Reiff wished to take at the dining table, but which Young, "having got into it (possession being nine points of the law), kept it"; Reiff, having spoken "excitedly" to him, was then sent Young's card.[13] Although seemingly melodramatic, the situation was serious for Reiff. Duels were frequent, so much so that publications such as John Lyde Wilson's *Code of Honour,* brought out in 1838 and reprinted in 1845 and 1858, attempted to curb the practice by imposing conventions on when—and when not—a duel should be fought. It is not clear from Reiff's account quite how the challenge from Young was resolved, but prompt action by William Harrison in calling the company's manager, Brough, who in turn found the clerk to the boat, produced a (probably) worried official of the steamboat anxious to avoid bloodshed aboard the vessel. Overall, the event shows Reiff to have been hotheaded but not malicious, and the rest of the company both concerned for and supportive of their musical director.

One of the central threads that winds itself through the narrative of the diary is that of slavery. Reiff's own recorded attitude to the issue is ambivalent, a position which may reflect both a lack of personal maturity and the reactions of a northerner when confronted with its reality. Reiff had clearly read or was familiar with Harriet Beecher Stowe's 1852 antislavery novel, *Uncle Tom's Cabin,* for the diary contains at least two direct references to characters from Stowe's text, Aunt Chloe and Legree. What is clear from the diary is how prominent a place the issue had in day-to-day discourse. Although Reiff makes nothing particular of it, the congressmen he hears on his visit to Washington held views ranging from the moderate to the

13. Page 32.

extreme on both sides of the question, a panoply of opinions on the matter that represents a miniature overview of a country whose union was, during this period, under constant strain.

Reiff records encounters with slaves as indoor servants, in which he dwells on their cheerfulness, servility, and honesty, and in one case, on some "very pretty young slaves; it must be acknowledged that a pretty Negro may sound strange to Northern ears."[14] At one point, he leaves the house without his pocket book, but when he gets it back, "not a dime had been taken. If this had been North, would the servant have returned it? Of course not."[15] He goes so far as to suggest to the reader of the diary that it would be desirable for him to purchase a slave and take him back to New York: "He was a most excellent polite and obliging waiter; I should liked to have bought him" from his owner, "Mr Danforth, a merchant of N.Y. City."[16] The insouciance with which he floats this idea is breathtaking, and as we discover later, he shared his views with his friends: on 23 February, he noted that "Arch [Johnston] is quite shocked at some slave selling he saw on board the boat, and with it, generally, thinks I am degenerated completely as regards slavery."[17] His reaction to the slave auction he encounters in Mobile does, however, reveal that he is not as cheerfully unfeeling on the issue as his other remarks suggest; he described the auction as "the worst place in which I have seen slavery to see human beings (with a soul) sold together with steamboats, horses, &c."[18] He describes one female slave as weeping "most bitterly," which he found "heart-rending"[19]; whether or not these tears were genuine is unknown. Walter Johnson, citing this sale,[20] notes that such tears and hard-luck stories told from auctioneers' rostra were sometimes fictitious, and were designed to inspire in potential purchasers exactly the response felt by Reiff, who had no experience with slave auctions and clearly believed the sales pitch in its entirety. Like many northerners, he seems to have had few qualms about the business of slavery when the matter was on a personal level, but when confronted with the reality of an auction, he saw the trade for what it was.

Reiff's casual racism found in the text makes reading the diary today a

14. Page 132.
15. Page 131.
16. Page 67.
17. Page 81.
18. Page 76.
19. Page 76.
20. Walter Johnson, *Soul by Soul*, 127–28.

distinctly uncomfortable experience; indeed, he employs language now regarded as unacceptable in any forum. But as with some others before him
traveling in pre–Civil War America, Reiff seems more interested than re-
pelled by the mixture of race, class, and profession he encounters on the
trip. The passengers on a western steamboat were a democratic mix of all
types—"gamblers, roustabouts, alligator-horses, slaves, and slave holders,
and worst of all, spitters"[21]—and did not suit many European travelers who
found the company and the river, Dickens's "foul stream,"[22] problematic.
Reiff, however, is endlessly curious about his fellow travelers and about those
he meets on the shore. Like Karl Arndt, he encounters not only Germans
and Frenchmen but "also Irishmen, Spaniards, Italians, and many thousands
of Negroes and slaves."[23] At St. Louis Cathedral, where he "heard nearly
every language spoken under the sun except English," he noted that "around
the altar were kneeling promiscuously whites, Creoles, Quadroons, Spaniards, &c."[24] On another occasion, he remarked of a rail journey he took
that "we were the only pure white men in the car. Some Creoles, & Indians,
semi-French and Negroes. Though only going a short distance some of the
passengers began to gamble; the Indians smoked."[25] We see his views on race
merge with those of class and profession, with the lowest rung in his personal inferno reserved for Smith's "spitters."

Reiff's general good humor and positive outlook tend to obscure the
dangers of the journey on which the company had embarked, for the reader
is told of ice and snags and other natural obstructions along the rivers. There
is also the danger that the boilers of the boat would explode; Reiff visited the
boiler room and discussed this very matter with the engineer. But dangerous
though they were, the biggest threat came not from the boilers themselves,
but from the possibility that the captain of the boat would risk the lives of
all on board trying to outdo a rival riverboat in speed and style. Although
the most famous race—that in 1870, between the *Natchez* and the *Robert E.
Lee*—was some years off, riverboat races were already legendary events in
the world of nineteenth-century Mississippi River boat travel.[26] At the start
of his journey, Reiff's boat passed the *A. L. Shotwell,* the boat that, during the

21. Thomas Ruys Smith, *River of Dreams*, 80.
22. Dickens, *American Notes for General Circulation*, 30.
23. Arndt, "A Bavarian's Journey to New Orleans and Nacogdoches in 1853–1854," 323.
24. Page 49, herein.
25. Page 52.
26. Hunter, *Steamboats on the Western Rivers*.

winter of 1853, competed with the *Eclipse* on the run between New Orleans and Louisville; the events were still fresh enough for Reiff, a New Yorker, to note the incident. So when, on the return journey, Mr. Andrews captaining the *Thomas Swann* took on the reputedly very fast *Princess*, Reiff was right to feel concerned. Not only was it a night race, but it was also terrible weather: "the wind was blowing a perfect gale, the rain came down in torrents, and the vessel shook terrifically." The captains of both boats indulged in spoiling tactics, and the *Swann* "nearly ran the 'Princess' down who, seeing that we would pass her, several times ran athwart our bow." During the race, Ghor came to Reiff, telling him "do not go to bed, for we are in imminent danger ... twenty chances to one, you will be blown up."[27]

Reiff was, though, unimpressed by all the fuss; when the *Princess* was passed, he recorded that there was "such a blowing of the whistle, ringing bells" that it quite baffled description. But his comment that the boat was shuddering with the amount of steam it was carrying gives some insight into the dangers riverboat passengers in these circumstances unwittingly encountered. And as it happened, the boilers of the *Princess* exploded in 1859, and the vessel sank with substantial loss of life. There were also dangers to be found on the shore. On one or two occasions, Reiff dwells on the rough-and-ready population they encounter on shore—"we walked through the woods about half a mile—getting dark—and I have about $50 in my pocket and these miners being a desperate set, I concluded to return"[28]—and in one case, describes a murder that took place next to their moored steamer in the lawless river town of Cairo. The circumstances were prosaic enough; the little Reiff records suggests that a brawl took place between two riverboat men in which one of them stabbed the other to death. The subsequent diary entry describes a lynch mob, and the citizens' arrest of the supposed culprit, in a manner that indicates a tribal loyalty of every crew to the riverboat on which they were currently employed.

Even with an event such as the Cairo murder, though, the irrepressible Reiff finds a moment of humor, noting that the passengers "were so dreadfully affected with the murder case (a perfect thrill of horror having run around the Ladies' Cabin when the story was related), that nothing would do to express their profound grief but a half a dozen of quadrilles, which they danced in the most bewitching manner."[29] Dancing was a frequent eve-

27. Page 83–84 herein.
28. Page 27.
29. Page 31.

ning entertainment on board, murder or not, and Reiff, as a musician, was at the center of these activities: "During the evening a dance was got up, a fiddler and a guitarist being on board. They are awful dancers. I was in fact made Floor Master and entered upon the labours of my new role with all proper dignity."[30]

On another occasion, Reiff notes that "during the evening the 'Stars' sang some glees" and that "dancing, political discussions, card playing, story telling, &c., filled up the balance of the evening." "Card playing" was, in most cases, gambling, with "Even the Pynes & Harrison, Stretton and Captain Tilman, set down to a game—in the Ladies' Cabin."[31] But it did not suit everyone: "An old lady, aged 66, came on board at Memphis, who is going to Texas to her son's, she had never even *seen* a steamboat before—and is perfectly shocked to see people play cards."[32]

There was "a tremendous quantity of card playing," although not always for money; Reiff noted that although he occupied himself "during the evening by playing whist," he felt constrained to add "but not gambling." The boat, however, observed the Sabbath: "no gambling today, it is the only thing that makes the day differ from the others in the week." Other onshore (or off the boat) entertainments included skating, drinking, and visits to the theater. These are mentioned only as passing references in most instances, but Reiff gives one extended account of a visit to the Gaiety Theatre in New Orleans. He was impressed with the house—"it is not as wide as Niblo's, but about as deep, having but two tiers of boxes; is beautifully fitted up. Good seats and well lighted"—but is astonished at the theatrical bill: "The performance was *Azuel, the Prodigal Son*, during which was a 'tableau vivant' of the crucifixion! Which was *encored!!* In New York—with all its wickedness—it would be hissed off the stage. Only to imagine a man to make up for such a part as 'Jesus Christ.' And today, I heard they are about producing a tragedy called the Messiah! I think I shall go and see it, if only for the horror of the thing. Only to think that this should be in the enlightened (!) America; it's absolutely dreadful."[33] Unfortunately, there is no account of the projected visit to the *Messiah*.

From a musical point of view, though, the diary is sketchy on the detail of the tour, but as any musician would have to, Reiff continued to attend to

30. Page 22.
31. Page 22.
32. Page 36.
33. Pages 44–45.

the mechanics of his career. Throughout the trip, he dealt with a number of agents or promoters who would like to sign him up, and indeed, his charm and talent ensured that he received offers of work for subsequent seasons, however "pencilled" those offers might have been. He also dealt with Faulds, one of the country's most prominent music publishers, who had taken on one of Reiff's songs and appeared to want another. Reiff was also kept up to date by his father, who was active on the New York musical scene, and although Reiff makes us privy to few details, Anton Sr.'s frequently mentioned letters clearly contain professional advice and information, as well as the expected domestic details. There are also one or two occasions that suggest Reiff supplemented his income along the way by giving music lessons. In Washington, where Reiff recorded that he taught two ladies "one the Fairy Queen, and the other Clorinda in *Cinderella*,"[34] he suggested that he was able to cash in by teaching ladies the tunes they had heard at the operas the company performed, while at the same time maintaining the illusion that his pupils could be taught to perform to the same standard as, say, Louisa Pyne. However, Reiff was clearly an accomplished pianist as well as a violinist, so his activities need not have been limited to just teaching the songs from the shows but may have extended to piano lessons. There was, too, some social cachet to be had, when boasting of music lessons with the "Musical director of the Pyne Harrison Opera Troupe." Teaching was the carrot offered by the Mobile music storekeeper and music teacher, Mr. Snow, who Reiff reported was "very anxious for me to come here to teach."[35] Snow probably also desired to have another decent musician in town.

But perhaps the most frequent activity recorded in the diary is sightseeing. Much of it is doubtless brought on by a desire to occupy what would otherwise be very long and tedious days, and to deal with cabin fever expressed early on in the diary when Reiff notes, "We returned to our vessel— in fact, *our home* for how long, heaven only knows."[36] Given that many of the towns were both new and small, it is the buildings that captured Reiff's attention, particularly the churches, usually the most prominent buildings in places such as Vicksburg: "Several churches can be seen from the river. One (the handsomest) has a [drawing of a cross] on the steeple and is in all probability of Catholic persuasion."[37] The churches also provide some-

34. Page 152.
35. Page 67.
36. Page 21.
37. Page 86.

thing to do: "At night (a beautiful) evening, I went with the girls to a Presbyterian Church on Broadway near Fourth St; heard a pretty good sermon, subject 'Why do the wicked live?'"[38] One of his more extended visits was to a church in Mobile, "which was way down Government St., near Royale, a very fine church, white in colour, a gallery around it," where he heard a sort of know-nothing sermon.[39] Reiff, of German Protestant stock, seemed to attend church not only as a matter of faith, but as something to do. What we do learn is that he paid critical attention to the sermons he heard, and that he had a suspicion of anything Catholic—"The inside is something like St Patrick's, N.Y., but with those peculiar 'confession closets' common to Catholic churches"[40]—and comments unfavorably on the "theatrical" aspects of the French Catholic cathedral in New Orleans.

Reiff's sightseeing habits lead to the set pieces of the diary, such as the slave auction in Mobile and the murder in Cairo; to these we can add the later visits to Mount Vernon and to Arlington House, and an account of New Orleans's Mardi Gras, then—as now—one of the great features of New Orleans life.[41] Sadly, the year that Reiff attended was not thought to be one of the best, the *Picayune* remarking:

> The mummers yesterday presented but a low caricature on the merry maskings of former years, for the air was a trifle too hyperborean for outdoor sports and the custom is of itself falling into decline. Most of the few who were out, were mere lubberly boys, who crawled into kitchen wenches frocks and dealt with in vulgarities behind pasteboard faces. Notwithstanding the high price of groceries, they distributed their floury favours quite extensively, and when flour failed they had recourse to lime as a cheaper substitute. With the last mentioned article, we understand the eyes of several boys were severely, perhaps permanently injured. This is how Madi Gras was passed by the "lower ten."[42]

It is hard to know how much faith to put in such a report; one year's event was so often "not as good as the previous year's," but it is true that Reiff's account does rather convey the impression that it was an underwhelming experience.

As enchanting as Reiff found aspects of the Pyne-Harrison tour, there

38. Page 108.
39. Page 74.
40. Page 153.
41. Pages 57–60.
42. *Picayune*, 6 February 1856.

are repeated references to homesickness, to missing the family, and to his ill health. This last seems to be a mixture of poor digestion (brought on by bad meals) and the state of his teeth, which he had attended to in Paducah, Kentucky (where he had a tooth pulled), and New Orleans (where he had another filled). Other members of the troupe also suffer: "Stretton sick with a slight touch (I reckon) of fever & augue. Susan Pyne somewhat recovering from her neuralgia, and Harrison from his boil—Louisa Pyne laid up with boils—and Horncastle going about with an enormous stye on his eye."[43] Reiff comments on this catalog of woe: "Good party"! His eagerness to get home becomes apparent through the last entries, which become more and more telegraphese, and his final single word of joy at finally being back in New York—"Hurrah"—is emphasized by an exclamation mark. So captivating is this last section that the reader is caught up in the moment that heralds his arrival at "The Battery, New York!" by the boat, the *John Potter,* from which he "dashed for *Home* like lightning."[44]

By whom did Reiff intend his diary to be read? What audience did he assume? The visits to the "sights"—those to Mount Vernon and Arlington, for example—read rather like postcards or travelogues; they seem to be written with an eye to the general reader. And also written with the same eye are the humorous tales that appear in the narrative. As the following account shows, Reiff had a keen appreciation of farce, and a skilled pen with which to convey it: "I was awoke by a terrific cry of 'murder' and heard a tremendous struggle, just on the floor below. I was so nervous that I jumped out of bed—got hold of my pants upside down—tried to get them on—finally did—rushed out of my room, where I found the boarders tumbling out of their rooms in all sorts of 'costumes.'"[45] Similarly, he did little but rush about during the accident at the tram stop in New Orleans in which Frank Boudinot shut his thumb in a carriage door. Reiff tells us that his reaction was to look about as fast as he could "(which I have no doubt done a great deal of good)."[46] Here, the main revelation for both Reiff and the reader was that the virtuous Louisa Pyne had brandy in her basket, from which it was "miraculously produced in a twinkling." The humor of some of his tales is, as here, partly at his own expense.

43. Page 37, herein.
44. Page 160.
45. Page 137.
46. Page 80.

What is omitted from the diary is as significant as what is included. Not once in the entire text does Reiff comment on the works they performed, or on the performances they gave, and comments only rarely on the spaces in which they performed; the Odd Fellows Hall in Mobile is almost the only venue on which he remarks, and only then to suggest that the acoustics were not all they might be. This lack of professional detail might indicate a more general audience for his text. And given the fervor with which Reiff greeted letters from home, and the extensive replies he seems on occasion to have sent, it might be that it was his New York family and friends who were the intended recipients. Indeed, the endless noting of the weather, the comparison of the streets and buildings to those in New York, and the description of personalities are precisely the sort of detail which would interest an audience at home. And yet, there are one or two moments when it seems inconceivable that the intended reader was anybody other than Reiff himself. The one, and possibly two, visits to the brothel in New Orleans might, for example, have taken some explaining in a family context. Similarly, his account of going into manager Brough's "room at Barnum's finding him out (i.e. *not in*) I tried the door which was open; popped in (a la Paul Pry) went to the table where I saw a list of salaries"[47] is probably not something he would particularly wish to share, although given that his father was also in the business, the actual salaries may have been of some interest. And his very positive attitude toward slavery may well have gone down badly in the North; the suggestion that he would like to purchase a slave to take back with him is made with no apparent irony or sarcasm in a text where, at times, both these traits shine unambiguously through Reiff's words. There seems to be every indication, then, that the diary was a private document, written for later consultation and reminiscence, and kept perhaps to keep the boredom of a long trip at bay, where it is clear that the other passengers are not altogether to his liking.

47. Page 149.

Figure 1. Some members of the
Pyne and Harrison Troupe.

Clockwise from top: The bass, Franklin
Brinsmade Boudinot; the tenor, William
Harrison; the bass-baritone, George
Stretton, in character as Paul Pesta in
William Michael Rooke's *Amilie, or the
Love Test;* the mezzo soprano, Susan
Pyne; and the soprano, Louisa Pyne.

The Pyne and Harrison Troupe

Members of the Pyne and Harrison Troupe mentioned in the diary; the brackets indicate the style used by Reiff to refer to them. Additional performers noted with the troupe are also included.

Mr. Adkins ["Old Adkins"] appears to be a member of the company's orchestra or the troupe's administration; an older man of somewhat choleric disposition, he is mentioned in diary entries for New Orleans, Vicksburg, and Washington.

George T. Atherton ["A," "Atherton," "Geo"], the tenor who is recorded singing in New York in 1860 at the Plymouth Church on 29 March, and at the New York Harmonic Society on 28 May 1860. He seems to disappear after this date.

Benedict De Bar (1812–1877), a performer mentioned by Reiff but not in connection with the Pyne and Harrison Troupe; he took the role of Pedro in *Cinderella* in New Orleans. De Bar was the lessee and manager of the St. Charles Theatre; he came to New Orleans from England as an actor and later became the stage manager at the St. Charles for Noah Ludlow and Sol Smith, and on their retirements, took over their interests in New Orleans (in 1853) and St. Louis (in 1855).

Clementina Booth (Mrs. Junius Booth Jr., formerly Clementina De Bar, sister to Benedict De Bar), a singer not mentioned by Reiff but who took the role of Thisbe in *Cinderella* with the Pyne and Harrison Troupe in New Orleans.

Franklin Brinsmade Boudinot (1836–1864) ["Frank"] was born in Georgia but brought up in Washington, Litchfield County, Connecticut, and was educated at a local school, the Gunnery. He then pursued an acting career in New York, where he met fellow performer Georgiana Sophia Annie Gimber (1836–1887); they married on 2 August 1857. His military career began when he enlisted as a private in Company H, New York First Mounted Rifles, on 1 August 1862; but by the time he died at Yorktown in 1864, he had risen to the rank of captain. His manner of death is variously given as a fall from a horse or heart disease as a result of injuries received during battle. Samuel J. Nettleton commented: "He was endowed with rare musical powers, a powerful bass voice and an intuitive skill with musical instrument. More than 6 feet in height and standing very erect, with noble features and carriage of person. Pure in speech among his fellows; to know was to honor him." See numerous sources, including washingtoncivilwarsoldiers.weebly.com/frank-b-boudinot.html.

William F. Brough (1798–1867) ["Brough"] was the Pyne and Harrison Troupe's agent. A former opera star, he had, since the 1840s, been a "manager of operatic performances generally" (*Spirit of the Times*, 8 September 1855).

Mr. S. E. Brown sang with the troupe in St. Louis.

Mr. Burnet sang Mr. Bundle in *The Waterman* in Washington.

Mr. Duffield, a performer not mentioned by Reiff but who took the role of Alidoro in *Cinderella* with the Pyne and Harrison Troupe in New Orleans.

Jane Germon played Meg Merilles in *Guy Mannering* in Washington.

Mr. Ghor ["Ghor"], singer.

William Harrison (1813–1868) ["Harrison"], a tenor, made his debut at Covent Garden on 2 May 1839, was active in Bunn's Drury Lane seasons of the 1840s, and went on tour to New York with Louisa Pyne. He was her partner in the Pyne-Harrison English Opera venture in America and in the Royal English Opera Company after their return to London. After the latter failed, he continued singing although plagued with vocal problems.

James Henry Horncastle (1801–1869) ["Horncastle," "Chatel," "Horny"] was an English actor and playwright who worked on the New York stage at the

Olympic Theatre from 1837 to 1841, and whose writing credits included the opera *The Cat's in the Larder; or, The Maid with the Parasol* (a burletta on *La gazza ladra*), the burlesque ballet *Buy-it-dear, 'tis Made of Cashmere*, and the Civil War ballad "The Gallant Cannonier." As Reiff's comments make clear, Horncastle is older than the rest of them, portly, and a seasoned traveler.

Joseph Jefferson (1829–1905) played the role of Pedro in *Cinderella* in Washington.

Marion Macarthy, a performer mentioned by Reiff but not in connection with the Pyne and Harrison Troupe. She took the role of the Fairy Queen in *Cinderella* in New Orleans.

Fannie Morant played the page in *Maritana* in Baltimore.

Joseph Parker played the Marquis in *Maritana* in Baltimore.

Louisa Pyne (1832–1904) ["Louisa," "Miss L.P.," "Louisa P.y," "Miss L. Pyne," and possibly the "Old Lady"], a soprano, studied singing with George Smart and made her debut at the Queen's Concert Rooms; her stage debut was in *La Sonnambula* at Boulogne in 1849. She appeared regularly on the London stage and in 1854 went to New York where, after some successful seasons, she formed the Pyne and Harrison Troupe. She returned to London in 1857 and, from 1859 to 1864, managed the Royal English Opera Company with William Harrison. After this failed, she dissolved her partnership with Harrison and in 1868 married the baritone Frank Bodda (c. 1823–1892). Apart from an unsuccessful attempt to establish herself as a mezzo-soprano as her voice deteriorated, she thereafter devoted herself to teaching.

Susan (or Susannah) Pyne (1821–1886) ["Susan," "S. P."], a mezzo-soprano, made her debut with Louisa at the Queen's Concert Rooms in 1842; she thereafter performed on the London stage, and went with her sister to America in 1854. They worked closely together, and she was a member of the Pyne and Harrison Troupe on this tour. However, her roles generally appear to have been limited: she played the character role of Dame Van Winkle in George Bristow's *Rip Van Winkle*, for example—and did more concert work than her sister.

Mrs. Silsbee sang with the troupe in St. Louis.

Le Grand Smith ["Smith"] was probably a manager in an unspecified capacity.

George Stretton ["Strettoni," "Joe"], a bass-baritone.

Frank R. Swan ["Swan"], a singer.

Henrietta "Hattie" Vallée (1828–1894), a performer not mentioned by Reiff but who took the role of the Fairy Sunbeam in *Cinderella* with the Pyne and Harrison Troupe in New Orleans. She was an actress and second wife to Benedict De Bar, lessee and manager of the St. Charles Theatre; she retired from the stage in 1857 while they were still in New Orleans.

G. H. Warre ["Warre," "Warrie"], a tenor, who, performing on 10 October 1859 at the Volksgarten, 45 Bowery, New York, was billed as singing "with the Pyne-Harrison Opera Troupe."

SCENES IN THE BACK WOODS

The company had been playing at the Louisville Theatre, Louisville,
Kentucky, for the week starting 31 December 1855, and had given their usual
fare of The Crown Diamonds, Maritana, The Daughter of the Regiment,
Fra Diavolo, *and* The Bohemian Girl. *The last performance they gave before*
the diary opens was Louisa Pyne's benefit performance of La Sonnambula
on 5 January. The company then embarked on the steamer Thomas Swann,[1]
bound for New Orleans, at which point Reiff's diary opens.

TUESDAY JANUARY 8th   OHIO RIVER, BELOW LOUISVILLE, KENTUCKY

[1] The ice getting very thick. Last night men were engaged repairing our
wheel which had been broken badly, also the paddle box.[2]

Today two steamers passed going up the "T. C. Twichell"[3] and the "Te-
cumoba"[4] it is quite an event for a vessel to pass the passengers rush out to
see it as eagerly as if it was at sea.

After shoving through the ice till about twelve o'clock we stopped again
tied the vessel to a tree *in* the forest, and *on* the river's bank, about twenty-
two miles below Evansville at a place called Diamond Island Bend, Henderson County, Kentucky.[5]

1. The *Thomas Swann* (also *Swan*), launched in Wheeling, West Virginia, about 1853, was
mostly associated with the Ohio River.

2. The ice, which Reiff discusses in the early part of the diary, was responsible for the company being ten days late into New Orleans. See the *Picayune,* 23 January 1856.

3. "T. C. Twichell": "T. G. Wichell" in Reiff. He appears to have meant the side-wheeler the
T. C. Twichell launched in New Albany, Indiana, in 1854, and which disappeared from records in 1862.

4. No record of this paddlewheeler has been found. Reiff may have mistaken this one for
the *Tecumseh,* built in Cincinnati in 1852 and named after the Shawnee chief.

5. Diamond Island Bend was described as being a bend in which "sportsmen find the greatest pleasure in the fall, winter, and spring months," and in which "there are a great number of
sloughs and ponds" (Starling, *History of Henderson County,* 383).

Figure 2. *Interior of the Main Cabin of the Steamboat Princess,* 1861.
The type and layout of the accommodation of the *Princess* on some pre–Civil War
paddlewheelers can be seen in this painting. The *Princess,* built in about 1855 in
Cincinnati, Ohio, was the steamer that raced the *Thomas Swann,* in which Reiff
was traveling out of New Orleans on the evening of 26 February 1856.

After dinner (as the sachem of the "American Exploring Company")[6] I
suggested we should explore the wilderness to which we had arrived. We
started ashore, the ground was covered with snow about an inch in depth
the bank is about twenty feet high and precipitous. Nothing but a magnificent forest to be seen. The trees very large—saw the trunk of one lying just
on the shore which seems upon a rough guess (they call me Yankee[7] here,

6. "Sachem": "sarhem," in Reiff. "The supreme head or chief of some Indian tribes" (*OED*,
XIV, 329). The "American Exploring Company" is clearly an in-joke and may well have been
used more often in conversation than the diary suggests; Reiff later employs it in a very offhand
manner as the "AEC." It emerges that there are three men on this exploration: Reiff himself,
plus George Atherton and Frank Boudinot.

7. "Yankee" at this time still usually referred to a New Englander, an insult of unknown

so I am privileged to *guess*) to be about forty feet in circumference. Two immense sycamores looked not only astonishing large but exceeding picturesque. [2] After walking about half a mile we came to a corn field and three log cabins made of logs and clay—a rude sort of chimney at back—I bolted in immediately, my companions following—where I found a perfect Aunt Chloe,[8] a Negress slave called Aunt Polly, a young nigger about twenty, her son, and a frightened dog who no doubt thinking us ruffians so he gently retired behind the door.

The cabin was rude in the extreme; two beds but made cheerful by an immense fire in the capacious fireplace which contained about a half a load of wood (Cannous' load in N.Y.).[9] We duly appreciated the fire. Aunt Polly after biding us welcome, insisted upon *"something coming out dar"* which demand being reiterated two or three times, produced a large black head from under the bed, which she rapped with some considerable force with a good-sized stick. We found the head belonged to her next son (the brother of the first one we saw) about eighteen in years. He scrambled from under the bed and got out of the door in a wonderful expeditious manner, accelerated no doubt by the stick in his mother's hand—it was very amusing to us, but evidently no fun to the nigger. [3] We had scarcely been here half an hour 'ere a white lady (the mistress of Aunt Polly) came in and invited us into her cabin where was her sister a young lady named Mary and her husband. Their names were Mr and Mrs Rankins, Mary's name being the same. She was evidently very glad to see three Single Gentlemen. She asked us almost immediately if we were married! We arrived here at twelve, and at three we knew the Rankins familiarly enough for them to call us by our christian names.[10] We returned to our vessel—in fact, *our home* for how long, heaven only knows.

During the afternoon a steamer came up the river and hauled in about

origin, usually used by southerners. During the Civil War, the term came to mean any soldier in the Federal Army (*OED*, XX, 692).

8. Aunt Chloe, the good, faithful wife to Uncle Tom in Harriet Beecher Stowe's *Uncle Tom's Cabin*. She is considered by some critics to be a stereotype of "Mammy," the good cook and affectionate mother. Stowe's novel was published in parts beginning in June 1851, and in book form on 20 March 1852; it played a major role in galvanizing the antislavery movement.

9. "Cannous load" not further identified.

10. While etiquette books of the day—such as *Etiquette for Gentlemen* (1851) and *Etiquette at Washington* (1857)—do not specify at what point in an acquaintance the use of a Christian name might be the correct mode of address, Reiff's comment does emphasize that their use in this context was arrived at very quickly.

two hundred feet above us.[11] Any quantity of gambling going on board the vessel.[12] Even the Pynes & Harrison, Stretton and Captain Tilghman,[13] set down to a game—in the Ladies' Cabin.

During the evening a dance was got up, a fiddler and a guitarist being on board. They are awful dancers. I was in fact made Floor Master and entered upon the labours of my new role with all proper dignity.[14] Turned in about one o'clock. Dreamt Father was dead—awoke and found that his son was nearly so—from extreme cold;[15] the thermometer was at my feet about two hundred below zero. [5][16]

WEDNESDAY JANUARY 9th   OHIO RIVER

Very cold; thermometer 10 below zero. Called upon Rankins with Atherton & Horncastle then walked up the river road about a mile and a quarter. Stopped to a much more dignified looking cabin, where was a lady named Clay, a distant relative of Henry Clay[17]—her brother who was (we measured

11. Reiff mentions on the 12th that this paddlewheeler was the *Ohio*. There were two boats called the *Ohio* on the Mississippi in 1856, one built in Cincinnati in 1849 with a tonnage of 348, and the other built at Marietta in 1855. The size of the former makes it the more likely to have been the one to which Reiff refers.

12. Gambling was rife on the riverboats: "Any narrative of a week's life upon a Mississippi steamboat without gambling experience would not possess the flavour of reality" stated Julius Chambers (*The Mississippi River and Its Wonderful Valley*, 128), while Ernst von Hesse-Wartegg gives this account of gambling in the saloon on one of the larger late-nineteenth-century riverboats just outside Cairo: "At one end of the long space, male passengers played '*poker*,' the West's infamous game of chance. At the other end, females played the piano. Therefore, at one end we could lose our money; at the other our hearing and sight; so we avoided both. In the middle we remained in reasonable safety" (*Travels on the Lower Mississippi, 1879–1880*, 151).

13. "Tilghman": "Tilman" in Reiff; see also below for more details. Lloyd Tilghman (1816–1863) graduated from West Point in 1836, resigned from the First US Dragoons three months later, and went to live in Paducah, Kentucky, in 1852. He was recommissioned in 1861 at the outbreak of the Civil War and was killed in the Battle of Champion Hill. See various texts, including Rabb, *Confederate General Lloyd Tilghman*, 7–25.

14. The context here suggests that Reiff was given a role similar to what was later termed a "caller," not only encouraging them all to dance, but prompting the dance routines (*OED*, II, 790).

15. "Father" is Anton Reiff Sr. (1803–1880), a bassoonist with the New York Philharmonic and active on the New York musical scene. He is recorded as having family in Mainz, coming to New York in 1821, playing the oboe and French horn, and singing for many years as a tenor in the St. Patrick's Cathedral Choir. He was the first vice president of the New York Philharmonic Society. See Erskine, *The Philharmonic-Symphony Society*, 8–9.

16. Page 4 omitted in the MS numbering.

17. "A lady named Clay" not further identified. Henry Clay (1777–1852) was a distinguished

with a rule) six feet two and a half inches, but he was not as tall as the man whom I borrowed a hose from yesterday, and he says he's "nothin' to some folks around haar." We returned by a circuitous route through the forest which is filled with most magnificent birds, one especially being entirely red—absolutely beautiful. Many of the passengers are out hunting—there is plenty of deer, birds, possum, squirrel, &c. There are droves of pigs—they call them wild pigs, as they live continually in the forest.

Hounds are used to bring them in. We walked through the forest—about four miles—it was certainly a beautiful walk—the trees are very large and abounding in wild grape vines.

During the evening the "Stars" sang some glees—dancing, political discussions, card playing, story-telling, &c., filled up the balance of the evening. [6]

THURSDAY JANUARY 10th   OHIO RIVER

Cold; five degrees less than yesterday. Frank Boudinot yesterday afternoon went to Rankins; they enquired particularly about Tony and George.[18]

We went there during the afternoon they gave us some hickory nuts very large ones, we made a very pleasant call and I (being very modest) asked them if they would wash some collars for me, of course they would. They have had many visitors since we first went there, but none are as much at home.

It seems as if we were like "Arctic Explorers" Ice Bound—visiting the Natives Ashore—we are completely cut off from all communication with the World—nothing but ice on one side and forest on the other. Many jokes are cracked at night; some will ask where you are going to spend the evening—one suggests the Opera,[19] another Niblo's,[20] with a promise to wind up at Shelly's.[21]

Kentucky politician who served both in the Senate and in the House of Representatives, where he was also Speaker (Paul E. Fuller, "Henry Clay," *ANB*, V, 25–28).

18. Tony and George: the author and George Atherton.

19. "The Opera" in a New York context in 1854 is probably a generic reference to what had been marketed there as socially upmarket entertainment. The Astor Place Opera House, which opened on 22 November 1847 with Verdi's *Ernani*, had closed in 1852, and was replaced in 1854 with the less glamorous Academy of Music at 14th Street and Irving Place (Ahlquist, *Democracy at the Opera*, 134ff).

20. Niblo's Garden in the form referred to here was the second theater on the site, opened in 1849. By 1850, it was staging Italian opera, but its well-equipped stage also received English opera, plays, and other performances. Members of the company, including Louisa Pyne, performed there in 1856. See Ahlquist, *Democracy at the Opera*, 143–47.

21. The context suggests that "Shelly's" is an unidentified café or nightspot.

There is on board a Capt. Tilghman who was a Captain in Mexico on Taylor's line to Buena Vista[22] and then was partially with Scott[23] for a long time stationed at Jalapa—he is a native of Maryland, Graduate of West Point[24] (in 1836) an engineer, very intelligent, affable and unassuming gentleman—lives at Paducah, Kentucky.[25] He tells me that the recall of Scott from Mexico, was looked upon by the Legitimate Officers in Mexico as a contemptible piece of hasty tyranny on the part of Mr Polk.[26] [8][27]

He says had the war continued, the army would have revolted sooner than have marched from the City of Mexico under General Butler—who was a perfect old woman—he says he would willingly stake his reputation upon this assertion.[28] He said General Scott is no doubt the *greatest* living

22. Zachary Taylor (1784–1850), later twelfth president of the United States, led the army that fought several battles south of the Rio Grande, captured the important city of Monterrey, and defeated a major Mexican force at the Battle of Buena Vista in February 1847 (Elbert B. Smith, "Zachary Taylor," *ANB*, XXI, 410–12).

23. Union General Winfield Scott (1786–1866) arrived in Jalapa in April 1847, from the successful Veracruz campaign, which surrendered and was occupied on 29 March. At Jalapa, Scott waited, concerned about supply and the loss of seven regiments of volunteers, but then advanced on Mexico City. The campaign resulted in the Treaty of Guadalupe Hidalgo, signed on 2 February 1848. His own account appears in his *Memoirs of Lieut.-General Scott*, II, 430–538.

24. "On the advice of the young West Pointers on his staff, Taylor emplaced his two 18-pounder iron siege guns in the center of his line and blasted the advancing Mexicans with canister." See *American Military History*, 164.

25. Paducah, originally called Pekin, was settled around 1815 as a town of both Native Americans (headed by Chief Paduke) and settlers. The town in its present form was laid out from 1827 by William Clark (1770–1838), the superintendent of Native American affairs for the Mississippi–Missouri River region and named after the Indian chief; it was incorporated as a town in 1830 and chartered as a city in 1856. Its origins and prosperity can be attributed to its strategic location at the confluence of the Ohio and Tennessee rivers. (Robertson, "Paducah," *The Kentucky Encyclopedia*, ed. Kleber, 705–6).

26. James K. Polk (1795–1849), eleventh president of the United States, (correctly) feared Taylor as a possible presidential candidate, but attempts by Polk to undermine Taylor backfired when the latter emerged victorious (and with a reputation for great personal courage) from the battle at Buena Vista in February 1847. Taylor's presidential supporters included Alexander Stephens and Abraham Lincoln, who later that year launched a successful "Taylor for President Club." An account of Polk and the army can be found in Winders, *Mr. Polk's Army*.

27. Page 7 omitted in the pagination.

28. William Orlando Butler (1791–1880), to whom Taylor was ordered by President Polk to relinquish command of the army in 1848 in the face of complaints that Taylor had accepted a bribe of one million dollars to become president of Mexico. Daniel Harvey Hill noted that

General, and that Wellington pronounced him so (after himself) when he (Scott) had completed his Mexican Campaign.[29]

Upon his authority all of the officers—that is to say, Generals appointed by Polk, Pillow, Shields, Pierce,[30] &c were perfect ninnys as regards military knowledge—were obliged to consult their aids upon the most petty questions—Quitman[31] was an exception; Butler, he says, absolutely knew nothing; he says General Scott planned the Mexican Campaign at *New York!* and *Washington!,* he asked for eleven thousand men—but had thirteen—all told. States that Taylor was a very nice man, but not to be compared as a military man to Scott; that the soldiers nearly revolted when obliged to leave Taylor; that the credit of the Fall of Monterry belongs to Worth.[32] He also says the affection for Scott in the Army was astonishing. [9]

Atherton and I walked down about two miles along the river where we enjoyed a magnificent sunset—on the opposite side of the river is a small town called West Franklin.[33] Four steamboats are lying there. Amused myself during the evening by playing whist—but not gambling.

---

it was the result of intrigue and that the president was weak and childish: "the whole army is indignant" (Anderson, *An Artillery Officer,* 338).

29. In fact, the Duke of Wellington, with whom by his own account Scott was acquainted, nearly lost faith in Scott during the campaign, saying of the march on Mexico City: "Scott is lost. He has been carried away by success. He can't take the city, and he can't fall back on his bases" (Scott, *Memoirs,* II, 466n).

30. Gideon Pillow (1806–1878), soldier and politician, who saw himself as Polk's representative in the army; James Shields (1806–1879), a politician who resigned his political posts to fight in the Mexican-American War and who emerged a hero after a number of engagements including Tampico, Cerro Gordo, Contreras, Churubusco, and Chapultepec; and Franklin Pierce (1804–1869), a lawyer, and later fourteenth president of the United States, who fought in the Mexican-American War, rising to be a brigadier general, but whose war record was somewhat marred by being known as the "hero of many a bottle" (Larry Gara, "Franklin Pierce," *ANB,* XVII, 495).

31. John A. Quitman (1799–1858), a lawyer and governor of Mississippi (1835–1836, 1850–1851); from 1846, he served as a brigadier in the Mexican-American War, and after the fall of Mexico City, served as military governor until his discharge in 1848. See Robert E. May, "John Anthony Quitman," *ANB,* XVIII, 48–49.

32. General William Jenkins Worth (1794–1849) was assigned command of the Second Brigade by Zachary Taylor in the assault on Monterrey in 1846, and his tactics were generally held to have won the American victory. See Wallace, *General William Jenkins Worth,* 87–103.

33. West Franklin, Indiana, was laid out in 1837; see Leffel, *History of Posey County,* 115. Fourteen miles below Henderson, it was—in 1861—described as being "a small village" (Hawes, *Commercial Gazetteer,* 143).

FRIDAY JANUARY 11th   OHIO RIVER

Cloudy; all wishing for rain to break up the ice; looks more like snow. Weather moderating, Atherton & I walked through the woods about two miles southwest. Invited to tea at Rankins. Saw some most beautiful birds, one specimen was entirely a bright red, some others (partially) a beautiful deep blue.

Everyone (nearly) playing cards. Several offering bets that we will get off in forty-eight hours. Some men succeeded in crossing to the Indiana shore in a skiff—it was watched with much anxiety from both steamers—no doubt was a perilous undertaking under the circumstances. [10]

SATURDAY JANUARY 12th   OHIO RIVER RESUMED

Cloudy and much warmer.

At twelve noon we started through the ice leaving the "Ohio" to her glory alone.[34] The ice was really dreadful. The engineer says he has been running on this river twenty years and never saw anything like it before. A man is continually stationed in the hold at the bow to watch for any smash that may occur. I was all through the hold today, the ice crushing against the vessel sounds like artillery. Horncastle, an old traveller, much frightened. The ice a foot thick! In some places (in narrow passes), it was piled up three & four feet. I stood on the extreme bow of the vessel, thinking what we would have for supper—"Where ignorance is bliss, 'tis folly to be wise."[35] 'Twas so with me, I did not fear any danger.

Before starting the captain purchased a bullock and some pork. Our fare is not as good as it was.[36] An old captain who has been running on this river sixteen years is quite nervous; the ice cakes sometimes will not break but go under; you can then feel it rub against the keel the entire length of the boat.

About five pm, came to the Wabash River which divides Indiana and Illinois. The last house on the Indiana Shore is a miserable dilapidated looking

34. See note 11.

35. Thomas Gray, "Ode on a Distant Prospect of Eton College" (1742), lines 97–100.

36. For George Byron Merrick's colorful account of the food-preparation conditions aboard the steamboats, see *Old Times on the Upper Mississippi*. Merrick opined that if the chickens "were *dead* enough to stay on the platter when they got to the table that was all any reasonable steamboatman could ask" (128).

dwelling, not a cabin but a house.[37] At half past 6 pm, stopped at a place in Fulton Co., Kentucky, called Curlew Mines.[38] The vessel was not fasten'd to the shore before Atherton & I were ashore. There is a coal mine here, four or five cabins, saw several miners about twenty. We walked through the woods about half a mile—getting dark—and I have about $50 [11] in my pocket and these miners being a desperate set, I concluded to return; it was a most beautiful walk.

SUNDAY JANUARY 13th   OHIO RIVER

Cold & wind, cloudy. Started early passed through dreadful ice. One place resembled the "Narrows" N.Y. Harbour very much, could almost fancy myself there.[39] The scenery is very beautiful.

At noon having bent and nearly torn off our Catwater[40] was obliged to lay up at a place call'd Grand Pier Creek, Pope Co., Illinois. Could not get within 75 feet of the shore and was obliged to go over the ice. Got upon shore which is rocky and hilly—the creek running from the river winds through beautiful hills—Ghor & myself having walked up it on the ice (which is very smooth) about 3/4 of a mile—it cracked some, so we sagely concluded to return. Cleared off quite warm. No gambling today, it is the only thing that makes the day differ from the others in the week.

A steamer "Thomas Gibson" is lying here—has been for the last fine day.[41] Much smaller than our boat, went aboard and found (had practical proof) that they sell liquor on board. Many of the passengers skating on the creek. In the afternoon, borrowed a pair of skates and had a fine time on the creek; it is as smooth as glass.

37. "About five P.M., came to the Wabash River . . . but a house" inserted from 9v.

38. Rennick, *Kentucky Place Names,* 76, records this as an "abandoned coal town and extinct Post Office." It was named after the owner of the local mines, and the post office, established on 3 September 1858, became Curlew Mines in 1860.

39. The "Narrows" is the nickname of the strait that separates the boroughs of Brooklyn and Staten Island, and links the Upper and Lower New York bays, historically the most important entrance to New York City.

40. "Catwater" not further identified.

41. No trace of a boat called the *Thomas Gibson* has yet been found. However, a Thomas F. Gibson is recorded as the first mate on the *Lexington* when it exploded in 1855, and it may be that the boat to which Reiff refers was named after this victim.

Atherton and I took a walk in a north-easterly direction. Went to a farm-house; I pretended that I was an Officer of the boat and wanted to purchase some wood. [12] We went up on the hill to the left of the creek; found a deserted house with a few dishes on table, about four baskets of excellent walnuts (I tested them), and a file of the *L'Orleanian* newspaper.[42] There was also an orchard, three graves, and what had seemingly been a Barn.

Our boat laid here all night.

MONDAY JANUARY 14th   SMITHLAND—PADUCAH—CAIRO

Started at 7 am. Had snowed some during the night. Passed two pretty islands called "The Sisters" arrived at Smithland about eleven.[43] It is situated on south east bank of the Cumberland River, Livingston Co., Kentucky.[44] Atherton and I, of course, went ashore immediately. Walked along the levee towards (in fact on) the bank of the Cumberland river; it seems a very contemptible sort of place, rough looking people.

After leaving here, ice became very thick, all the way to Paducah where we stopped about 1 pm.[45] It is in McCracken County, about 4,500 inhabitants—looks quite like a city situated at the mouth of the Tennessee River. Rushed to a hotel,[46] and found what purported to be a *news*paper it *was all but* the news.[47] Captain Tilghman here left us taking me to a dentist—Dr.

42. *L'Orleanian,* the *Daily Orleanian,* or *L'Orléanais* was a bilingual newspaper published between 1847 and 1858 in New Orleans (Reinders, *End of an Era,* 231).

43. The Twin Sisters Islands, plus the Pryor and Rondeau islands, form part of a group known as the Ohio River Islands, just upriver from Smithland. Views—as they must have been when Reiff passed them—were painted in the 1860s by Lefevre James Cranstone; see Donald Smith, *Lefevre James Cranstone,* especially 10–24.

44. Livingston County, Kentucky, was formed in 1799; Smithland is the county seat (Ron D. Bryant, "Livingston County," *The Kentucky Encyclopedia,* ed. Kleber, 564).

45. See note 25.

46. Possibly the St. Francis Hotel, at that time the largest hotel in Paducah, was sited at the corner of Main and Broadway; contemporary advertising noted that its porters were "always on the lookout for boats day and night." The hotel is mentioned frequently in accounts of the Civil War; see, for example, Craig, *Kentucky Confederates,* 102, 137.

47. Which paper Reiff saw is unclear; possibilities include the *Paducah Journal* and the *Paducah American.* The *Paducah Herald,* the main midcentury Paducah paper, did not begin publishing until 1857 (Robertson, *Paducah, Kentucky,* 18).

Kidd[48]—who pulled my tooth which has tortured me ever since the evening I left Louisville. Saw a new Gothic brown coloured building, which is to be a bank situated on Broadway; it is a very nice sort of an affair.[49] [12ᵛ] Paducah is named after an Indian Chief and should be celebrated for being the house of so fine[50] a man as Captain Tilghman.

Stayed here about an hour—nothing particular occurred until tea time when the ice jarred the vessel so much as to nearly shake the dishes off the table. Arrived at Cairo about 7; it was intended for a large city, being at the mouth of the Ohio about two hundred houses will go up next year. The town is lower than the river (generally) it is protected by an immense levee.

Several of us went ashore; posted my letter home written on the 12th ult. Just crossed the street where there were several men standing with lanterns. Discovered a *man lying soaking in his blood,* having only a few minutes before been *murdered,* supposed shot. Stretton, I, and several others examined him, he was quite warm. Warre felt his breast. His left temple was the place where he received his wound; looked to me as if it had been done by a slingshot. He was a hand on board of a steamer. A friend of his wanted to get enough of us to tear down the "House" (a low tavern) where he had either been killed *at,* or by[51] someone who was there. Our party wanted to go in like bricks, but it fizzled out—it is said that no-one's life is safe at Cairo—in fact, the man lay[52] there half an hour before he was even removed from [13] the street. No *public functionary* appeared. I presume that nothing will be done about it. Many think that in all probability the murderer will go down the river on this boat as a large number of passengers have come on board, and another steamer will not be down for days.

48. Probably B. F. Kidd (1824–1870; see Oak Grove Cemetery, Paducah), a surgeon dentist with an office at Locust and Broadway; see *Williams' Paducah City Directory,* 60.

49. The Commercial Bank of Kentucky was sited at the corner of what was then Locust and Broadway; the other bank in Paducah, the Bank of Louisville, had opened in 1847 and was not "new." The Commercial Bank, which had opened in 1852, closed during the Civil War (*History and Families,* 14).

50. "Fine": obscured by an inkblot.

51. "By": "from" in Reiff.

52. "Lay": "laid" in Reiff.

TUESDAY JANUARY 15th   CAIRO

Last night, a party of men from the "Star of the West"[53] (the steamer to which the murdered man belonged) went to the tavern where he was kill'd, seized the tavern keeper, took him to a lonely spot, and there, presenting several rifles at his head (with sundry pistols), demanded who the murderer was, threatening instant death if he did not tell. After a little parley, he divulged. They then started after the murderer, whom they found, and delivered up to a Justice of the Peace.

There is some talk that the steamboat men will tear down the "House" today. Our Engineer says he never thinks of going into Cairo without his revolver.

We left this morning (after I had taken a walk) at half past ten, [it] snowing very fast. It looks (as you sail down the river) something like N.Y. that is, the situation.[54] It seems as if the Mississippi ran into the Ohio, instead of vice versa.[55] Last night the Illinois Central Rail Road[56] brought in four car loads of game of which our captain purchased a bountiful supply. [13ᵛ]

Our Engineer (a very clever fellow) says we carry on this boat a hundred and sixty pounds steam (160 lbs) to the square inch, this vessel not being allowed by law to carry more.[57] Borrowed an old hat of his, pretended

---

53. The *Star of the West* was launched in 1855 at McKeesport, Pennsylvania; she burned and sank at St. Louis in 1858.

54. Presumably Reiff is referring to the scene looking back toward Cairo as the boat moved downstream, with the Mississippi to the left and the Ohio to the right; he seems to have been comparing it with the view looking back toward Manhattan Island, with the Hudson on one side and the East River on the other.

55. Charles Dickens left a description of the junction which was not "at all inspiring in its influence. The trees were stunted in their growth; the banks were low and flat; the settlements and log cabins fewer in number; and their inhabitants more wan and wretched than any we had encountered yet" (*American Notes*, 30).

56. Cairo to Galena in northwest Illinois (with a branch line to Chicago) was the subject of the Illinois Central Railroad's original charter, issued in 1851. The ICR was the first railroad company to receive a land grant. The line, which was finished in 1856, gave Chicago a route to New Orleans by way of a railroad-operated steamboat line between Cairo and New Orleans. See Stover, *The History of the Illinois Central Railroad*, 28–30, 38–84.

57. Steamboats had always been plagued by exploding boilers; such accidents led to many fires and sinkings. The reasons for such accidents lay partly in the inadequate construction of

that I had lost mine—created considerable fun in the Saloon. I had forgot to mention that, last night, our passengers were so dreadfully affected with the murder case (a perfect thrill of horror having run around the Ladies' Cabin when the story was related), that nothing would do to express their profound grief but a half a dozen of quadrilles,[58] which they danced in the most bewitching manner. [14]

About ten miles below Cairo passed the "Shotwell"[59] the fastest boat on the Ohio or Mississippi (the rival of the "Eclipse");[60] [a] short distance farther met the "Virginia."[61] Half past 12 pm, stopped at Columbus, Kentucky, small place pop. 1000.[62] Could not get within 75 feet of the shore; it was quite amusing to hear our mate swear at the hands as they would fall getting over the ice—was not able to go ashore.

2 pm, stopped at Hickman, Kentucky, the county seat of Fulton Co. It is the starting point for a great stage route to Nashville, Tennessee. It is not on

---

the boilers themselves and their unregulated overcharging in order to increase the speed of the boats, and thereby their reputation for speed and profits. The public outcry was such that the government was forced to step against opposition from the boat owners, concern about private-property rights, and doubt as to why the explosions occurred. Congress passed two pieces of regulatory legislation, one in 1838 (which concentrated on the engineers) and the other in 1852 (which concentrated on the boilers themselves), which together established the first federal agency responsible for the regulation of a private industry, the Steamboat Inspection Service. See Hunter, *Steamboats on the Western Rivers;* John Brown, *Limbs on the Levee;* and Paskoff, *Troubled Waters,* for discussions of these issues, and for a contemporary account of the various disasters, see *Lloyd's Steamboat Directory,* 5–259.

58. A quadrille was a popular dance for four couples.

59. The *A. L. Shotwell* was built in New Albany, Indiana, in 1853. In May that year, she raced from New Orleans to Louisville in 4 days, 21 hours, and 30 minutes; the *Eclipse* (see note 60) set out to break that record a few days later, and timed it at 4 days, 9 hours, and 30 minutes. A week later, the *Shotwell* managed a disputed 4 days, 9 hours, and 29 minutes. See Harrison and Klotter, *A New History of Kentucky,* 129–30; Bogle, "The Eclipse versus the A. L. Shotwell," 125–37; and Twain, *Life on the Mississippi,* chap. 16, "Racing Days."

60. The *Eclipse,* a sternwheel wooden-hulled packet, was launched in 1854, California, Pennsylvania. Associated with Cox, Brainard and Company of Mobile, Alabama, she disappeared from the lists in 1860.

61. The *Virginia* was launched in 1853.

62. Columbus, Kentucky, the oldest town in the Jackson Purchase, was first settled as "Ironbanks"; it was renamed "Columbus" in 1820 and was until 1830 the county seat (Spence and Spence, *A History of Hickman County*).

bottom lands, exactly but partly on a hill.[63] A[therton] & I ashore, walked only a short distance. The ice is not so thick as on the Ohio but exceeding tough. Saw a St. Louis paper from which I heard that at New York on the 5th and 6th ult, an immense snowstorm occurred, and that, generally, it has been very cold in the North; glad I'm not there.[64]

A large number of passengers came aboard at Cairo.[65]

WEDNESDAY JANUARY 16th   MISSISSIPPI RIVER

We laid up last night somewhere in Missouri, but where I do not know. Took in a large quantity of wood. I went ashore up the high bank and into a partially finished log hut which was filled with sacks of what appeared to be corn.

Started this morning at daylight—after breakfast went on upper deck [15] where I remained until nearly dinner time. At dinner time a very important *thing* or event happened to me. A gentleman and myself having a dispute about a seat at the table which I claimed, he, having got into it (possession being nine points of the law), kept it. I spoke rather excitedly to him, but finally took a seat at the opposite side of the table. I had scarcely done so, before a waiter came to me with the gentleman's card (Colonel Young of California)[66] with the request *that I would meet him* after dinner—*with a friend,* as he would me—saying we could then settle our dispute. I sent word to him that I would see him after dinner—but felt somewhat anxious I must confess, for he was too big for me to *pummel* and, being a Graduate of West Point, I thought *possibly* a better shot, as I have not fired a pistol six times in my life and I was also afraid that he would possibly shoot me in the dispute which I saw was inevitable.[67]

I did not enjoy my meal as *much as usual* but put on a calm face and

63. Hickman, Kentucky, was once called "Mills Point" and was nominated the county seat in 1845. The hill to which Reiff refers is one of the five bluffs above the river on which the town now stands. See Ron D. Bryant, "Hickman," *The Kentucky Encyclopedia*, ed. Kleber, 427.

64. The papers that Reiff might have seen include the *Daily Missouri Democrat*, the *St. Louis Leader*, the *Daily Pilot*, and the *Morning Herald*.

65. This confirms the rumor Reiff reports on Thursday 15 January.

66. "Colonel Young" not further identified.

67. See Wilson, *The Code of Honour*, 8–10, for some guide to dueling in the South. In Wilson's terms, Young's quarrel with Reiff did not warrant a duel; the etiquette required him not to send a challenge in the first instance, but to consider the matter carefully with his second before taking action. However, in the rest of his conduct—not challenging the transgressor in

listlessly cracked some almonds for my dessert [for] at least five minutes.

The best of the joke (it had like to have been a serious one) was that I discovered he *was not in my seat,* but another man was—However, after telling him so—we kept disputing [16] whether my man was entitled to a seat.

In two minutes, I was (to use Swan's words) completely surrounded by Brass Buttons, several of his friends, all military men. Stretton, seeing me in a dispute—with a friend came to my rescue—then Swan, and several others. My challenger said—I had[68] also yesterday insulted one of his friends— (I began to think that there was a dead set against me) I demanded that I should be set face to face with the man. The Colonel then began to talk about the customs in this county (quite a crowd being now about us, and he evidently taking me for an Englishman) said he was a New Yorker by birth. He was quite nonplussed when I told him that I was a native of New York, and as good an American as he was. He then somewhat abated at finding that I had friends as well as he. Swan said "If any man gets in my *seat* I'll *haul* him out"; it finally was settled by the clerk of the boat telling us we must desist.[69]

The Pynes saw that I was in some difficulty, they found Harrison and told him. He got Brough—who it was sent the clerk to us. At night, I was in my seat by times, and strange to say, the *Colonel sat next to me,* was very clever, told me how much money he had made in California, &c. ($400[,]ooo). [16ᵛ]

Went into the Engineer's Room and saw a number of slaves dance and sing as they do on the plantations.[70] [17] The boat jerks so badly as to be almost [impossible] to write.[71]

---

public, sending a note in the language of a gentleman (in this case, his card), and so on—Young appears to have followed it to the letter.

68. "Had": "have" in Reiff.

69. Steamboat clerks were third in rank to the captain and the pilot and were responsible to the owners for the business end of the venture, including the recruiting of passengers, the collecting of fares, and the hiring and firing of deckhands (Kotar and Gessler, *The Steamboat Era,* 266).

70. The slaves here were probably the boat's firemen. The firemen worked for the engineer, and below Louisville, most of them were slaves. Fredrika Bremer recounts a journey in the 1850s in which she saw one fireman standing astride a large pile of firewood and throwing down the wood from the top. "The slave at the top of the wood pile sang out a stanza and the other firemen echoed a chorus, all in perfect time to their movements. The whole scene 'was so accordant and well arranged, that it would have produced a fine effect upon any theater anywhere'" (Gudmestad, *Steamboats and the Rise of the Cotton Kingdom,* 41 and n26).

71. "The boat . . . to write": contemporary marginal note by Reiff.

Left Kentucky and Missouri behind us and came to Tennessee and Arkansas. Arkansas seems to contain some most beautiful land, soil very deep. Saw a very large plantation, the negroes' houses making quite a village. Passed a "Cotton Gin."[72] A most beautiful day, the sunset really magnificent.

During the past few days saw several bald eagles, they "sail" most beautifully.

Today saw immense flocks of wild geese; they fly very high. Also passed a flock of cranes on sand bars. Ducks have absolutely swarmed, the past three days.

The sun much warmer—but a cold wind blowing.

Arrived at Memphis, Tennessee, at 1 am.

We have broken our wheels so badly especially on the starboard side as to render it necessary to lay up for the night.

The ice today cut a hole into us—but it was easily stopped. [18]

THURSDAY JANUARY 17th   MEMPHIS

Got up early and went ashore. Memphis stands upon a high bluff, a short sort of levee, then you pass through a cut up hill, where you find the first street—very wide the space between the deep cuts being a "Cotton Mart." Saw several carts laden, come down the different streets, one with six oxen.

Walked through the town to the Post Office, in Jefferson Street one block from Main.[73]

There is a park on Main St. about as large as St. John's, N.Y., but not as handsome.[74]

72. A machine that separates the cotton fibers from the seedpods; the machine that Reiff saw was probably a variant of the machine "invented" by Eli Whitney in 1793; the disputes over just who invented the machine dragged on for years. See Lakwete, *Inventing the Cotton Gin*, 177–92.

73. The post office, which opened in 1823, would see the hoisting of the Union flag from its roof in the Civil War, when the town surrendered to Federal gunboats on 6 June 1862 ("Jackson's Monument at Memphis," *Harper's Weekly*, 5 July 1862).

74. St. John's Park was a square in TriBeCa, New York. The property of Trinity Church from 1705, it was held as farmland until 1800, when Trinity built an elegant new chapel in 1807, St. John's, to the design of John McComb Jr. (1763–1853) and his brother Isaac; in the process, the square became a private park. In the period in which it was known to Reiff, it was used for church and public events. Also see Burrows and Wallace, *Gotham*, 374, 457–58.

We (Atherton and I) also went into an Engine House, and into the Veranda Hotel, where I found a piano, the first I've seen since leaving Louisville.[75] Went into a very fine book store—where was a magnificent Bible.

The weather today is perfectly charming. How different it must be in New York.

The sky remarkably clear.

Left Memphis about eleven. Saw in a newspaper here that Nagle of the Broadway Theatre died suddenly a few days ago.[76]

Memphis from the river slightly resembles Albany, N.Y.

Saw several large plantations.

Passed one steamer aground (laden with cattle) and many others going up the river. [18ᵛ]

Atherton and I became acquainted with a young gentleman of New York City named Stephen K. Lane[77]—he is travelling for pleasure going to Natchez—he has promised to positively call upon us in New York. [19]

Several times today—when the river was a mile and half wide—we would pass within fifty feet of the shore; the channel is so peculiar. Saw a number of snags.[78]

At 7 pm, hauled up on the Arkansas side of the river to wood.[79] I shall certainly never forget the first time I stepped my foot on Arkansas soil if only

75. This confirms the possibility—suggested by Reiff's 8 January report of dancing to a fiddle and a guitar—that the boat had no piano (even in the Ladies' Saloon) for entertainment.

76. William S. Nagle (1830–1856): "On Monday evening last, Mr. WILLIAM S. NAGLE, who has been for the last six years assistant Treasurer of the Broadway Theatre, died suddenly at the early age of 26 years. On Friday and Saturday he attended to his duties, apparently in perfect health. He was indisposed on Sunday, and on Monday he was a corpse" (*New York Times,* 17 January 1856).

77. "Stephen K. Lane": Stephen S. Lane (or possibly also "Lane," "Love," or "Laue," but Reiff's entry for 10 February suggests "Lane"). However, later in the diary it becomes clear that this is Stephen Knowlton Lane (1833–1896), who was born in New York, became a member of the New York Produce Exchange, and who later served as mayor of Bayonne, New Jersey, from 1879 to 1883 (Whitcomb, *First History of Bayonne,* 80).

78. Snags—a tree or part thereof which is sunken, or which floats just above the water—were a constant danger to shipping. If struck hard enough, they were capable of sinking a vessel (*OED,* XV, 822).

79. This seems to have been at Dunn's Wood Yard, below (and on the opposite side of the river to) Commerce, Mississippi; see *Lloyd's Steamboat Directory,* 194.

for the beautiful night it is quite mild and moonlight. The stillness of the night (Hang it! there go those horrid geese with their shocking quack, they are on the hurricane deck in coops) but the evening is certainly beautiful. All the passengers going ashore, even our rheumatic Parson Dr Phillips.[80] We all went to see (hard by) an immense ox who is six feet, seven inches in height and did when fat weigh *5,200 pounds!* He was raised in Kentucky.

Men are endeavouring to repair our wheels which are again broken.

FRIDAY JANUARY 18th   MISSISSIPPI RIVER

Started at half past six—a most beautiful morning—passed a tremendous snag. Thermometer (at eight A.M.) at 40 degrees above zero.

At nine, we arrived at Helena, Phillips Co., Arkansas, situated on a bluff, very rich soil. We walked through [the] village. There are *two* churches here, and one in the course [19(2)] of erection.[81] The streets run as if from a point.

We took on board about fifty oxen. There was much difficulty in getting them on; the Second Mate was thrown by one and trampled on, hurting his ankle, it was miraculous that he was not killed. It was very amusing to see Stretton with a club assisting the men—one ox jumped ashore twice, being quite raving (and no wonder, from the manner in which he was beaten) he howled and made a dash up the bank but was finally drag'd on board by main force.

The soil here is the most perfect rich mould.

The ice here is in very small cakes.

An old lady, aged 66, came on board at Memphis, who is going to Texas to her son's, she had never even *seen* a steamboat before—and is perfectly shocked to see people play cards.

There is an old man who is also going to Texas—with his granddaughter—he never wears an overcoat or cloak and gets off the boat at every opportunity—in fact, it seems as if a majority of our passengers are going to

80. "Dr Phillips" not further identified.

81. One of these was probably the First Baptist Church of Helena, established in 1852, and the other, St. John's Episcopal Church, established in 1853. The one Reiff saw being constructed must be the 1856 frame church that replaced the first Catholic church in Helena, built between Columbia and Franklin streets, and Porter and Perry streets, which was burned in 1854 by the anti-Catholic Know Nothings. Reiff would discuss them with Bishop Spalding on 19 February.

Texas. The most important man aboard (after Gibsoni)[82] is a nigger over-seer of some slaves. Passed several boats. [20] Went all night, the first time since we started.

SATURDAY JANUARY 19th   MISSISSIPPI RIVER

Raining. Promenaded the deck for quite a long time. Stretton sick with a slight touch (I reckon) of fever & augue. Susan Pyne somewhat recovering from her neuralgia, and Harrison from his boil—Louisa Pyne laid up with boils—and Horncastle going about with an enormous stye on his eye. Good party.

A tremendous quantity of card playing today.

12 pm. Rain turned to snow—became so thick that we could not see twice the length of the vessel. We wanted wood [and] blew the whistle for some; men on shore came out with lights.

Stopp'd at a miserable place or so.[83]

We are now between Mississippi and Louisiana. People here say it has been the coldest winter for thirty years. Snow being in Louisiana an *event* in its history. Darkies don't know what to make of it. There is a gentleman on board who left New York two days after we did Louisville—was twice the time (in consequence of snow drifts) he ought to have been getting to Cincinnati—staid there two days—went to Cairo, where he joined us. [20ᵛ]

We got the mails at Cairo, and I have often looked wistfully at the mail bags as I expect there are some letters in there for me.

The mules got off in Mississippi. The poor creatures had been standing for two weeks, they scampered, rolled, and frisked about with most wonder-ful agility—some endeavoured to get aboard again.[84] [20(2)]

82. "Gibsoni" not further identified. He may be the "Gibson" who takes items to New York for Reiff (see page 70). The Italianization of his name follows the form used by Reiff for Stret-ton's nickname, "Strettoni."

83. Settlements to which Reiff could be referring include Victoria, Mississippi; Napoleon, Arkansas; and Greenville, Mississippi. There are other minor landings and settlements that might also qualify as "miserable places"; see *Lloyd's Steamboat Directory*, 196, 198.

84. "The mules got off in Mississippi . . . some endeavoured to get aboard again": separately dated the 19th, this has been inserted from 19(2)v.

Figure 3. *Cairo. Mouth of the Ohio.* A "pastoral" view of the rough-and-ready river town of Cairo sited at the confluence of the Mississippi and Ohio rivers. Cairo was typical of many of the towns Reiff visited: small but flourishing, and with a period of boom followed by a general decline ahead of it.

SUNDAY JANUARY 20th   MISSISSIPPI RIVER, VICKSBURG TO NATCHEZ

Clear and cold—high wind. Froze[85] last night (not me) but water on the deck. Steve, George, and I walked the deck had a good talk about New York—read our letters to each other.

Had service in the morning, Rev. Gibbs preaching.[86] Scenery very monotonous—low, flat cotton trees, and sand bars. Passed Vicksburg during the night. About 3 pm, stopped to take in wood at a very muddy bluff. The men had terrible work to clamber up the hill; very funny to see them get stuck in the mud, the mate swearing as usual. The trees here have a peculiar sort of moss growing on them which has a very strange appearance.[87]

85. Reiff has no detail on how the company managed the cold.

86. "Rev. Gibbs" not further identified.

87. Spanish moss (*Tillandsia usneoides*) noted also by others: "Some kind of lichen clothes the swamp-forests in mantles of unwholesome richness. It hangs in festoons and pendants; it droops or forms itself into jagged projections; it enlaces the tree-branches and hangs to them,

The sky is perfectly beautiful. A plantation about a mile down the river looks quite enchanting with its white houses and sycamore trees, the sun shining on them, the whole *coup d'oeil* is charming.[88]

Arrived at Natchez,[89] 5 pm. It is situated mostly on a bluff—they speak of Natchez on the *bank* and Natchez on the *bluff.* The principal part of the town cannot be seen from the river; along the bank it is a horrid-looking place, some[thing] like Pittsburgh is, along the banks of the river. [20(3)]

We here parted with Steve who had arrived at his destination, and I must say that a more open hearted, good natured, gentlemanly little fellow, I have seldom—or ever—met with. I trust we may be better acquainted. I am glad to say that he is a Gothamite.[90]

Beautiful sunset. Service in the evening by another minister, Rev. Gibbs and Mr Phillips having left us at Natchez. We kept going all night.

MONDAY JANUARY 21ST   MISSISSIPPI RIVER, NATCHEZ TO NEW ORLEANS

Windy, clear, and cold. Froze last night. We were taking in wood at a plantation when I arose, went ashore saw the first post & rail fence since I left Delaware. I met a very intelligent slave [who] said he was raised in North Carolina, [and] belonge[d] to a "Member of Legislature" who was going to "Baton Rouge."—said he had to cut a "cord of wood" today,[91] that he could

---

and winds around the trunk, and at last, so they tell, it kills the tree" (Sala, *America Revisited,* 277–78).

88. In using the term "coup d'oeil," Reiff is taking in the scene at a glance, literally at "a stroke of the eye" (*OED*, III, 1046).

89. Natchez, Mississippi, was established in 1715 and was the state's capital until it was replaced by Jackson in 1822. Natchez was the principal port for the trade from the plantations, and the town that Reiff saw was greatly enriched by the plantation owners, who built mansions in the city. It was reputed to have more millionaires living there before the Civil War than any other town in the United States.

90. The term "Gothamite," or New Yorker, comes from "Gotham," first used to describe New York in the 11 November 1807 edition of Washington Irving's *Salmagundi,* a satirical magazine whose title comes from an early seventeenth-century salad of many and disparate ingredients (*OED*, VI, 702).

91. A cord of wood was 128 cubic feet, corresponding to a woodpile 4 feet wide by 4 feet high by 8 feet long. However, different US states had different measures, so it is not clear whether the slave and Reiff understood quite the same thing in this conversation. See *OED*, III, 924.

do it by two o'clock—whatever he does after that was for himself.[92] [He] said he earned 75 cents every day last week for himself—lik'd his master but hates all overseers.

Several very beautiful plantations hereabouts.

The country is very flat—a "levee" all along, then plantations, which are generally lower than the river. Backed by forest, swamps, not a hill to be seen. Sugar plantations' houses built of brick for preparing the sugar. [20(3)ᵛ]

Our pilot (the oldest one) says he never felt so cold a winter or had such a trip before, and he has been on these water[s] over twenty years. [20(4)]

Arrived at Baton Rouge 12.45 pm.

This is the capital of the state. The State House stands so as to be seen coming down the river—and for a long time after you pass the town.[93] It is built of "Iron" part of which came from England—it looks like a marble building—it's very handsome[94]—somewhat resembles the N.Y. Arsenal without its wings, extends back.[95] A.M.S. Barracks is at this place, long low

92. The system the slave describes here was called "overwork," a well-understood system which did not work to the slaves' advantage. See Follett, *The Sugar Masters*, especially 140–41.

93. The building was designed by James H. Dakin (1806–1852), an American architect who championed the Gothic style. In 1847, Dakin won a competition for the new statehouse of Louisiana with a daring Gothic design, a style he chose "because no other style . . . could give suitable character to a building with so little cost" and because to use a Classic style would give a building "which would appear to be a mere copy of some other edifice already erected and often repeated in every city and town of our country" (Dakin, Diary Mss 509).

94. Not everyone agreed with Reiff, Twain commenting: "Sir Walter Scott is probably responsible for the Capitol Building; for it is not inconceivable that this little sham castle would ever have been built if he had not run the people mad, a couple of generations ago, with his medieval romances. The South has not yet recovered from the debilitating influence of his books. Admiration of his fantastic heroes and their grotesque 'chivalry' doings and romantic juvenilities still survives here. In an atmosphere in which is already perceptible the wholesome and practical nineteenth-century smell of cotton factories and locomotives; and traces of its inflated language and other windy humbuggeries survive along with it. It is pathetic enough that a whitewashed castle, with turrets and things—materials all ungenuine within and without, pretending to be what they are not—should ever have been built in this otherwise honourable place; but it is much more pathetic to see this architectural falsehood undergoing restoration and perpetuation in our day, when it would have been so easy to let dynamite finish what a charitable fire began, and then devote this restoration money to the building of something genuine" (*Life on the Mississippi*, 369–70).

95. The Arsenal in Central Park, at East Sixty-Fourth Street and Fifth Avenue, was built between 1847 and 1851, to the design of Martin E. Thomson (1786–1877). See Todd, *New York's Historic Armories*, 40.

white buildings,[96] near to which is General Taylor's former residence, a small white frame house near the river's bank.[97] Am perfectly surprised to find that he should live in such a little house; I certainly live in a much better house.

The town has a "French Aspect" [with] quite a number of brick buildings—it is situated on the left bank of the river—at a slight curve on ground a little elevated. After this, a succession of beautiful plantations.[98]

The weather astonishingly cold [and] windy. The river is now frequently two miles wide, not a particle of ice.

From here down pass'd most beautiful plantations, which certainly look charming the river seemed like a great canal; the land is lower than the river.

At night saw a beautiful fire caused by [20(4)^v] burning stubble (old sugar cane). Arrived at New Orleans, Tuesday 22 Jan'y at 3 am.[99] [20(5)]

TUESDAY JANUARY 22nd NEW ORLEANS

Left steamer "Swan" with Brough. The first part of the city struck me as somewhat resembling New York. Was surprised to find no raised levee, as I

96. The buildings Reiff saw were the Pentagon Barracks, constructed under the supervision of James Gadsden (1788–1858), between 1819 and 1825. The four buildings form the sides of a regular pentagon which is to the river on the fifth (Lane, *Architecture of the Old South: Louisiana*, 62).

97. Zachary Taylor (1784–1850), twelfth president of the United States. The house, which Taylor himself drew, stood on bluffs downriver from the barracks; it was demolished in 1859. See Bauer, *Zachary Taylor*, 112; he cites Thorp, "General Taylor's Residence in Baton Rouge," 765.

98. From here to New Orleans, the boat was passing down what was called Plantation Alley, a line of plantations that stretched from Baton Rouge to New Orleans.

99. The group, which was ten days behind schedule, were tracked by a no-doubt anxious theater manager, the *Picayune* of 22 January 1856 announcing that "they have been telegraphed as having passed Baton Rouge yesterday." The *Picayune* of the following day listed not only the main singers, but also noted that they had "auxiliaries," and in the course of the three weeks in New Orleans, would be performing "several of the most popular and favourite English operas . . . in the most attractive style." In other words, operas in English was the focus of the season's marketing. The reporter also commented: "On their passage down the river, the members of this talented troupe have given great pleasure to the party on board, by their liberal and courteous manner in which they yielded to the general wish to hear them sing; and, just before arriving at the end of their tedious voyage, the passengers pressed a unanimous vote of thanks to them for their kindness, and the delight at the performances given." This report suggests that the company gave more substantial performances than just the dancing and occasional song recorded by Reiff. It is also a contemporary acknowledgment that the river journey could be tedious.

had always supposed there was. Went to "St. Charles Hotel," a magnificent marble building, immensely high pillars in front; the steps go from under a sort of doorway.[100]

The levee is very wide, a portion of it about half its width (along the river) has a board flooring upon which is piled (promiscuously) cotton, flour, &c. The city is perfectly flat. In rainy weather the water will scarcely run any way, but soaks in the earth; of course, there are no cellars here!

Visited the French Opera at night.[101] *Lucia* was played, very good performance.[102] Mme Corson, the prima donna,[103] though nothing great is a very pleasing singer—the orchestra (of about 36) very good. The ladies in the theatre were dressed magnificently. They have what is called the parterre as sort of first tier, at the back of which are "stalls," private boxes which have a sort of window which can be shut down; in fact, it looked like anything but an "American Theatre"! Some of the "Ushers" were Negroes, but all spoke beautiful French. [20(5)ᵛ]

St. Charles Street runs nearly north and south—Royale St. commencing at the north end—the French part is north of Canal St. Julia St. crosses St.

100. The second hotel of that name—the first burned to the ground in 1851—was opened in 1853 and was designed by Isaiah Rogers (1800–1869) and George Purvis; it was demolished in 1894. The interior was as extravagant as Reiff's description of the exterior although it appears to have had its foibles; the hot and cold running water only ran in the basement (where the baths were located), and the steam engine which heated the water shook the whole building (Cable, *Lost New Orleans*, 114). According to the *Picayune* of 23 January 1856, Louisa Pyne (and her servant), Susan Pyne, William Harrison, and "a lady" all stayed at the St. Charles. Brough is listed as staying at both the St. Charles *and* the City Hotel (the latter is more likely). Reiff is not mentioned.

101. This was at the Théâtre d'Orléans, first opened in 1815, and then rebuilt after a fire in 1819, when the management was taken over by John Davis and then his son, Pierre. The theater was the major New Orleans venue for opera in French, and the company was the rival for many years of James H. Caldwell's St. Charles Theatre's operas in English. It made a considerable contribution to opera in the United States, presenting 109 different operas in nineteen seasons, some of them American premieres. The building Reiff knew was succeeded by James Gallier's French Opera House in 1859. See *GDO*, III, 984.

102. The opera *Lucia* was Gaetano Donizetti's opera *Lucia di Lammermoor*, a setting of a libretto by Salvatore Cammarano, based on Walter Scott's novel, *The Bride of Lammermoor*. The opera premiered at the Teatro di San Carlo in Naples on 26 September 1835. The advertised cast members were Mms. Laget-Planterre and Gambier, Messrs. Duluc, Junca, Crambade, and Laget (*Picayune*, 22 January 1856).

103. "Mme Corson" not further identified.

Charles running from the Mississippi to the "New Basin"—nearly in a north-west direction.[104] What seems strange here is to see the water in the gutters running from the river; it is pumped out at the back of the city by a steam engine. Another strange sight I witnessed: horses dragging an engine to a fire with some of the firemen very coolly taking a ride! It is stranger to me than it would be to an European. [21]

Figure 4. *Saint Charles Hotel*. A grandiose building and institution, the first hotel opened in 1837, only to be destroyed by fire in 1851. The building that replaced it, pictured above, opened in 1853 and was in a similar style to the first, although it lacked the outsized dome that towered over the portico. Reiff called there on 22 January 1856, and Louisa Pyne, her servant, Susan Pyne, William Harrison, and "a lady" from the opera company all stayed there.

104. The "New Basin" was a boat turning-basin at Rampart Street and Howard Avenue that was the terminus of the New Basin Canal. It was built by the New Orleans Canal and Banking Company, which was incorporated in 1831 with a capital of $4 million, with the aim of building a shipping canal from Lake Pontchartrain to the Uptown or "American" part of the city (Campanella, *Time and Place in New Orleans*, 70).

WEDNESDAY JANUARY 23rd   NEW ORLEANS

Crossed a wide street with a small park all along (unfinished) in the middle of it called Canal St., and as in the French part of the city which is narrow; [it] has a decided "Francais" appearance—*ici tout ilsa Français*[105]—No such thing as a row of uniform buildings are to be seen, each and every house seems to have been built without reference to any other. Met any quantity of Creole women; they wear no bonnets, but handkerchiefs on their heads *à la Française*. They speak French generally much better than they do English—all the niggers here speak French—those that do not, are an exception to a general rule.

Went to the Gaiety Theatre.[106] It is not as wide as Niblo's, but about as deep, having but two tiers of boxes; is beautifully fitted up. Good seats and well lighted. The performance was *Azuel, the Prodigal Son,*[107] during which was a "tableau vivant"[108] of the crucifixion![109] Which was *encored!!* In New York—with all its wickedness—it would be hissed off the stage. Only to imagine a man to make up for such a part as "Jesus Christ." And today, I heard they are about producing a tragedy called the Messiah! I think I shall

105. "Ici tout ilsa Français" is not French of any standard kind; the sentence may be of Creole structure, and have the sense of "everything's French round here."

106. Gaiety Theatre (formerly the Varieties Theatre) stood on Gravier Street between Baronne and Carondelet streets. The building Reiff visited had been opened in 1855 under the management of Dion Boucicault (1820–1890); its predecessor, the Varieties, was burned to the ground on 21 November 1854. The programs offered under Boucicault's management included comic opera, burletta, and ballet (Huber, *New Orleans*, 146). See also Melebeck, "A History of the First and Second Varieties Theatres of New Orleans."

107. Advertised as "the great biblical drama . . . or the Son of Israel." The bill was limited to one work only "so that the extreme purity and nobility of the subject may be unmingled with any other emotion" (*Picayune*, 23 January 1856). Reiff paid 75 cents to attend the evening's event.

108. For staging these, see Frost, *The Book of Tableux and Shadow Pantomimes*; for their history, see McCullough, *Living Pictures*.

109. Louis Keller (with his company of performers) produced a series of "religious pictures," a series of these tableaux: *The Simple Jewish Customs, The Luxurious Egyptian Idolatry, The Mysteries of Iais, Mythological Tableaux, Religious Pictures, Joy in Heaven,* and *Return of the Lost Sheep. The Crucifixion* was a new addition for that evening. See Palmquist and Kailbourn, *Pioneer Photographers*, 367; McCullough, *Living Pictures*, 38–61, with a photograph at figure 11 of Keller's "Washington Crossing the Delaware" of 1851; and Lawrence, *Strong on Music II*, 727, for an account of their performances later that year.

go and see it, if only for the horror of the thing. Only to think that this should be in the enlightened (?) America; it's absolutely dreadful. [22]

THURSDAY JANUARY 24th NEW ORLEANS

Walked through some parts of the French Quarter—the names of the streets are quite funny to an American, *viz:* Rue l'Union—Rue Poydras—Rue Phillippe—Rue d'Englien[110]—Rue Royale—Rue Dauphine—Rue Bourbon—Rue Orleans. "Great Men St." is in the French Quarter. Children in this part of the city speak French as if it was their native language and English an acquired one—they speak both well, but when playing together always speak French.

Quite cool for this time of year, here.

[Performance: *The Crown Diamonds,*[111] St. Charles Theatre.][112]

FRIDAY JANUARY 25th NEW ORLEANS

The Custom House on Canal St. which is building here, is truly grand. It is an immense building; the scaffolding around it is quite wonderful in itself.[113] The building is built of Quincy granite from Massachusetts, it has

110. "Rue d'Englien": Rue d'Enghien.

111. *The Crown Diamonds* (*Les Diamants de la couronne*), composed by Daniel Auber with a libretto by Eugène Scribe, premiered at Paris's Salle Favart on 6 March 1841. Cast was Lacatarina: Louisa Pyne; Don Henrique de Sandoval: William Harrison; Rebaledo: Joseph Stretton; Diana: Susan Pyne; Campo Muja: James Henry Horncastle; Don Sebastian: Mr. Duffield (*Picayune*, 24 January 1856).

112. The St. Charles Theatre, the second on the site, was constructed in 1843 for the theatrical partnership of Noah Ludlow (1795–1886) and Solomon Smith (1801–1869) and was the center of their Mobile–New Orleans–St. Louis circuit. In 1853, it was taken over by the actor Benedict "Ben" De Bar (1812–1877) as lessee and manager for eight very successful years until the outbreak of the Civil War in 1861. De Bar had also been stage manager for Ludlow and Smith. See Huber, *New Orleans*, 145–46.

113. Begun in 1849, interrupted by the Civil War, and completed in 1881, the Greek Revival building with neo-Egyptian details was used in part as an office by Major General Benjamin "Spoons" Butler (1818–1893) during the Union occupation, and in part as a prison for Confederate soldiers. A great dome was planned, but the great weight of the existing building caused the foundation to settle, and the dome was never completed. (In 1940, the building had sunk thirty inches, while the street level had been raised three feet.) Of particular interest is the famed Marble Hall, an architectural wonder. See Poesch and Bacot, *Louisiana Buildings*, 201–3.

been over nine years building and will probably take as many more before it is finished.[114]

[Performance: *Maritana,*[115] St. Charles Theatre.]

SATURDAY JANUARY 26th   NEW ORLEANS

In the American part of the town there [is] an immense quantity of dentists—The amount of business on the levee seems quite wonderful; principally cotton—the numerous steamboats and ships gives the place a decided mercantile look. [There are also] drays—no carts à la New York. Some parts of the levee I find is much higher than others; the ships lie up nearly (in some places) above one's head (the water line) when walking on the street. [22[v]] Opposite the French Cathedral is a very fine park something similar to St. George's in N.Y.,[116] interior of F.C. [23]

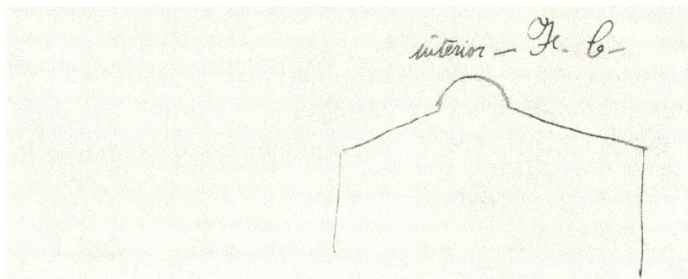

[Performance: *The Bohemian Girl,*[117] St. Charles Theatre.]

SUNDAY JANUARY 27th   NEW ORLEANS

Fine Day. At a little past seven was in the French Cathedral. The front has the appearance of some antique European cathedral (three steeples) some

114. In fact, it was not completed until 1881 (Poesch and Bacot, *Louisiana Buildings,* 201–3).

115. *Maritana,* composed by William Vincent Wallace with a libretto by Edward Fitzball, premiered at London's Theatre Royal, Drury Lane, on 15 November 1845. Cast was Don Cesar: William Harrison; Don Jose: Joseph Stretton; Charles II: James Henry Horncastle; Maritana: Louisa Pyne; Lazarillo: Susan Pyne (*Picayune,* 25 January 1856).

116. Reiff appears to be referring to New York's Stuyvesant Square, the fashionable square into which the congregation of the Episcopal Church of St. George had relocated into a new building in 1846–56, designed by Charles Otto Blesch and Leopold Eidlitz.

117. *The Bohemian Girl,* composed by Michael William Balfe with a libretto by Alfred Bunn,

few Moorish arches in it—but it seems something like an "olla podrida" of all styles.[118] On the inside, it has galleries which seem to be exactly mid-way between the floor & roof supported by plain pillars—the roof is this shape.

The arch, being clear from floor to ceiling, the galleries are under the lower portion of the roof. The organ was a very commonplace one, got twenty that are better in N.Y. Outside the "French Cathedral" is a bulletin board on which is posted notice of auction sales, &c., &c.[119]

From there walked over to the French Market on the River Street—it was certainly a very strange sight.[120] "Café, Café" was shouted to me by Men, Quadroon,[121] &c., for every market in this place has a number of coffee stands.

With the exception of one or two butchers, I did not hear any English spoken from the moment I entered the market until I left it.[122] Everything, and more besides, seems to be sold in these markets. One stand with poodle dogs and others with sour kraut, candles, candy, rabbits, birds, calico, cakes,

---

premiered at London's Theatre Royal, Drury Lane, on 27 November 1843. Cast was Thaddeus: William Harrison; Count Arnhem: Joseph Stretton; Devilshoof: James Henry Horncastle; Arline: Louisa Pyne; Gipsy Queen: Susan Pyne; Florestein: Mr. Duffield (*Picayune,* 26 January 1856).

118. The French cathedral—the Cathedral Church of St. Louis—occupies a site in Jackson Square that has been occupied by the Roman Catholic Church since 1718. It became a cathedral in 1793, and the building Reiff saw was primarily the result of designs by J. N. B. de Pouilly (d. 1875), and construction work using these plans in 1849–1850. "Olla podrida" is a Spanish stew with central ingredients of pork and beans, but unspecified other ingredients of meat and vegetables. Reiff appears to be calling it a mish-mash of stylistic elements (*OED,* X, 780).

119. "Outside the "French Cathedral . . . &c., &c"": this sentence appears on 23v.

120. The French Market in this form began in 1791 and, by the time of Reiff's visit, had gone through several iterations; see Magill, "French Market Celebrates 200th Anniversary," 7–10. George Sala noted in 1880: "As for the confusion of tongues in the market, it was simply delicious. French, Italian, Spanish, Portuguese, Dutch and 'Gumbo' contended with each other for supremacy; but French predominated." See Sala, *America Revisited,* 323–24.

121. A "quadroon" was the offspring of a mulatto, with a quarter Negro blood (*OED,* XII, 962).

122. Frederick Law Olmsted noted: "there were not only pure old Indian Americans, and the Spanish, French, English, Celtic and African, but nearly all possible mixed varieties of these and no doubt some other breeds of mankind" (*A Journey in the Seaboard Slave States,* 583).

pies, &c. &c. It seems so curious to hear the women quarrelling with the butchers in French. Outside the market were several tents with oysters; men were crying "Bon Marché" as loud as they could yell. Outside of the markets, Negroes, Negresses, and Quadroons have things in large baskets for sale; they (the people) squat down upon the ground.[123] The butchers' stalls are very close together. [24]

Figure 5. *Noon on Sunday at the French Market in New Orleans.* Reiff visited the French Market on Sunday, 27 January 1856, and saw stalls with "poodle dogs and others with sour kraut, candles, candy, rabbits, birds, calico, cakes, pies, &c., &c."

Nearly every person in the market seemed to be talking at once. The chattering of these French people would do credit to an army of monkeys; it seems anything but Sunday.[124] Here all seems "confusion, worse confounded."[125] Saw *considerable* quantities of "vermicelli" macaroni, &c., done

123. "They (the people) squat down upon the ground": "they (the people squat down upon the ground)" in Reiff.

124. "The creoles . . . go to Mass and also go to the market, which, on Sunday morning, is crowded, more noisy and fuller of negro and creole gaiety than on any weekday" (Nichols, *Forty Years of American Life*, I, 193).

125. John Milton, *Paradise Lost,* II.966.

up in paper for sale. A number of stands had nothing but bread to sell. Potatoes were piled on plates as we sometimes do with oranges in the north. It is customary to drink coffee when going to the French Market; it is thought to be the best in New Orleans. I did not indulge, but for the sake of escaping the horrid yelling of one woman I purchased some sort of French cake. From here returned to the Cathedral which was now crowded—wedged in between a nigger wench and a Creole—heard nearly every language spoken under the sun except English—around the altar were kneeling promiscuously whites, Creoles, Quadroons, Spaniards, &c. People walk in and out whenever they get tired—which (by the way) seems very often to be the case. Outside children were playing, men smoking in fact, France again. Returned towards my home—saw a gentleman and lady who were pricing some looking glasses, I watched them, [one] quarter of an hour afterwards, they were going to church—saw them go in—I went in, it was an American Church, the minister was preaching in broken English, evidently a Frenchman or a German.[126] [25]

MONDAY JANUARY 28th   NEW ORLEANS

Being very busy, did not go anywhere on Monday.
[Performance: *The Bohemian Girl*, St. Charles Theatre.]

TUESDAY JANUARY 29th   NEW ORLEANS[127]

Atherton and I visited the City Hall a beautiful building on Charles St., opposite a park. It is built of marble, granite steps—an entry way runs directly through the building, rooms each side, it is high.[128] We then walked up Charles St. to the railroad; saw many very nice dwelling houses with cedars

126. Reiff appears to be describing the third building of Christ Church, the first Episcopal congregation in the then largely Catholic New Orleans. This Gothic-style church stood on the corner of Canal and Dauphine streets and was built under the supervision of James Gallier the younger (1829–1870), to the design of the architect and diarist, Thomas Wharton (1814–1862). The building Reiff entered was given up in the 1880s and subsequently demolished (Cable, *Lost New Orleans*, 159).

127. "29th": mistakenly given the date of the 28th by Reiff.

128. The fine Greek Revival City Hall was proposed by the architect James Gallier (1798–1866) and finished to his design by 1850. See Poesch and Bacot, *Louisiana Buildings*, 198–99.

(very dark green) trimmed in the shape of a pineapple—looked beautiful. Quite warm, country very flat. Passed several little canals along the sides of the road; ditches are dug to somewhat drain the water off, not withstanding it is very muddy. After going about two and a half miles, we turned towards the river, passed several orange trees (which are in full blossom) got (an orange) it was very sour; the sweet ones having been picked some months since. We went home along the levee, passed three markets, at one place saw niggers compressing cotton bales for shipping, very interesting; first put it in, then a steam engine presses it, cords are then put around, it is released from its pressure, and is ready for shipping.

The ships look very fine along the levee—two or three abreast all their bows up stream.

Some of the street lamps (especially on the levee) are very peculiar large posts with a sort of arm to it the lamp is let down (to be lighted) by ropes— too much trouble to get up there with a ladder. [26]

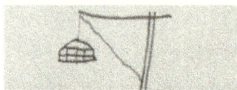

Visited the French Cemetery; the graves or vaults are all above ground, the coffins are put in end ways.[129] The tombs were dressed in the most extraordinary manner—looked as if some crazy person had done it. Many had a peculiar sort of wreath hanging on to them—one grave had two beautiful large china vases between two and three feet high, another (the end where the coffin had been put in) was so arranged that it greatly resembled the proscenium of a theatre.

This is a Catholic ground—there were inumerable crosses all about—on many graves were small crosses with Christ crucified—.

There was one high pile for some Portuguese society and another for firemen—French firemen![130] The ground was covered with small pebbles and shells to keep it from being muddy. Little cupids were on some graves and as they were made of plaster which the rain had partly destroyed, the appearance of some of them was ludicrous in the extreme.

129. This is St. Louis Cemetery I, opened in 1789, today surrounded by Basin, Tremé, and St. Louis streets; when Reiff visited, it had to a large extent already been superseded by the 1823 St. Louis Cemetery II (Huber, *New Orleans Architecture*, III, 4–5).

130. The Society Tombs were those for groups of people who did not have a family vault. The Portuguese Society Tomb to which Reiff refers was constructed in 1850 (Huber, *New Orleans Architecture*, III, 9).

The whole affair struck me as being decidedly more *funny* than solemn.
[26 1/2]

[Performance: *The Bohemian Girl*, St. Charles Theatre.]

WEDNESDAY JANUARY 30th   NEW ORLEANS

[Performance: *Cinderella*,[131] St. Charles Theatre.]

THURSDAY JANUARY 31th   NEW ORLEANS

[Performance: *Cinderella*, St. Charles Theatre.]

FRIDAY FEBRUARY 1st   NEW ORLEANS

An uncommonly warm day. Atherton and I started to go to the Battle
Ground[132]—on our way saw a young Indian boy—lying in a beastly state
of intoxication—he had the most beautiful head of hair I ever beheld—it
was slightly curly and very long. Arrived at the "Gulf Rail Road Station,"
a miserable-looking place and more *miserable-looking cars*.[133] They were
absolutely filthy, the platforms run to a point—the seats had immovable

131. *Cinderella; or, The Fairy and Little Glass Slipper*, an opera after *La Cenerentola, ossia
La bontà in trionfo*, composed by Gioachino Rossini with a libretto by Jacopo Ferretti after
Charles Perrault's 1697 story, *Cendrillon*, premiered at Rome's Teatro Valle on 25 January 1817;
by 1855, this version—*Cinderella; or, The Fairy and Little Glass Slipper* and described as a
hodgepodge—was being attributed to M. Rophino Lacy. Cast was Prince: William Harrison;
Dandini: Joseph Stretton; Baron: James Henry Horncastle; Pedro: Ben De Bar; Alidoro: Mr.
Duffield; Cinderella: Louisa Pyne; Clorinda: Susan Pyne; Fairy Queen: Marion Macarthy;
Thisbe: Clementina Booth; Fairy Sunbeam: M'lle Vallée (*Picayune*, 30 January 1856).

132. The site of the battle of New Orleans on 8 January 1815 at Chalmette, which saw a
decisive defeat for the British under Major General Sir Edward Pakenham (1778–1815), commander of the British forces at the Battle of New Orleans, and a triumph for the American
forces, commanded by Major General Andrew Jackson (1767–1845), later seventh president of
the United States. It was the last major battle of the War of 1812, and while technically unnec-
essary—the Treaty of Ghent that ended the war had been signed on 24 December 1814—the
victory was decisive in building the image of a new, go-ahead America opposing an older,
conservative Britain. See, among other discussions, that by Remini, *The Battle of New Orleans*, chap. 9.

133. Reiff and Atherton are arriving at the Mexican and Gulf Railroad Company's terminus
on the corner of Elysian Fields and Good Children Street (now St. Claude Street). The company operated from 1837 to 1867, and the line ran from this depot to Shell Beach. See *Crescent
City Business Directory*, 45.

backs—we were the only pure white men in the car. Some Creoles, & Indians, semi-French and Negroes. Though only going a short distance some of the passengers began to gamble; the Indians smoked.

We had the windows open the sun shining brightly in, very warm—an engine—a mean looking one (built in Philadelphia by Norris) managed to get us four miles in half an hour. When we were informed we had arrived at our destination—got out (in a swamp) met a fellow with a gun—seemed to be frightened at us—probably thought we were going to kill him—walked towards the river found an old Negro guide who showed us about—he said that he was raised in Virginia, but has been here a long time; his present master is a French Creole, he doesn't like him because he does not give him (the Negro) enough to eat—said he would like to be free.

He seemed to have very little to do—was a perfect specimen of a Negro— spoke so I could scarcely understand him—when he spoke of Virginia—he said America—as if [27] *this* was some Foreign Place. Showed us the embankments which are now about three to four feet high and about a mile long—the canal is now almost entirely filled in—the ground is swampy and level—it is about half a mile from the river—we were shown the tree under which General Pakenham was carried after having been wounded[134]—it is a beautiful live oak, it was in full leaf; I pulled a handful of the leaves off. The birds were singing gaily and the sun shone brightly—it was so warm that standing perfectly still (in the sunshine) I was so warm that for comfort's sake I was obliged to take my coat off and go in my shirt sleeves. About an eighth of a mile from the "Pakenham Tree," there is a monument about being erected in commemoration of the battle—they were working at the base (which is of brick) at present about five feet high. The monument is to be 150 high it is about forty feet at the base—the material is to be marble and granite. Nigger masons, with one (a regular Legree)[135] white boss, were[136] to work on the monument.[137]

134. Pakenham, a brother-in-law of the Duke of Wellington, was killed in the final battle on 8 January 1815 (H. M. Chichester, rev. Roger T. Steamer, *ODNB*, XLII, 422–23).

135. Legree is a character in Harriet Beecher Stowe's *Uncle Tom's Cabin*. A northerner, he is the vicious white plantation owner to whom Tom is sold by Augustine St. Clare's widow, and who reneges on the slave owner's pledge to free Tom.

136. "Were": "was" in Reiff.

137. Called the Chalmette Monument, it was built by Newton Richards, a builder responsible for many of the monuments in Louisiana's cemeteries. The brainchild of the Young Men's

From here walked down to the river, passing some beautiful plantations. The houses (generally) having orange tree hedges which grow about twenty feet high. The leaves were perfectly green—and the trees were full of oranges (sour ones) they looked charming. About the houses were generally magnolia trees in full leaf—the leaves are of very dark sombre green. [28] Walked up along the levee about a mile the river was as placid as a lake, not a ripple to be seen, the warm sun. Beautiful plantations on both sides of the river, the Negro cabins (painted white or whitewashed) the new young grass, the gardens of green salad, &c., the orange trees full of fruit, the dark magnolia trees—the wild cactus, and (pineapple shaped) cedars gave the whole an enchanting aspect, and this the 1st of February!

We had now arrived at a large sugar factory.[138] Popped in on the ground floor, the engine and place for grinding the cane; then the second floor, where the sugar was in large earthen pots, *sugar loaf shape*. Men were digging it. I tested the different kinds of sugar pretty thoroughly. On the next floor were all sorts of things. One sort of boiler for boiling the sugar, the drippings being molasses.

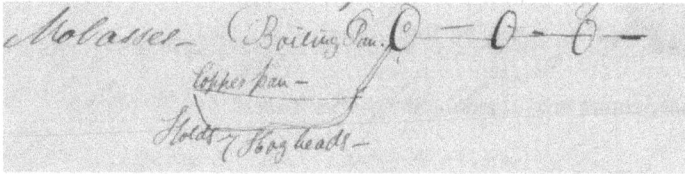

On the fourth floor, men were refining the sugar in large flat tanks, about twelve feet long, five wide and three deep, skimming the dirt off with copper ladles. Several of the workmen were Germans. From this building, we obtained a grand view of the country and the city in the distance.

We walked home along the levee; the road from here to the city is lined with small but rich plantations. The houses all having fine [29] door yards at least three hundred feet deep. The hedges being generally (nearly always)

Jackson Committee formed in an effort to create a memorial commemorating the battle's heroes, it was conceived in 1839, but not completed until 1908. See Samuel Wilson, *Plantation Houses on the Battlefield of New Orleans*, 35.

138. These were frequently referred to as "Sugar Houses"; the later (and illuminating) account of a visit to a sugar plantation by Ernst von Hesse-Wartegg comments on attempts to divorce sugar production from the growing of sugarcane (*Travels on the Lower Mississippi*, 201–5).

orange trees and magnolia trees. Met many slaves all of whom spoke French; met one who spoke such bad English as to be scarcely able to understand him. On our way, came to two convents; a Nigger was sitting by the gate of the first one (he could not speak any English), he told me (in French) that it was a convent kept by Mlle St. Clair.[139] A high board fence was around the grounds which prevented me seeing what it was like—this one (so the Nigger informed me) was for the rich people, the second for the poor. This (the last) having an open paling fence, I reverentially looked in—the grounds seemed very fine, magnolia trees, oranges, cedars, &., and a good comfortable looking house.

We next (about a mile further) came to a M. S—— Barracks.[140] Went in under an arch way it was about four acres surrounded by two storey (yellow) brick buildings. We found a German woman in the principal building, and by aid of some extraordinary motions, &c., (for she could speak nothing *but* German) we found out that there were no soldiers there at present, but that there would be on the tomorrow—from New York, they drill soldiers here. [29ᵛ]

We got home at nearly three o'clock having come down New Levee St. Felt very tired, have walked about seven miles.

Very warm—the nights, however, get very cool.

[Performance: *Cinderella*, St. Charles Theatre.]

SATURDAY FEBRUARY 2ⁿᵈ   NEW ORLEANS

Pleasant day. In the morning (with Anderton, prompter)[141] saw the celebrated "Bearded Woman" and an immense giantess over seven feet high.

In the afternoon went to see the "Thomas Swan" sail. Mrs. Andrews (Captain's Wife), Hester (the screecher) his niece, Meriman, Cosgrave, and Fulton (Engineer) all very, very, clever, treated us (Swan, George, and me)

139. The convent for "rich people" Reiff saw was the Ursulines' convent, which had moved out of the French Quarter in 1824 to a riverside site, where they remained until 1912 (Campanella, "The Ursuline Nuns' Lost Landmark on the Mississippi River," 14–15).

140. Reiff appears to be visiting what (since their capture by Federal forces in 1862) are now known as the Jackson Barracks. They were constructed under the 1832 Federal Fortifications Act between 1832 to 1836, as the "New Orleans Barracks," and were first occupied by troops in 1837 (National Register of Historic Places).

141. Anderton, the prompter of the St. Charles Theatre.

to champagne. Fulton says he will try and get down here before we go, so that we can go up with him. Vows he will try, if he *"bursts his boilers."* Shook hands with me very warmly, said he would make me a "coal ring."[142] He's a fine open hearted, good fellow, and a very handsome man withal.

We watched the "Swan" till she was out of sight—felt quite an affection for the old boat which had brought us down through such enormous ice. The Captain and pilots hallooa to us, when they were out in the stream. [30]

Henry's birthday.[143] I was thinking about him, just after supper while walking on the veranda in front of the house—without even my hat on! It was so very pleasant.

[Performance: *Cinderella*, St. Charles Theatre.]

SUNDAY FEBRUARY 3rd   NEW ORLEANS

Atherton and I went to the French Market. Last night the weather changed suddenly (rained), and this morning it is quite cool.

Saw the same things at the market as last Sunday with the addition of twenty-five Indians; they were on the levee, had mostly baskets for sale. They were wrapped up in dirty blankets and seemed to suffer from the cold. I quite pitied them.

We went to mass at half past nine.[144] Sat upstairs, could not help remarking that the chairs near the altar were mostly occupied by Negroes; they were also in the majority upstairs. The priests came in—eight boys following—they seemed to march in and all three officiated at once. The choir consisted of male voices entirely; they sang some very good chorales. The organ struck me as being better than it did last Sabbath, especially the low pedal C which is a beautiful note; the Organ has about 25 stops and two banks of keys.

The singing was nearly all in the key of C, and even the priest in his chants sang in C. Once or [30ᵛ] twice he modulated into G, but apparently getting frightened, he almost immediately came back to that horrid C again. When the minister began to preach, Atherton and myself, presuming that

142. A "coal ring" (here, literally, a ring) seems here to be made out of jet, a type of lignite, and a gemstone of organic origin. Long used in jewelry, it was used as a mourning stone in the nineteenth century (*OED*, VIII, 223).

143. "Henry" not further identified, although possibly Henry Horncastle; Reiff does not refer to him elsewhere as "Henry," and the context suggests someone removed from the scene.

144. At the French Catholic cathedral. See note 118.

possibly the sermon would do us but little good (being in French), got disgusted with these foreigners—and evaporated.

The paintings over the arch (through the centre of the church) are very beautiful but give it a theatrical aspect; the "fixings" about the altar were very showy; the windows are stained glass with a cross as the principal figure in the glass.

At half past 11, went to a fire in Chartres St., about two streets above Canal. It was almost out! The engines were similar to the N.Y. ones—the firemen sang a sort of chorus while at work. Billiards saloons, and all such things, in general, were open.

MONDAY FEBRUARY 4th   NEW ORLEANS

Very cold; ice in the gutters. In the afternoon (alone) took a long walk up Canal St. Saw a large yard for storage of cotton and some cotton presses—the yard was covered with small pebbles to prevent its being muddy.

Turned down towards "French Town" and walked out on the Shell Road; it is very level, the land all about being swampy—looked very pretty—the "veranda houses," the distant woods, very flat of course, &c., &c., &c. [31]

Coming back, I saw a large building to the right of Canal St. Went to it, it stood back from the street about 75 feet with a fine door yard. Walked in, found a man who told me it was the Charity Hospital.[145] Having assured[146] there was no contagious disease in the building, I visited one of the wards; there were about twenty-five patients. The head of the beds were turned towards the wall; at the foot of each bed was a small placard telling who, when entered and the disease of the patient. One Frenchman (who was sitting up in his bed) struck me as being particularly melancholy; his hair was cropped short, he seemed as if he had been of a very lively disposition, and that as if the fact of being obliged to be in bed was enough of itself to make him ill.

I remarked to the Paddy who was showing me the Elephant[147] "that as he has left the door open that it probably made the sick very uncomfortable." He replied: "Oh no, these are quite healthy fellows." He wished to show me

145. This was the fourth Charity Hospital, built in 1834 on what is now Tulane Avenue. The Sisters of Charity were paid by the state, and an outbuilding housed the insane. See "The New Orleans Charity Hospital," *Harper's Weekly*, 3 September 1859, 569–70.

146. "Assured": Reiff appears to mean "ascertained," or "assured myself."

147. "Paddy": Slang for Irishman (*OED*, XI, 55). The reference to being shown the "Ele-

some more wards in the more-sickly department, but the unfortunate looks of these poor sick creatures had quite satisfied me, so thinking I had sufficiently "supped of horrors,"[148] I declined making any further researches.

There are some wards (where you get better attendance) which charge a dollar a day. The building is something longer than the N.Y. Institution for the Blind[149]—but deeper, it has large side wings which [31ᵛ] run back from the building about 125 feet, the building is four stories high—a large yard the whole covers about three acres of ground. Saw men carrying immense kettles of tea, saw at least six casks (ordinary sized ones) of tea pass me in these kettles. From the kitchen (in one wing) to the other wing there is a small railroad—the victuals is put in a small car—which has shelves—and then a couple of men pull it across the yard. [32]

[Performance: *Cinderella*, St. Charles Theatre.]

TUESDAY FEBRUARY 5ᵗʰ   NEW ORLEANS

Mardi Gras.[150] Somewhat cool—in the morning saw all sorts of queer costumes (masked) in the streets. This day, they generally flour the Niggers and common people, and in fact everyone is in danger more or less. Was much amused by seeing two Quadroons flour each other in Royale St., also

phant" is possibly a play on "to see the elephant," a slang expression recorded as current in 1835, and meaning "to see life," or "to gain knowledge by experience" (*OED*, V, 134). Reiff seems to have met a particularly garrulous person keen to "educate" him.

148. "Supped of horrors" is probably a version of "supp'd full with horrors," from *Macbeth*, V.v.1.

149. The New York Institute for the Blind was opened in 1832 by Samuel Akerly, John Dennison Russ, and Samuel Wood on the Bowman estate now near Ninth Avenue and Thirty-Fourth Street. The building to which Reiff refers was the 1837 building, designed by the architect Martin Euclid Thompson (1786–1877); see Adele Hast, "Martin Euclid Thompson," *ANB*, XXI, 567. Reiff's father, Anton Reiff Sr., was on the original teaching faculty and worked there for forty years (Blumhofer, *Her Heart Can See*, 88).

150. "Mardi Gras": appears in a separate heading in Reiff. The origins of the New Orleans Mardi Gras lie in traditions brought to Louisiana by French settlers. Called Fat Tuesday in English, and observed as Shrove Tuesday, it is the day before Ash Wednesday. However, there has long been a Mardi Gras season, from Epiphany leading up to Lent, and by 1743, there are records of costume balls, and later processions and the wearing of masks in the streets. By 1833, money was raised to support an official Mardi Gras celebration. The Mardi Gras as described by Reiff (including the throwing of flour) is corroborated in other sources; see, for example, Creecy, *Scenes in the South*, 44.

by two Frenchmen in costumes and masks, one as a woman, the other as her Cavalier. They ventured into Canal St. [where] a lot of American Boys flew at the man and pummelled him with large sticks.[151] They retreated up to Carondelet St.,[152] where cavalier made a stand, but was obliged to again flee. When he got to the corner of Baronne St. (at the Episcopal Church), his mask was torn off, his nose streaming with blood. Atherton, I, and several others interfered, when the boys said: "He's no business in Canal St." and seemed quite indignant that they could not beat poor Frenchy as much as they pleased. It seems that it is a custom among the boys (the American ones) if they catch a French boy as mask this side of Canal St., they kick him like fury.

Saw a queer dress (burlesque) a man in woman's guise on horseback.

All the Niggers suffer today; they are quite white with the flour thrown on them. In fact, all New Orleans is besprinkled with flour. [32ᵛ] There were six mask balls in the evening.[153] To the one at the St. Charles, I received an invitation ticket. N.B. A Season Ticket to a series of balls, this being[154] the only one I will be able to avail myself of. I went at little past eleven (disguised with a pair of huge whiskers and a pair of spectacles) found a very poor attendance. Sat in the boxes for at least an hour, all the ladies on the floor were masked excepting two, one of whom was very beautiful.

Horncastle was disguised as a Yorkshire man; after I found *him out,* we walked around the room. The Pynes and Harrison, with Barney Williams and wife,[155] were in the boxes. I afterwards went to them (but not until I

---

151. The 1856 Mardi Gras was a particularly violent one, and the processional floats were thought poor; one response to this was the establishment for the next year of the Anglo-American carnival organization "The Mystic Krewe of Comus," a "secret society" with a closed membership which promoted more elaborate floats and costumes. See Reid Mitchell, *All on a Mardi Gras Day,* 23–28, 38–50.

152. "Carondelet St.": "Candolet St." in Reiff.

153. The six balls were the one that Reiff attended at the St. Charles Hotel; the Mardi Gras Masked Society Ball at the Théâtre d'Orléans; the Grand Military Masquerade and Fancy-Dress Ball at the Pelican Theatre; the Grand Military, Mask and Fancy-Dress Subscription Ball at the Odd Fellows Hall; the Fancy Dress and Masquerade Ball at the Union Hall; and the Young Bachelors' Fancy Dress Ball at the Masonic Grand Lodge Hall.

154. It is not known who sent Reiff a ticket.

155. The comedic duo was Barney Williams (1823–1876, born in Ireland as Bernard O'Flaherty) and his wife, Mary. Although he emigrated to New York as a young man (and had an early career as a negro minstrel, a clogger, and in circus routines), he was regarded as em-

had shaved); they pointed out to me (as they said) [Marion] McCarthy[156] and Mrs De Bar.[157] I sought McCarthy, but it proved to be someone else, the supposed Mrs De Bar. I picked her pocket of her handkerchief and, instead of finding (as I had expected) marked Harriett, it was Lisette, evidently another mistake.[158] I began to get *riled* against these two ladies who were so extremely anxious that I should come, and they would not make themselves known. Almost determined to go home, but [33] while walking through the room, a "Mask" poked me in the region of the ribs and said "Mr Reiff, if you dance as well as you conduct an orchestra, I should be pleased to dance with you." She was with a gentleman, and before I could see her, another lady with light hair said: "You are looking very well Mr. Reiff, very pretty tonight, pray who curled your hair?" This was more than I could bear—as I had not the most distant idea who they were—while standing in the room while cogitating who they were, I was suddenly seized from behind by two ladies (masked, of course). They were dressed magnificently, the tallest in pink and white, whom I immediately recognised as Marion McCarthy and the other as Mrs De Bar. In fact, they made themselves known to me; they positively assured me (and I afterwards found out it really was so) that they had just come in from Odd Fellows Hall.[159] While walking around the room

---

bodying the soul of Ireland; indeed, the *Picayune* in 1854 found him to be, "in the presentation of the genuine Paddy, the *true Irish peasant.*" The husband-and-wife team (he married Maria Pray in 1850) on occasion advertised themselves as the "original impersonators of Irish and Yankee life," and were often pictured as a duo, including one woodcut in the *Illustrated London News,* 26 July 1856.

156. Marion Macarthy suffered a nervous breakdown—apparently from having to learn a large number of Shakespearean parts in rapid succession—and ended her days in a mental asylum; see Logan, *Before the Footlights and Behind the Scenes,* 446–47. She played the Fairy Queen in the Pyne and Harrison Company's production of *Cinderella*; see 30 January 1856.

157. Henrietta "Hattie" De Bar (1828–1894), née Vallee, born in Philadelphia. She was an actress and second wife to Benedict De Bar, lessee and manager of the St. Charles Theatre; she retired from the stage in 1857 while they were still in New Orleans (Brown, *History of the American Stage,* 94).

158. "Lisette" was McCarthy's role in the burletta *The Swiss Cottage.*

159. Situated on the corner of Camp and Lafayette streets, the Odd Fellows Hall was built in 1852 to the design of George Purves (d. 1883); see Lane, *Architecture of the Old South: Louisiana,* 114. Described by the *New York Times* as "the most magnificent building in the city except the St. Charles," it burned to the ground on 7 July 1866. Reiff would perform there when the company returned from Mobile.

with them, some young sprigs who recognised Marion M (by her curly hair) requested to dance with her, but she invariably replied that she was engaged to me. Of course, I was obliged to dance with her after that, which was particularly unfortunate as I had previously promised (Mask No 1 in blue tuck up) to dance with her this very dance, and besides, I was obliged to leave Mrs De Bar in the middle of the room. Impudence, however, got me through. I afterwards vowed to Mask No 1 [33ᵛ] that I had been looking all over for her, could not find out who she was.

Mrs De Bar and Marion M. completely took possession of me; it was rather distressing as Mr Ben De Bar[160] was in the boxes. However, managed to get off home without anything particular happening.

Jim Otis[161] was there, said to Harrison, Williams, &c., that he had known me since I was a boy. Anderton was very clever, &c. [34]

[Performance: *Cinderella*, St. Charles Theatre.]

WEDNESDAY FEBRUARY 6ᵗʰ   NEW ORLEANS

Beautiful day. Writing all day.

[Performance: *La Sonnambula*,[162] St. Charles Theatre, Harrison benefit.]

THURSDAY FEBRUARY 7ᵗʰ   NEW ORLEANS

Atherton and I went to Algiers or Gretna on the opposite side of the river.[163] It lies low; the buildings are mostly of wood, one story with the conical shape roofs. One of the best, and in fact about the only, fine building in the place,

160. Benedict De Bar (1812–1877), the lessee and manager of the St. Charles Theatre; he came to New Orleans from England, as an actor, and later became the stage manager at the St. Charles for Noah Ludlow and Sol Smith, and on their retirements, took over their interests in New Orleans (in 1853) and St. Louis (in 1855). He left New Orleans at the outbreak of the Civil War (Ben Alexander, "Benedict De Bar," *ANB*, VI, 307–8).

161. James F. Otis, the American music critic.

162. *La Sonnambula*, with music by Vincenzo Bellini and a text by Felice Romani, premiered at Milan's Teatro Carcano on 6 March 1831. Cast was Elvino: William Harrison; Count Rudulpho: Joseph Stretton; Alessio: James Henry Horncastle; Lisa: Susan Pyne; Teresa: Mrs. Booth; Amina: Louisa Pyne (*Picayune*, 6 February 1856).

163. Algiers was established in 1719 and was originally owned by Jean Baptiste Le Moyne, Sieur de Bienville (1680–1767); it was not annexed to New Orleans until 1870. Gretna, slightly upriver, was founded in 1836 (then called Mechanicsham). See Seymour, *The Story of Algiers, 1718–1896*.

was the Opelousas Railroad Depot.[164] It was of brick with handsome iron arches to support the roof; the large and side doors of the depot were of slats or lattice-work, so as to admit of plenty of air.

We also saw a large foundry—it had a decided Southern look. Everything seemed slovenly about it—they were casting while we were there. The building and grounds (yard) I should say covered about three acres. The price of the ferry was five cents, very cheap for here; I expected it would have been a dime at least.[165]

[Performance: *The Daughter of the Regiment*,[166] St. Charles Theatre, Pyne benefit.]

Friday February 8th   New Orleans

Beautiful day; overcoats obsolete. Had a tooth fill'd by Dr. Knapp (next door to my hotel) one of the first dentists in New Orleans.[167] He has letters from Henry Clay, Andrew Jackson,[168] &c., speaking in the highest terms of his skill. I presumed, therefore, he must be good, and therefore cheerfully paid him the $8.00 he asked me.[169]

In the afternoon, I dined with Anderton (prompter); he lives with a Mr John M. Powell, the marine editor [34v] of the *Picayune*. The house, at 43 Perdido St.; his place of business, 51 Camp St.

164. The New Orleans, Opelousas, and Great Western line was begun in 1852, and expanded after the General Assembly of Louisiana authorized the issuance of state bonds in 1853; the route started in Algiers. See Reed, *New Orleans and the Railroads*, 108–20.

165. The ferries began operating between New Orleans and Algiers from about 1827, and from New Orleans and Gretna (then called Mechanicsham) in 1838.

166. *The Daughter of the Regiment* (*La fille du régiment*), with music by Gaetano Donizetti and a text by Jules-Henri Vernoy de Saint-Georges and Jean-François Alfred Bayard, premiered by the Opéra-Comique at Paris's Salle de la Bourse on 11 February 1840. Cast was Tonio: William Harrison; Sergeant Sculpizio: James Henry Horncastle; Hortensius: Ben De Bar; Marie: Louisa Pyne; Marchioness: Susan Pyne (*Picayune*, 7 February 1856).

167. Frederick H. Knapp, Dental Surgeon, at 155 Canal Street; his advertisement claimed that "his prices are the same that he has charged for the last fifteen years" (*Picayune*, 28 January 1856, and others).

168. Andrew Jackson (1767-1845), later seventh president of the United States, was the American general at the Battle of New Orleans in 1815. See Robert V. Remini, "Andrew Jackson," *ANB*, XI, 732–37.

169. Eight dollars in 1856 was the equivalent of some two hundred dollars today. See Inflation Calculator.

As his "*establishment*" is very common thing in the South,[170] and would be a wonder in the North, I shall devote a few words to it. After drinking a glass of whiskey with Anderton, we were asked in a little back room to dinner. It was plainly furnished, but with a very good French "boudoir piano."[171] The dinner was "quasi Français"; soup, claret wine, &c.[172] After dinner, a very dark Quadroon came in with a little boy. I found out that the first was Powell's mistress and the latter his little son! The boy was quite pretty, of course a half white and black.

His mistress played the piano for me—and done it very nicely too. I then played, and while at a set of variations, I heard someone bounce in the room laughing in the most boisterous manner. Turning round I beheld a most beautiful girl, not only as regards her face but of the most exquisite form. I was introduced, and I must say she would have thrown Lady Gay Spanker quite in the shade had the latter lady been present.[173] She was going to ride in the afternoon—asked me if I rode *well!* Told her I thought I could hold on. She had first been to see a tiger (!) which has been bought for her as a sort of lap dog; she said he was perfectly [35] docile, and she did love it so. She said it put its head in her lap and purr'd just like a cat. She was kind enough to offer when I returned to New Orleans to show me—not the elephant— but the tiger. I declined most modestly, although told her I should be most happy to meet the mistress of the beast (tiger).

I concluded she *was* a fast girl; she evidently knew something of me (by some words she dropped during our conversation) and I supposed very probably she was one of the Masks who spoke to me the other night. After

170. "Common thing in the South": "common in thing the South" in Reiff.

171. The London piano maker John Hopkinson (d. 1886, active in London from 1849) was one of the first to advertise a "Boudoir Piano." The term has meant various things, but in all cases appears to mean a less than full-sized model of whatever style was being referred to, a model suitable for a private sitting room. See "A History of John Hopkinson, Piano Manufacturer."

172. Reiff appears to be suggesting that the meal was served *à la française,* a method of serving in which a large number of dishes were placed on the table, from which the diners then served themselves. This method may well have seemed archaic to Reiff, the New Yorker; *service à la française* was being replaced by *service à la russe,* in which one course followed another (*OED,* I, 290).

173. Reiff appears to be referring to the character of Lady Gay Spanker, from Dion Boucicault's 1841 farce, *London Assurance.* Lady Spanker is an overdrawn horsey character, whose laugh "rings loudest in the field," and who falls immediately in love with Sir Harcourt Courtly; as Reiff later observes of this young lady, she is a "fast" woman.

smoking a cigar and being invited to come there on my return from Mobile, I vamoosed.

[Performance: *The Daughter of the Regiment,* St. Charles Theatre.]

SATURDAY FEBRUARY 9th   NEW ORLEANS

Four years ago, I commenced my engagement with Purdy.[174] It is a most beautiful day. Today is to be inaugurated the celebrated equestrian statue of Jackson in Jackson Square in front of the French Cathedral. Most of the procession formed in front of my windows on Canal St. George and I wended our way through the crowd towards the square.[175] Met in Royale St. about three hundred boys in a procession, they yelled on a very high key quite unlike the shouts of boys in the North; it was perfectly hideous.

The appearance of the streets (Royale in particular) was very novel, the French and American flags—the verandas filled with Americans, French, Creoles, Quadroons, Niggers, &c. [35ᵛ] The square was jammed; even the steeple of the Cathedral was full and the peculiar buildings each side of it were crowded.[176] Atherton and I getting jammed up in the crowd completely surrounded by *anything* but Americans—the odour *was not like* strawberries, in fact, more like garlic. In Canal St. we saw some companies carrying

174. Alexander H. Purdy (d. 1862). During the period 1850 to 1857, he managed New York's Chatham Theatre (1839–62), on Chatham Street between Roosevelt and James, which during his tenure was known as Purdy's National Theatre. The building was extensively renovated in 1852, and it appears from this remark that Purdy must have employed Reiff there as part of his reopening plans; Purdy was nothing if not a grandiose showman and was responsible for introducing *Uncle Tom's Cabin* on the stage. The heavy emphasis here given to the appointment by Reiff coupled with his age (he would then have been twenty-two) suggests that this was his first professional engagement (Wilmeth and Bigsby, *Cambridge History of American Theatre,* I, 88).

175. Jackson Square was formerly known as the Place d'Armes, and the statue to which Reiff refers was cast by the American sculptor Clark Mills (1810–1883); Mills's equestrian statues of General Andrew Jackson are also in Washington, DC, and Nashville, Tennessee. See Cowan, *New Orleans Yesterday and Today,* 42–45. A listing of those in the procession and a note on the order of events can be found in the *Picayune,* 6 February 1856.

176. The "peculiar buildings" were, to the left of the cathedral, the Cabildo (1795–99), and, to the right, the Presbytère (1791–1813); both buildings were designed by Don Gilberto Guillemard, but both were extensively remodeled in 1847 to their present-day appearance. See Barbara SoRelle Bacot, "New Orleans after the Fires," in Poesch and Bacot, *Louisiana Buildings,* 37–42. Wharton gives this account of the affair: "Then we threw ourselves into the vast human

their arms, lying back of their shoulders on their knapsacks. Recognised Hewitt among the Continentals[177]—the bands were very shy.[178]

Figure 6. *Inauguration of the Jackson Statue, New Orleans.* The cast of Clark Mills's equestrian statue of Andrew Jackson was erected in Jackson Square (formerly the Place d'Armes) and was dedicated on 9 February 1856. Reiff saw the procession assembling and attended the dedication, commenting that it was rather "bad . . . that the statue is galloping up the country going *from* the battle ground" of New Orleans. The engraving shows, anachronistically, part of the old front of the cathedral, rebuilt in the 1850s.

---

stream and moved down Chartres Street to the 'Cathedral Square' where we took up an advantageous position clear of the crowd and saw the long 'cortege' as it filed past us into the square with rich banners and excellent music. . . . The Pontalba Buildings, their long galleries filled with the richest costumes sparkling in full sunshine, and gay military uniforms, and gilded banners grouped around the 'Monument' in the Centre, or glancing among the beautiful evergreens and foliage of the Square" (Wharton, *Queen of the South,* 110).

177. See Reinders, "Militia in New Orleans," 33–42.

178. Reiff presumably means they played little.

In the afternoon we went around into the square. The statue is certainly beautiful; it struck me, however, as rather bad, however, that the statue is galloping up the country going *from* the battle ground. It is, however, done (I suppose) that his face may be seen from the river. It was exactly four o'clock by the Cathedral clock while I first looked at the "staty."[179]

Went to the French Opera—*Moïse*[180] was done,[181] the orchestra and chorus were excellent. The mechanical and scenic department was also good. The *prima donna* had a shocking shrill voice, the tenor looked like a great butcher; he sang flat. Junca (*Moïse*), the baritone, was very good. [36]

SUNDAY FEBRUARY 10th   NEW ORLEANS

A most beautiful day.

Atherton and I got up early, run up town to see Steve Lane (who met Adkins[182] yesterday and told him he was going to New York today). We found the steamer Cahawba.[183] Steve was on the dock, and since he left us on the "Swan" at Natchez, he has got married! The villain! Miss Euphemia Fox![184] He brought his wife on deck as the vessel was going out. We saw her from the levee, she is rather pretty, somewhat petite. We bid him goodbye with hopes to meet at dear New York.

At 4 pm, left New Orleans by the Pontchatrain Road; the cars were very Southern in appearance; airy, light, and small seats. The weather was magnificent; I sat with the window open a beautiful [breeze] was blowing which

---

179. "Staty": statue.

180. The opera was the 1827 *Moïse et Pharaon,* an opera in four acts by Gioachino Rossini, derived from his own earlier *Mosè in Egitto.* A benefit performance for M. Grant that the *Picayune* for 9 February 1856 announced for seven o'clock, also gave the performers as Mesdames Laget-Planterre, and Gambier; and Mons: Duluc, Junca, Crambade, and Laget. The company, under Charles Boudousquie (1812–1866), is also discussed in *Dwight's Journal of Music,* IX, no. 11 (1856), 88.

181. "Done": "did" in Reiff.

182. "Adkins" not further identified, but he is a member of the company, possibly a musician, noted both at Vicksburg (30 March) and Washington (18 April).

183. The *Cahawba* was built in Cincinnati in 1847 but seems to have run from New York to New Orleans, sometimes via Havana. Her arrival in New Orleans is reported in 1852, and at Port Royal in 1863.

184. "Euphemia Fox": "Euphinia" in Reiff. Fox married Stephen K. Lane on 6 February 1856 in Natchez. See note 77 on Lane.

made it delightful. After about a quarter of an hour's ride, the locomotive Liberty brought us to the Lake Pontrachtrain, where we embarked on board the steamer "California" for Mobile.[185] Land cannot be seen (from here) on the other side. We started at quarter to five; our steamer is about two hundred feet long, with one boiler and an upright working beam. She is something between a "steamboat" and a "steam ship";—Ladies *State Rooms* on the after part of the upper deck, gentlemen's *berths* on the forward part of ditto. We supped in the Gentlemen's Saloon, which has also berths all along; it is situated where the Ladies Saloon is, on North river boats. [36ᵛ] Two sea gulls followed the vessel for miles; it is astonishing what power of endurance they have. After supper (which was very fair) we saw an enormous fire—(some miles distance of course) it seemed at least a half mile in length—could see it, progress, looked like a huge serpent crawling along the water.

The sunset (the first I've seen at sea) was truly grand! There were some clouds, but fortunately were not so low as [to] hide this interesting sunset. The sun seemed to set upon the water; it was a deep, bright red colour. I never saw anything like it; if I had seen anything like it in a painting, I should have pronounced it over drawn.

I turned in berth 91, where I slept very comfortably. About 4 a.m. awoke; the vessel was pitching about but gently. At 6, we were sailing up the Mobile Bay. Saw several ships at anchor, the city looks very pretty. [37]

MONDAY FEBRUARY 11ᵗʰ   MOBILE, ALABAMA

Put up at Mrs Ackerman's Boarding House on St. Louis St.[186] The house stands back from the street about fifty feet—with a fine door yard. It is three stories high, and a garret, with three verandas in front which can be enclosed with green blinds, the whole giving the establishment a country aspect.

Yesterday at the lake I beheld the first sloop since leaving Providence, R.I. Upon landing at the wharf (there is no levee here) the city strikes the beholder as a miserable dirty hole.[187] The "Battle House" on Royale St is the

185. The wheeler *California* was built in 1850 in New Albany, Indiana; the advertisements in the *Picayune* for the ships sailing at this date recorded that it was captained by a Mr. Myers.

186. "Ackerman" was probably Mrs. J. C. Ackerman, who was also advertising boarding at the Kennedy House (*Mobile Daily Advertiser*, 12 February 1856).

187. Many of the buildings described by Reiff were damaged or destroyed in the explosion caused by the ignition of some Confederate ammunition; it devastated much of the area,

principal (and only decent) hotel in the place; it is of white marble, a plain, but good, building.[188]

I have forgot to mention that when I stopped in New Orleans' Canal St. Hotel, there was a very interesting slave there, Denis by name, a waiter at the table. He is owned by one Mr Danforth, a merchant of N.Y. City.[189] Denis wanted to buy my fiddle—I played a little for him one day. He was a most excellent polite and obliging waiter; I should liked to have bought him, he was very sorry when I told him I was going away. I told him he would have one less to wait on: he said: "My young Massa, I likes to wait on such a good gemman as you, cause you dos'ent swear at me."

Denis was quite deserving this notice. [37ᵛ]

Introduced to a Mr. Snow who kept a music store in Dauphin St., near Royale;[190] he is very anxious for me to come here to teach, says he will answer for my doing well. He teaches himself.

TUESDAY FEBRUARY 12ᵗʰ   MOBILE

The streets are not paved here at all. Very ill with a severe colic and bilious attack. Managed to write a letter home. Odd Fellows Hall is situated on Royale

---

and in 1866 the damage was still evident to Trowbridge. See Trowbridge, *The Desolate South*, 216–19.

188. The Battle House, which takes its name from James Battle and his two half-nephews, John and Samuel, was built on the site of the 1812 military headquarters of Andrew Jackson and opened in 1852. It was designed by Isaiah Rogers (1800–1869); the building Reiff knew was destroyed by fire in 1905. The hotel still operates. See Gould, *From Fort to Port*, 148–49.

189. The slave owner here was possibly Joseph Lewis Danforth (1821–1887) of Louisville, Kentucky. A Louisville native merchant, he studied at Harvard, had business experience in Philadelphia and New Orleans, and returned to Louisville to establish the partnership of Danforth, Lewis and Company, which later became J. Danforth and Son. The New York connection may be derived from the fact that, by 1856, he had abandoned wholesale trade and had become deeply involved in the city's insurance industry, representing firms from around the country, including those from New York (Johnston, *Memorial History of Louisville*, I, 397).

190. Joel H. Snow (d. ca. 1896), "teacher of music," 25 Dauphine Street. He was labeled "Professor" in *Daughdrill and Walker's General Directory for the City and County of Mobile, for 1856*, 100, and the *Directory* for 1870 adds his Christian name. 25 Dauphine Street was the store; for an advertisement, see the appendix to *Daughdrill and Walker's*, 22. It was described elsewhere in the press as the "Musical Exchange and Piano Forte Warehouse," and was still listed in the directory in 1895.

St.;[191] a long entry way leads to the room which is nearly square, with a small staging backed by an arch; through the back of which the performers enter. The Hall will seat between six and seven hundred. It has rather too much reverberation; there are no galleries. A Custom House is building, corner of Royale & St. Francis Sts. It is about a hundred feet wide and 150 deep, one story is up, the material dark granite.[192] Saw several Alabama River steamboats sail. [38]

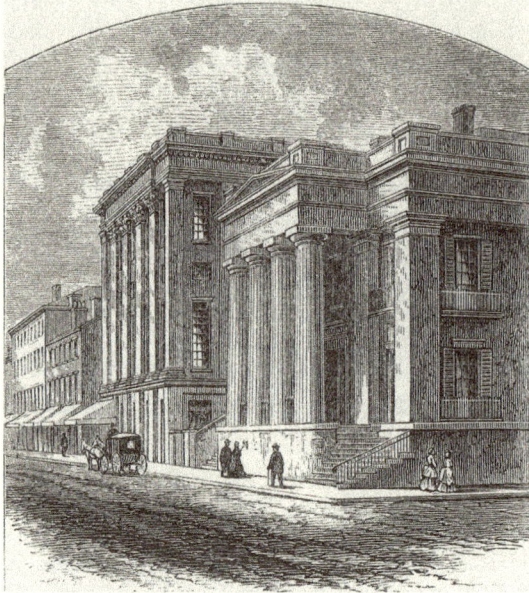

Figure 7. *Bank of Mobile and Odd Fellows Hall—Mobile, Alabama.* The Odd Fellows Hall on Royale Street in the center of Mobile was the venue for four concert performances the opera company gave in the city. Three were evenings given in costume of "gems" from *La Sonnambula, The Bohemian Girl,* and *The Crown Diamonds,* and the fourth was one of "Musical Morceaux." Reiff felt that the hall had "rather too much reverberation."

191. Robertson's 1856 map of Mobile shows the probably new Odd Fellows Hall to have stood on Royale Street, between Dauphine and Conti streets. It is listed there until 1875, when it appears to have been rebuilt.

192. The building Reiff saw was completed later that year and demolished in 1963; the architect was Ammi B. Young (1798–1874), supervising architect of the US Treasury Department, charged with overseeing federal buildings constructed throughout the country (Gould, *From Fort to Port,* 136).

[Performance: Concert, Gems from *La Sonnambula,* Odd Fellows Hall.][193]

WEDNESDAY FEBRUARY 13ᵗʰ   MOBILE

A most enchanting day.

Feeling much better (thanks to the medicine). I arose about ten and sallied forth for a walk—went up Conception St. out of Town—towards the suburbs. All the houses have pretty door yards before them. At the end of the town—which ends suddenly—is a very pretty pine wood, through I went, but not without getting very muddy, for it is a perfect swamp; all sorts of rank weeds growing which are peculiar to the South. The wood is about half a mile long—it took me nearly an hour to get through it—and not only my boots but my pants were in an awful plight. Stopped at a nigger house where I got a good drink of water. Told me there was a better road to the city towards the bay. A short walk brought me to a magnificent view of the bay looking out into the Gulf. Counted sixteen sails in the river bay and gulf. It was uncommonly warm with a nice breeze from the [sea]. Wished I could have Father & Mother here to enjoy it. A large plantation was just at the back, a nigger (about 20 years of age) was collecting some wood loading a small cart with a mule before it. He worked very slowly; at the North a man would have done three to his one. I had quite a talk with him and also with a little darkie about Ambrose's age, who wore no hat.[194] N.B.—little niggers seldom have hats here in the South. [38ᵛ] They both were perfect specimens of Southern Negroes. After lingering here for an hour I returned to the city by another—and a dry—road to Mobile. It was so very warm that I found shirt-sleeves more comfortable than a coat. The trees are very tall and straight. The trees are green all the year round; passed several (and one particularly handsome) magnolia trees. After getting through the woods, found a small stream running directly across the road; by throwing over sticks into it and laying a small board (which I fortunately found) over it, I succeeded in getting across, but not without wetting my feet, which, however, got dry again in half an hour. Went to the river, got on board the schooner "Mary Baker"

193. Although they were concert performances, *La Sonnambula, The Bohemian Girl,* and *The Crown Diamonds* were all given in costume. See the *Mobile Daily Advertiser,* 10 February 1856.

194. Ambrose Reiff, Reiff's younger brother.

of Philadelphia where I watched the vessels coming up to the city, among others a small steamboat from the Gulf named the "Junior." Opposite here is a long strip of low sandy land which seems to form the river; it was covered with crows. [39]

Government St. is one of the finest in the city, running from the river. On the corner of it and Royale, stands the Court House, a building resembling the N.Y. Custom House, but with a large dome on the top of it.[195]

Saw in one of the back streets a rather nice-looking cemetery, nothing peculiar about it except the pine trees.[196] Received a letter from Zeke.[197]

THURSDAY FEBRUARY 14th   MOBILE

St. Valentine's day. Boudinot & I went walking in the northwest part of the city, then down to the river. Saw some very large cotton yards with the usual sort of houses or sheds all around them.[198] Large quantities of cotton were in the buildings and yards. Got on board of an old steamer. The weather is certainly most charming. While playing the piano in Snow's, a number of very handsome ladies passed and re-passed the door. About the docks the city seemed particularly lively; several river steamers about sailing. [39ᵛ]

[Performance: Concert, Gems from *The Bohemian Girl*, Odd Fellows Hall.]

FRIDAY FEBRUARY 15th   MOBILE

A lovely day. Bought a compass, sword-cane, and a little cane for Ambrose; Gibson's[199] going to N.Y. tomorrow and will take. Wrote Father a letter six

195. This building, which can be found on the 1856 Robertson map of Mobile, was designed by William S. Alderson and built by James Barnes. The building replaced the earlier structure that burned down in the early 1850s. See Gould, *From Fort to Port,* 131–32.

196. Reiff, taking in Government Street, seems to be visiting the adjacent Church Street graveyard. It was opened on land acquired by the city of Mobile in 1820, but had been in use as a burial ground from 1819, when Mobile was in the grip of a yellow fever epidemic. See Sledge, *Cities of Silence,* including page 92 for the Church Street Graveyard deed.

197. "Zeke" (also "Ezhl" 28 and 30 March and "Zkl" 10 April). Probably Ezekiel A. Harris, a librarian at 108 Hammersley (now West Houston), New York. On 28 March, Reiff meets "Ezhl's" brother, Thomas Harris, at St. Louis; this is probably Thomas J. Harris, a lawyer, who lived at the same address, 108 Hammersley, New York. See H. Wilson, *Trow's New York City Directory.*

198. It is not possible to identify just which yards Reiff was visiting; Robertson's 1856 map of the city lists twelve different cotton presses operating.

199. For "Gibson," see note 82.

pages long. Walked up (southwest) St. Louis Street a few blocks, where one street to the northwest are three long low white buildings which I've been told are hospitals.[200]

About 6 pm dropped into the Jewish synagogue in Jackson, near St Louis St.[201] The men were sitting with their hats on; in the centre was the sort of pulpit. When the minister was holding forth and sort of chant[202] which seemed to mostly consist of these intervals:

which the congregation seemed to respond to—it was very curious to me being the first Jewish ceremony I have ever seen. The minister had on a white gown similar to an Episcopal parson—but his common street hat gave him a very singular, if not a comical, appearance. [40]

[Performance: Concert, Gems from *The Crown Diamonds,* Odd Fellows Hall.]

SATURDAY FEBRUARY 16ᵗʰ   MOBILE

A warm and most charming day.

Hired a horse in Jackson St. near St Francis; made for the magnolia grove, [but] not before I drove at a good canter through Royale St., passed the "Battle House," went up to Lawrence St., which runs into the Bay Road. It commences through a beautiful wood, a good road mostly pine trees (Southern Pine—a pitch pine). The Bay Road runs in a south-easterly direction along Mobile Bay. After going about a mile, passed a dilapidated house formerly

200. Reiff is referring to the United States Marine Hospital (built between 1838 and 1842), the Mobile City Hospital (built between 1833 and 1836), and the Providence Infirmary (built in 1854–55), buildings that stand in a group on St. Anthony Street. The Marine and City hospitals, built side by side, are both Greek Revival buildings, and were in use as hospitals until the second half of the twentieth century. The former was designed by architect Frederick Bunnell, and the latter by Thomas S. James. See Erwin Craighead, "Dropped stitches from Mobile's past," *Mobile Register,* 2 February 1929. The Providence Infirmary was built opposite the City Hospital, to be run by the Sisters of Charity; the hospital moved to Spring Hill Avenue in 1901. See Gould, *From Fort to Port,* 143.

201. The synagogue on Jackson Street was the home of Congregation Sha'arai Shomayim, one of the oldest Jewish congregations in the United States and the oldest in the Alabama; it had opened on 10 March 1853. The congregation had been served by their first leader, Mendes da Silva, in December 1846. See Olitzky and Raphael, *The American Synagogue,* 31.

202. "Chant": "chat" in Reiff.

a toll gate, and came to the water side, where I struck a plank road; my horse was a most excellent one, the road was nearly level. The view on the bay, beautiful; two ships, and a brig were sailing in the bay, several vessels (among them a steamer) were in the offing, not a cloud to be seen. Oh! if only Father & Mother and many of my dear friends in New York (Ezke, of course) were here to enjoy it. Saw a Negro ploughing.

To describe this splendid ride would require a much more able pen than mine. Toll gate 20 cents. Suffice to say the road was excellent, the view lovely, and the weather all the most fastidious could ask for.

About five or six miles from the city is the grove at the entrance of which the plank road stops.[203] There are two or three houses here—met a very intelligent man, who answered all my questions—and they were not *few*. Rode along in the grove after resting my good horse, who I ridden very fast. Went along slowly through the grove—the magnolia trees are certainly very [40ᵛ] beautiful. I cannot describe this ride; I wished for *all* my friends to be here. Rode back more gently. If anything, it was somewhat too warm, but I find in Mobile there is always a pleasant breeze coming in from the Gulf. The inhabitants say the weather here is never as sultry as it is in New York from the fact of always having this Gulf breeze.

Mobile seems to be on the south-west side of the bay; three or four miles below the city, is a long, low, flat island extending several miles above the city. It forms two rivers, one each side of it, so Mobile actually is not upon the bay, but upon Mobile River which runs to the south-west of the island, and the water (on the other side) is called Spanish River, up which vessels (that is to say ships) bound for Mobile frequently[204] go to get to the city. As the water is much deeper there than in Mobile River, they (the vessels) are obliged to go up Spanish River about 18 miles and then come down Mobile River, which is much deeper in this part than it is at the mouth.

Returning from my ride, I galloped at a tremendous speed down Government St. to Royale, then dashed down Dauphin to Snow's store, who insisted upon my coming in and playing for some young ladies; of [41] course, after a tremendous deal of coaxing, I consented. From here called upon Harrison at the Battle House, and from thence home.

Horncastle dined with me today, and enjoyed himself very much especially on the veranda or gallery.

203. Wooden-plank roads were favored by turnpike companies.

204. "Vessels (that is to say ships) bound for Mobile frequently": "vessels (bound for Mobile) that is to say ships, frequently" in Reiff.

SUNDAY FEBRUARY 17th   MOBILE

Beautiful day, but a somewhat cold wind. Felt very unwell, costive[205] and bilious. In the morning with Snow went to a Presbyterian Church, corner of St. Francis & ———, near the park,[206] where I played the organ. Heard a very poor sermon.[207] The organ good: 2 banks of keys, 27 stops, one octave in the pedals. The church very plain.[208]

Dined with Snow at the Battle. After dinner we went up Dauphin St. about a mile, until we came to a Mr Price's mansion, which stands back some thirty feet from the street; it is in the suburbs of the town.[209] Was there introduced to Mr & Mrs Price, Miss Mary Price,[210] and Miss Ashmore, a younger sister of Mrs Price. They are all originally from New Jersey, New Brunswick,[211] which I, of course, was well acquainted with, so I very soon got into the good graces of the old gentleman, and extolled Jersey (Brunswick in particular) to the skies.[212] He seemed to like me very much, and in a twinkling, his daughter came in with some beautiful cake of which I partook

205. "Costive": constipated (*OED*, III, 991).

206. The Second Presbyterian Church stood on the corner of Francis and Conception streets (Gould, *From Fort to Port*, 116).

207. The incumbent at this time was the Reverend Robert Nall, whom Reiff hears preaching later that day at the First Presbyterian Church (Marshall, *The Presbyterian Church in Alabama*). Nall was probably not the preacher mentioned by Reiff here.

208. The Presbyterian Church was constructed by I. P. Pond, E. W. Erwin, and B. H. Scattergood, and was a temple-style Greek Revival building. Now demolished, it can be seen on the 1873 bird's-eye map of the city by Erghotte Krebs.

209. Caleb Price Jr., who dealt in hardware at 72, 74, and 76 Water Street, and with a residence "north of Dauphin"; see *Daughdrill and Walker's General Directory for the City and County of Mobile, for 1856*, 87. Price was born in New Jersey in 1814 or 1815, and died in Mobile in 1882; his death certificate gives the date as 21 February. He arrived in the city after 1852, and appears in the 1855–56 city directory, where he is listed living in the country; given Reiff's description of his house in the "suburbs," this may be the same one. Price was later appointed mayor of Mobile, an office he held from 1868 to 1870. See *Mobile Register*, 12 June 1983; this article details land Price owned at 88 Government Street, a site that is too close to the city to be "in the country" and is likely to have been a city residence. If, as the article suggests, Mrs. Price was "Lavinia," her maiden name is likely to have been Lavinia Ashmore; see "Miss Ashmore, a younger sister of Mrs. Price" in this diary entry.

210. An article in the *Mobile Register*, 12 June 1983, gives the name of a Miss Price as Annie Marsh Price (1854–1901). This is not the Miss Price of Reiff's acquaintance.

211. New Brunswick, New Jersey, established 1730.

212. Reiff mentions on 26 April that he was "reminded of Grandfather's place in Jersey," suggesting that his familiarity comes from this family connection.

most bountifully (simply because the young lady said she made it), a servant followed with the wine which was most excellent. Several gentlemen called in during the afternoon. [41ᵛ] They (the Prices) insisted upon our remaining to tea, and could not help remarking that they were particularly attentive to me, for instance. Mary, who presided at the tea tray, sent the waiter with my cup first; we had a regular jovial time as if we were old acquaintances.

After supper, church was in order. Off we went, Snow taking Mary, I, Sarah Ashmore, and Price, his wife. We beat the Old Fogies getting to church which was way down Government St., near Royale, a very fine church, white in colour, a gallery around it.²¹³ Seemed to be (inside) of Egyptian style of architecture, especially back of the pulpit. The ceiling was made in diamond shape. All four disciples of young America bolted into the Price's pew, so when he arrived he was obliged to take another seat. The Parson (who by the way was not Dr Mandeville²¹⁴ whom we expected to hear, but a Dr Noll)²¹⁵ preached a sort of know nothing sermon and once when he said foreigner, I told the girls he pointed at me, but afterwards remarked that it must be them because they had come from Jersey. After getting home (Prices) we had some hickory nuts (brought from the North) which the young ladies kindly cracked for us.

Music next in order "Old Hundred,"²¹⁶ "Wake, Isles of the South,"²¹⁷ &c., was played by me and sung by Mary, her mother, and Snow; so the time passed till 11 pm, when Snow and I left, and so ends one of the pleasantest

213. Government Street Presbyterian Church, now at 300 Government Street, is today one of the best-preserved examples of Greek Revival architecture in Alabama. Built from 1836 to 1837, the consensus of opinion is that James Gallier and Charles B. Dakin designed the exterior, and that Charles B. and James Harrison Dakin were responsible for the interior; see Sledge, *The Pillared City*, 53–54.

214. The Reverend Henry Mandeville (1804–1858) was a professor at Hamilton College in Clinton, New York, and a minister of the Collegiate Church in New York City. He accepted the ministry at the First Presbyterian Church in Mobile, where he caught yellow fever during an epidemic and died (Find A Grave).

215. "Noll": possibly "Nall." This would be the Reverend Robert Nall, the incumbent of the Second Presbyterian Church at Francis and Conception streets. See note 207.

216. "Old Hundred" is a hymn attributed to the French composer Loys Bourgeois (ca. 1510–ca. 1560) from the *Pseaumes Octante Trois de David* (1551) and is usually sung to a paraphrase by William Kethe (d. 1594), "All People That on Earth Do Dwell."

217. The text of "Wake, Isles of the South" was written by William Tappan (1794–1849) in 1822, while the musical setting, written in 1848, was by William Hauser (1812–1880).

calls in two months. [42] Snow remarked to me that Price is worth over a hundred thousand dollars; what could he possibly mean by telling me that? The remainder of our conversation I shall not record.

Figure 8. "Husbands, wives, and families sold indiscriminately to different purchasers, are violently separated; probably never to meet again," 1861. On 18 February 1856, Reiff encountered an outdoor slave auction on the corner of Royale and Government streets: "This auction to me was the worst place in which I have seen slavery to see human beings (with soul) sold together with steamboats, houses, &c., as was the case today, seems absolutely horrible."

MONDAY FEBRUARY 18th   MOBILE

Beautiful day. Saw a slave auction on the corner of Royale and Government Streets, opposite the Court House.[218] One woman who was sold very much excited my pity. Her master was in debt and was obliged to sell her to pay some mortgage. She had always lived with the family, she was about 35

218. This sale was probably conducted by auctioneer A. Brooks, whose premises were advertised as being in Royale Street, opposite the courthouse. No located advertised sale quite fits Reiff's description, but his later reference to "satisfying a mortgage" suggests that he may have been referring, in part, to a sheriff's sale at the courthouse at noon that day of a slave named Rose, auctioned to satisfy a claim against the estate of the late William Oswald (*Mobile Daily Advertiser*, 16 February 1856).

years old. Her grief (to mewas heartrending; she wept most bitterly. She was knocked down for $700, thought to be very cheap.[219] A very good looking nigger was bought for $875 by a brutish-looking fellow who told him to go up to his store and tell them that he was just bought, and his clerks would give him something to do.[220] This auction to me was the worst place in which I have seen slavery to see human beings (with a soul) sold together with steamboats, horses, &c., as was the case today, seems absolutely horrible.[221]

In Snow's store, where I *accidentally* stopped, Mary P., Sarah A., and Mrs P. *accidentally* dropped in, and, of course, I had a good time, playing, chatting, &c. The ladies were dressed most magnificently, splendid and extravagantly. After the concert I again (happened to be at the door) saw them as they were leaving the room. [42ᵛ]

I had nearly forgotten to say that on Sunday, I stepped into the Cathedral which is in a street near Dauphine (crossing it) the building on the outside is not finished, it is about 175 feet deep, very wide, of brick the front will be plastered the inside is pure white.[222] The ceiling being three arches, the centre one quite large, the two side ones smaller. The middle aisle is very wide, above at say thirty-five feet, the floor was marble laid in diamond form. The church was very plain for a Catholic one, no pictures, banners, &c. It is, however, a very handsome building; the arches are supported by ten large pillars, five on each side of the church. One thing struck me as being very peculiar; the church (not being completed) there was not a single cross on the outside of the edifice.[223] [43]

[Performance: Concert, "Musical Morceaux,"[224] Odd Fellows Hall.]

219. In today's market, Measuring Worth shows that the 2014 real price of a commodity at this time to be $20,200.

220. Measuring Worth suggests that this would be $24,500 in today's money.

221. Johnson in *Soul by Soul,* 127–28, cites this scene in the context of a discussion about slave-auctioneering practices. He suggests that, on occasion, tears of this type were part of a sales pitch designed to evoke in the buyers exactly the sort of feelings described by Reiff.

222. The Catholic cathedral was begun in 1834 to the design of Claude Beroujon (1797–1875), a former seminarian turned architect, but not consecrated until 1850, when, as Reiff noted here, the building was still unfinished. Its present form is largely the result of subsequent additions and alterations (Gould, *From Fort to Port,* 114–16).

223. The building still stands but was badly damaged by fire in 1954.

224. *Mobile Daily Advertiser,* 16 February 1856. "Morceaux," translating literally as "morsels," suggests an evening of extracts from larger musical works. Benefit: Louisa Pyne.

TUESDAY FEBRUARY 19th   MOBILE TO NEW ORLEANS

Left Mobile on steamer "Cuba," bound for N.O.—a somewhat cloudy day. The "Cuba" is a very fine vessel, nearly new, the Engine built by Pease & Murphy, New York. Our state rooms are the most complete things of the kind I ever saw; a marble top washstand with all the appurtenances,[225] a covered, sort of small, sofa, an excellent looking glass, a lamp so arranged that the rolling of the vessel will not overturn it, two chairs, two berths. The room, being situated upon the upper deck, from the window an excellent view may be obtained; I (with Stretton) was ticketed for No. 4.

Snow came down to see me off.

Our vessel is loaded with cotton, which is so piled that it is almost impossible to get about on the main deck—small passages are left through which only one man at a time can go—We have also a large number of passengers. My companions were fearful that I would be left, and as I met one after the other (after the steamer started) they would [say] "why here's Reiff now." Miss L. Pyne said she certainly thought I was left behind. [43ᵛ] Left the Dock at 10 mins past 2 pm.

The sail down the bay was exceeding pleasant. Our dinner was most excellent; even the "Old Lady"[226] said she had never eaten such roast beef in America—any further proofs concerning the good dinner would [be] superfluous.

About half past five we came to the "Pass" which is the "inside" route to N.O.; the outside (the way in which we came from N.O.) is by the Gulf. The "Pass" is very narrow; though the width of the water from shore to shore is between 15 and 20 miles, the "Pass" seems to be about a hundred feet wide and is indicated by stakes driven in the bottom. A small flat island less than an acre is here—with a rickety-looking dwelling upon it and an outhouse or so. A dredging machine was fastened to one of the piles about 500 hundred feet from the island.

The "Man of the Island" receives a certain sum from the A.L. Government to keep this pass open; the island is rock.[227] [44]

Another smaller island was seen to our right about a half a mile distant.

225. "Appurtenances": "apurtenauces" in Reiff.

226. This seems to be a reference to Louisa Pyne.

227. "A.L.": possibly "H.L." or "U.S." in Reiff, but presumably an abbreviated form of "Alabama."

We went very slowly through the "Pass" which is about (indicated by the piles) three quarters of a mile long; to come through it at night is almost impossible. It looks very curious to find it so shallow in so tremendous an expanse of water. Had a long talk with Bishop Spalding of Kentucky—he is a Catholic—seems to be a very well-informed gentleman, told me he was a Native of Kentucky.[228] He blames the K. N——'s for the riot at Louisville last summer.[229] He spoke very well, though (like most priests) he is evidently of the fanatical order. We had also talking with us a very intelligent man who has travelled greatly in Central America, Mexico, &c.; between him and the Bishop, I passed the time very agreeably. The Bishop has been lecturing in Mobile.

Swan and I (just after sun down) were sitting in the bows, on some cotton bales speaking of our homes—when we were aroused by smelling something burning. Upon looking around, we saw the cotton was on *fire!* Just [45] inside the doors (which shut out the forward part of the vessel) some men were pulling a bale from the inside—they got it upon the outside but were unable to throw it overboard in consequence of its being so *much* on fire. Swan made a terrific dash and over the peculiar stairs (they are like a one-sided stoop in N.Y.) he *was,* in the shortest space of time; he dashed through the cabin, into his stateroom. The passengers, seeing this, some of them bolted

228. Martin John Spalding (1810–1872), Catholic bishop of Louisville, Kentucky (1850–1864). On his accession, his diocese comprised the whole of Kentucky; a man of immense energy, he had, before he met Reiff, visited every Catholic institution in the diocese, resumed the building of the Cathedral of the Assumption in Louisville, persuaded the Holy See to divide the diocese in two, and traveled to Europe to attempt to solve the shortage of clergy in the diocese. After the Louisville Riots—see note 229 below—he called for calm and forgiveness. A set of Spalding's printed lectures with handwritten addenda for the period 1850–65 are in the archives of the University of Notre Dame, CDBL 10/45 folder.

229. The 1855 riots in Louisville, also known as Bloody Monday, grew out of an election rivalry between the Democrats and the supporters of the Know Nothing Party, Reiff's "K. N——'s." The editor of the *Louisville Journal*, George D. Prentice, had written a series of anti-immigration articles which attributed subversionary attitudes to Catholics, and the fury of the rioters was directed at any German and anything Irish; a conservative estimate puts the number killed at twenty-two, with much property destroyed, with the new Catholic cathedral (see note 228) narrowly escaping destruction. Spalding (and others) put the number at around one hundred. There are many accounts of these events; for a contemporary one, see the *Louisiana Daily Courier* and the *Louisiana Daily Journal* for August 1855, and for a modern one, see Lee, *Kentuckian in Blue*, chap. 4.

out, and we had quite a panic on the forward part of the vessel, the *Ladies,* fortunately, knowing nothing of the matter.

I was, only for [an] instant, a little nervous; it was when I looked to see how near land we were; in one direction only could I see land, and that was almost imperceptible from the distance it was away! My next glance at the laden vessel (cotton, cotton, and only two small boats to save us);[230] however, it was only momentarily for I thought it would get put out *somehow,* which was done in an admirable manner by the men with large buckets of water. [46]

They then searched among the cotton for above an hour; one bale had a place burnt nearly through it. Shortly after, supper was disposed of, then I took to the deck [and] had a long talk with the Bishop and an Alabama gentleman upon the subject of slavery. The latter said he knew my countenance well, this being the second person who insists upon knowing me. About ten, the steamer "California" from N.O. bound for Mobile passed us. I retired at half past twelve, where, in the most comfortable bed since I left Hare's, I slept well and soundly despite the fire excitement.

We arrived at 10 mins past four at the Lake Landing. I did not awake until 6 am, when I found a furious north-east rainstorm raging. Most of the passengers had gone. The rain and wind was terrific. On board was a little girl about five years old who had been put in charge of the stewardess by its mother at Mobile. The child had a bad hand and it had been sent to N.O. to have its hand amputated. Its father was to receive it at the boat, but it rained, and in consequence he did not come down; it was to be sent to him. What a horrible affair. [47] The little dear was running around the vessel without anyone to look after it.

At half past eight, we ran through the rain down the pier towards the train of cars about three hundred feet, and in a few minutes, started. The rain now came down a perfect sheet of water. Frank Boudinot, while endeavouring to shut the car door, smashed his Larboard thumb. Every[body] flew. Brandy was miraculously produced in a twinkling from Louisa P.y's basket—a handkerchief from Susan's—Smith seized[231] him—and I looked

230. "Boats to save us); however, it was only momentarily for": "boats to save us, however, it was only momentarily) for" in Reiff.

231. Le Grand Smith, the manager of the Pyne and Harrison Company; see Lawrence, *Strong on Music II,* 540.

about as fast I could—(which I have no doubt done a great deal of good). Of course, Frank (though suffering intense pain) soon got better, and I have no doubt that we would have cured him in a very short space of time, when, unfortunately, we arrived in New Orleans, and he went to a *doctor* and, as a matter of course, it is now problematical whether it will ever get well at all.

Got into the St. Charles carriage where I breakfasted (not in the *carriage*, but in the Hotel); arrived at my rooms where Atherton was waiting, expecting me. [49][232]

In the afternoon, Atherton and I took a walk up to the "New Basin" which is the head of a canal which runs from Lake Pontchartrain. Schooners and sloops were laying here, giving at quite a different aspect from the river. We then went to the Old Shell Road just passed inside of the Toll Gate; the shells are broken up fine. Went back passed over a small bridge across the canal, passed the "Gas House" extending an entire block; low, painted yellow.[233]

WEDNESDAY FEBRUARY 20th   NEW ORLEANS

Done nothing but write today (warm).
   [Performance: *La Sonnambula*, Gaiety Theatre.]

THURSDAY FEBRUARY 21st   NEW ORLEANS

Was to the St. Charles Theatre; [Marion] McCarthy, Anderton, and Charles glad to see me.
   [Performance: *The Crown Diamonds*, Gaiety Theatre.]

FRIDAY FEBRUARY 22nd   NEW ORLEANS

Very warm day.
   Soldiers formed in line on Canal St. Saw an Irish company[234] march-

232. Page 48 omitted in the MS numbering.

233. James H. Caldwell (1793–1863), the founder of the original St. Charles Theatre, was also the founder of the New Orleans Gas Light Company; see *Norman's New Orleans and Environs*, 144–45; and Thomas Brown, *History of the American Stage*, 61.

234. Possibly the volunteer militia the Irish Emmett Guards and Emeralds, active in New Orleans at this time. See Reinders, "Militia in New Orleans, 1853–1861," 36.

ing through the small alley which runs from the St. Louis Hotel (rue St. Louis).[235] On Canal St., saw a German company, which reminded me of N.Y. Washington Riflemen.[236] Of course, saw quite a number of Frenchmen. In Lafayette Square, saw the beautiful block of marble which the Continentals are about sending to Washington.[237] [49ᵛ] A beautiful day; very warm. All the Flags hoisted—quite a holiday. The steamer "Swan" arrived.

[Performance: *The Bohemian Girl*, Gaiety Theatre.]

SATURDAY FEBRUARY 23ʳᵈ   NEW ORLEANS

Met Arch Johnston in Gravier St. Of course, was much surprised; he's out here on some law business of Pecks.[238] Came down on the "Belle Sheridan" which boat is very much like the "Swan."[239] A man named Murphy[240] (who came with him from St. Louis) told me they had a high time in the cars, drinking, &c. Arch is quite shocked at some slave selling he saw on board the boat, and with it, generally, thinks I am degenerated completely as regards slavery. [50]

Took Arch to the "Swan" and introduced him to Walker, Mrs Andrews, & Hester, who looks quite fat and pretty.

235. The St. Louis Hotel was the deluxe hotel of the French Quarter; designed by J. N. B. de Pouilly, it opened in 1838, burned down in 1840, and was immediately rebuilt. It was a glamorous center of Creole society, but—renamed the Royal—it never recovered from the economic effects of the Civil War and was demolished 1912. For the early history, see Poesch and Bacot, *Louisiana Buildings*, 178–79.

236. Reiff could have seen a variety of German militias; see Mehrländer, *The Germans of Charleston, Richmond and New Orleans*, 114–15, with table 119–24. Mehrländer remarks that "Nowhere else in the South did foreign militia units enjoy greater social attention than in New Orleans. Ethnic representation was important here, not only to show strength in relation to the native majority, but also to show the group's influence as compared to the many other nationalities."

237. This appears to be a donation for stone for the Washington Monument, built at intervals between 1848 and 1885 to the design of the architect Robert Mills (1781–1855); the states and territories, and indeed, other groups, were encouraged to donate commemorative blocks of stone that were 4 feet by 2 feet by 12 to 18 inches, for the interior walls. Reiff saw the monument on 11 April, and commented on the variety of stones received. See Emery, *The Washington Monument*, which details the inscriptions on the stones inside the monument.

238. "Arch Johnston" not further identified.

239. The ferryboat *Belle Sheridan* was built in New Albany, Indiana, in 1854.

240. "Murphy" not further identified.

I went to a ―――― with A[rch] and Powell[241]—and—[242]

[Performance: Concert,[243] Gaiety Theatre.]

SUNDAY FEBRUARY 24th   NEW ORLEANS

Beautiful day.

Took a long walk up town (southwest). Went into an Episcopal Church (up Camp St.);[244] it looks something like Chapin's, N.Y.;[245] then, nearly opposite, into a very plain Catholic Church.[246] From thence, came down Magazine (the next st. towards the river), returned into Camp St. about two squares above Odd Fellows Hall, where is the church which we (A, B & I) have called Rutger's St. Church; it is, I believe, St Patrick's, it is a very pretty church, somewhat plain for a Catholic Church; saw Bishop Spalding coming out.[247]

In the afternoon Johnston and I had a walk. I with him called upon M[ar-

---

241. Presumably John Powell, the marine editor of the *Picayune;* see 9 February.

242. This is clearly a visit to a brothel; see also a return visit at note 248.

243. *Picayune,* 22 February 1856. The concert included "'Farewell benefit for Louisa Pyne and positively the last appearance of the Pyne Harrison Opera Company'.... [First Part]— 'The Grand Overture by the orchestra conducted by Mr. A. Heiff [Reiff] . . . After which the comedy of 'Still Waters Run Deep'—Characters by Messrs. J. S. Browne, J. E. Owens Copley, and Mrs Place . . . To be followed by a Grand Concert in two parts, consisting of the following selections—Glee: 'When winds whistle cold,' by the Chorus. Song: 'Lo, the Factotum,' Barber of Seville. Mr Stretton. Ballad: 'O say of Dublin,' Miss Pyne. Ballad: 'We may be happy yet,' Mr Harrison. Buffo Song: 'Lord Lovell,' James Henry Horncastle. Second Part—Overture: 'Barber of Seville.' Glee: 'Spring's delight,' by the Chorus. Song: 'Let me like a soldier fall,' Mr Harrison. Scotch Ballad: 'Hunting Tower,' Miss Pyne. Air: 'The Muleteer,' Mr Stretton. Trio: 'Tune on old Time,' Miss Pyne, Mr Harrison and Mr Stretton. Buffo Song: 'Something Pekooliar [*sic*],' Mr Harrison." The comedy was Tom Taylor's 1855 play, *Still Waters Run Deep.*

244. The Episcopal Church of St. Paul built in 1853; the congregation moved to Lakeview in the 1950s.

245. The church on Broadway of the Fourth Universalist Society, who had had as their pastor since 1848 Edwin Hubbell Chapin (1814–1880); in 1866, the church moved to the corner of Fifth Avenue and Forty-Fifth Street.

246. The building of St. Patrick's Church (at 724 Camp Street) was started in 1840 to the design of Charles B. Dakin (1811–1839) and James H. Dakin (1806–1852) and was completed by James Gallier; the sophisticated and elegant structure still survives. See Poesch and Bacot, *Louisiana Buildings,* 208.

247. See notes 246 and 228.

ion] McCarthy, then went alone to P——o St——.[248] Stopped with Arch (at the St. Charles) all night. [51]

MONDAY FEBRUARY 25th   NEW ORLEANS

Rainy—in the morning. Dined with Arch at the St. Charles Hotel, took him to Jackson Square.[249]

TUESDAY FEBRUARY 26th   MISSISSIPPI RIVER

Heard that only a portion of us were to depart today, upon which I got into a most intolerable bad humour. Endeavoured to have my stay prolonged—but it was no go. [52] Left New Orleans at 10 mins past 5 pm on board steamboat "Thos: Swan." State room 40 in company with George Atherton. Johnston, Caffe,[250] Peri,[251] Murphy, &c. came to see me off. I was in a terrible bad humour. The "Princess" started just ahead of us.[252] At the end of the city, saw some men dumping stable manure into the river; they do not use it here (in this part of the country).

The "Princess" stopped at a wood yard; we passed her—then came the tug-of-war. The "Princess" has the name of being the fastest boat on the river; our boat increased her steam fearfully. About 9 pm., the "Princess" passed us, their passengers cheering, while we felt down-hearted. They had pine wood which does not emit but few sparks, while our boat (burning cotton wood), the sparks came out of the pipes in such myriads and a heavy wind prevailing, it blew the sparks in such a manner that the pilots could not keep the vessel to its proper course. Many of the passengers were much frightened, and when I was going to bed—(my state room being [53] directly over the boilers) Ghor came to me and said "Tony, do not go to bed, for we

248. "P——o St——": Perdido Street. On this occasion, the text has not been expanded to emphasize that Reiff is being coy; this is probably the brothel Reiff appears to have visited the day before; see note 242.

249. Preston, *Opera on the Road*, 271, includes a rogue entry for this date. This appears as "Monday 24th," with a full performance of *Barber of Seville*.

250. "Caffe" not further identified.

251. "Peri" not further identified.

252. The *Princess*, built in about 1855 in Cincinnati, Ohio, was destroyed in 1859, when she exploded off Conrad's Point near Baton Rouge, killing seventy people; see accounts in the *Picayune*, 2 March 1859, and *Weekly Advocate*, 6 March 1859.

are in imminent danger. At least do not take your clothes off; twenty chances to one, you will be blown up." I promised him, Adkins, and Mrs Bevans I would not,[253] but the moment I got my room to myself, I jumped into bed, of course having first divested myself of clothing—where I calmly awaited the *"busting business."* Atherton shortly afterwards turned in. The wind was blowing a perfect gale, the rain came down in torrents, and the vessel shook terrifically, caused, however, more by the tremendous amount of steam she was carrying than anything else. We nearly ran the "Princess" down who, seeing that we would pass her, several times ran athwart our bows. Notwithstanding however, between 11 and 12 pm, we *passed her.* Such a blowing of the whistle, ringing bells, quite baffles description.[254]

WEDNESDAY FEBRUARY 27ᵗʰ   MISSISSIPPI RIVER TO VICKSBURG

A beautiful clear morning. The "Princess" out of sight. Was in the "Pilot House" nearly two hours this morning, the scenery excruciatingly monotonous. Had a long talk with the Mate; he says [54] that our late trip from Louisville (we were the last vessel down) was the most terrible one he ever saw, and he has been steamboating on these waters for twenty years.

Saw a new method of wooding.[255] We ran up to a flat boat loaded with pine wood—where the following conversation ensued:

Captain—How much?

Boatman—$4.00

Capt.—Will you tow?

Boatman—Yes.

253. "I promised him, Atherton, and Mrs Bevans I would not": if Reiff's insertion sign for "I would not" is followed, the sentence reads: "I promised him I would not Atherton and Mrs Bevans." The insertion mark for "I would not" appears to be in the wrong place.

254. Ghor was right to be nervous; steamboat races were extremely dangerous, as John Henry Vessey's account from Memphis suggests: "I saw two steamers leave for Vicksburg, one waiting for the other to start fair and have a race. They are such a rascally set for so long as they have insured the boat they care precious little for their own lives or for those of their passengers, only that they can get to New Orleans in such a time, for if the coals won't do, they think of nothing of piling on tar bands and putting a nigger on the safety valve" (*Mr. Vessey of England*, 102 [23 April 1859]).

255. Wooding up was always an issue for steamboat traffic. Charles Lyell (1797–1895), the noted British geologist, recounts his efforts to get a steamer from downriver to Natchez. Having hailed a steamer, *La Belle Creole,* and been told it was bound for Bayou Sara, he relates that the captain then "asked if we had any wood to see, and on learning there was none, sailed away" (*A Second Visit to the United States of North America,* II, 190).

Figure 9. *"Wooding Up" on the Mississippi.* Frances F. Palmer's 1863 lithograph shows the *Princess* at a landing, loading wood. Palmer produced both day and night versions of this subject, the night version here showing not only wooding up, but a number of dangers of riverboat travel, including a snag, and a scene that would become pitch dark when the clouds close over the moon. On 20 February 1856, Reiff records the *Princess* stopping at a woodyard before a dangerous night race out of New Orleans against Reiff's boat, the *Thomas Swann.*

In an almost incredible short space of time, our deck hands jumped on the flat boat and began pitching the wood in, the Mate helping them by swearing as hard as he can. The wood is measured with a long pole; we tow the boat along. Wood is generally about $2.75 a cord—the highest I have seen was $4.50 cents and the lowest $1.75.[256]

We have few passengers, though new ones seem to be getting on at all sorts of out of the way places, a white flag being the signal for the boat to stop. [55]

THURSDAY FEBRUARY 28th   VICKSBURG

Got up at 5 am. The boat had just arrived at Vicksburgh, Miss. It is very prettily situated on a slope, the back portion of the city being quite high. I went ashore and walked through one of the principal streets, but it was too

256. Measuring Worth gives today's real prices of a commodity in this transaction as follows: $4.00 = $115, $2.79 = $80.40, $4.50 = $130, and $1.75 = $50.40.

early for the stores to be open, just daylight. Several churches can be seen from the river. One (the handsomest) has a cross on the steeple and is in all probability of Catholic persuasion.[257]

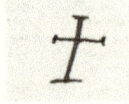

The river is about a quarter of a mile wide here. There is no town on the opposite bank, nor even a plantation. The river here runs nearly north & south, slightly to the southwest. About quarter of a mile above the city, the river takes a sudden turn, so much so as to run in exactly an opposite direction, leaving a strip of land about the fourth of a mile wide something in this manner so that if a bird were to start from one side to the other, he would land on the same side—provided it flew about a mile.

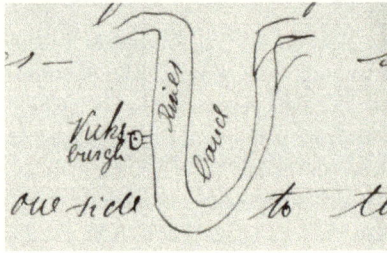

At night, we pulled up at a wood pile, where A. and I went ashore "*to see the Country*" as [56] . . . [55ᵛ] "*Napolean*" Oaks. A short time since a family feud broke out here, and at the end of the difficulty, six men were shot dead and twelve others were wounded.

Some people cooking their breakfast on the bluff; the woman (of the family) was making a sort of "sloe cake" which she baked in a spider.[258] She seem[ed] to carry all sorts of things in her pocket. They had made a fire alongside of a tremendous log. The father was holding a rather small child—which he wrapped in a blanket to keep warm—there w[ere] two or three other boys. For poverty, I've not seen a sight to equal it for a long time. They were Americans. . . .

257. The Catholic church that Reiff saw in Vicksburg was blessed in 1849; it replaced an earlier frame church built on Walnut Street in the 1840s during the time of Father M. D. O'Reilly (Pillar, *The Catholic Church in Mississippi*, 10, 43; Gleeson, *The Irish in the South*, 74–93). ·

258. A spider was a long-handled, footed skillet that stood just over the coals for hearth baking (*OED*, XVI, 216).

THURSDAY FEBRUARY 29th–
SATURDAY MARCH 8th   VICKSBURG TO ST LOUIS[259]

MONDAY MARCH 10th

[Performance: *La Sonnambula*, St. Louis Theatre.][260]

TUESDAY MARCH 11th

[Performance: *The Bohemian Girl*,[261] St. Louis Theatre.]

WEDNESDAY MARCH 12th

[Performance: *The Crown Diamonds*,[262] St. Louis Theatre.]

THURSDAY MARCH 13th

[Performance: *Maritana*, St. Louis Theatre.]

FRIDAY MARCH 14th

[Performance: *The Daughter of the Regiment*,[263] St. Louis Theatre.]

SATURDAY MARCH 15th

[Performance: *The Crown Diamonds*, St. Louis Theatre.]

MONDAY MARCH 17th

[Performance: *Guy Mannering*,[264] St. Louis Theatre.]

259. Manuscript missing pages 56 to 74, covering 1 to 28 March, in Reiff. The company arrived in St. Louis on the night of the 7th (*St. Louis Globe-Democrat*, 8 March 1856).

260. Managed at this time by H. L. Bateman.

261. William Harrison was ill for this performance, and the opera was not heard "in entirety" (*St. Louis Globe-Democrat*, 20 March 1856).

262. "To conclude with a characteristic dance by Mons. [Hippolyte] Monplaiser and Madame Olocco" (*St. Louis Globe-Democrat*, 12 March 1856). The Monplaisir Ballet Troupe, an ensemble of French dancers including Hippolyte and his wife, Adele, crossed over with Pyne and Harrison, and for that week St. Louis had the semblance of opera in some of the larger theaters in major cities where both troupes could be employed on a regular basis. See Preston, *Opera on the Road*, 294.

263. "The performances were proceeded by the play of the Old Guard" (*St. Louis Globe-Democrat*, 15 March 1856).

264. *Guy Mannering; or the Gipsy's prophecy, a musical play*, an adaptation by Daniel Terry,

TUESDAY MARCH 18th

[Performance: *The Barber of Seville*,[265] St. Louis Theatre.]

WEDNESDAY MARCH 19th

[Performance: *Maritana*,[266] St. Louis Theatre.]

THURSDAY MARCH 20th

[Performance: *The Bohemian Girl*, St. Louis Theatre.]

FRIDAY MARCH 21st

[Performance: *The Love Spell*,[267] with *No Song, No Supper*,[268] St. Louis Theatre.]

SATURDAY MARCH 22nd

[Performance: *The Daughter of the Regiment*, St. Louis Theatre.]

---

premiered at London's Theatre Royal, Covent Garden, on 12 March 1816. The music was by Thomas Attwood and Henry Rowley Bishop. Cast was Julia Mannering: Louisa Pyne; Lucy Bertram: Susan Pyne; Dandle Diamont: Henry Horncastle; Henry Bertram: William Harrison; Dominic Sampson: Mr. S. E. Brown; Megg Merriles: Mrs. Silsbee. "In consequence of the extreme length of the Opera, there will be no afterpiece." The press noted that this was the re-engagement of the Pyne & Harrison Company (*St. Louis Globe-Democrat*, 17 March 1856).

265. *The Barber of Seville, or The Useless Precaution* (*Il barbiere di Siviglia*), with music by Gioachino Rossini and a libretto by Cesare Sterbini, premiered at Rome's Teatro Argentina on 20 February 1816. No cast given. In previous performances the present members of the troupe played Almaviva: Harrison; Bartolo: Horncastle; and Rosina: Louisa Pyne. See dramatis personae in *The Barber of Seville* with music by Rossini and an English libretto by John Fawcett (1768–1837).

266. The evening will "conclude with a grand pas de deux, by Mons. Monplaiser and Madame Olocco," and "In consequence of the extreme length of the Opera, there will be no afterpiece" (*St. Louis Globe-Democrat*, 19 March 1856).

267. *L'elisir d'amore* (*The Love Spell*), with music by Gaetano Donizetti and a text by Felice Romani, premiered at Milan's Teatro Canobbiana on 12 May 1832. Cast was Adria: Louisa Pyne; Wemorini: William Harrison; Dr. Dulcamara: George Stretton (*St. Louis Globe-Democrat*, 21 March 1856).

268. *No Song, No Supper*, with music by Stephen Storace and a text by Prince Hoare, pre-

MONDAY MARCH 24th

[Performance: *Cinderella*, St. Louis Theatre.]

TUESDAY MARCH 25th

[Performance: *Cinderella*, St. Louis Theatre.]

WEDNESDAY MARCH 26th

[Performance: *Cinderella*,[269] St. Louis Theatre.] [75]

THURSDAY MARCH 27th   ST LOUIS

Wrote two letters home, one containing a V——.[270] Corrected the proof sheets of my song "There be none of beauty's daughters."[271] Ballhouse wishes me to write another before I go.[272] Hoped today to hear from Gallatin.[273]

The following conversation occurred today between Horncastle and Warre. Horncastle rooms with me, Warre's room is only separated by a folding door:

Warre/	Hello!	Horncastle, are you up?
Horncle/	No!	
Warre/	Is Tony up?	

---

miered at London's Drury Lane Theatre on 16 April 1790. Cast was Margaretta: Louisa Pyne; Dorothy: Susan Pyne; Crop: Henry Horncastle; Robin: William Harrison. "In consequence of the extreme length of the Opera, there will be no afterpiece" (*St. Louis Globe-Democrat*, 21 March 1856).

269. "Mr Whytal, the scenic artist of the St. Louis Theater, has acquitted himself handsomely and achieved quite a triumph for Mr Bateman" (*St. Louis Globe-Democrat*, 26 March 1856).

270. "V——" is presumably an "anonymous" Valentine, if somewhat late.

271. "There be none of beauty's daughters" is a twenty-six-line poem by George Byron, a very popular text for setting as a song; there are over a hundred extant settings, including those by Fanny Mendelssohn, Charles Parry, Roger Quilter, and Charles Stanford. No copy of Reiff's setting of the song has as yet come to light.

272. The music publisher J. Ballhouse of St. Louis (fl. 1855–56), whose publications included music of black composer Sam Postlewaite and is clearly publishing Reiff's song; see above note and Krohn, *Music Publishing in St. Louis*, 39.

273. "Gallatin" not further identified.

Horncle/   Yes, he turned out like a brick—about an hour & a half ago. Ran around with his bare shanks awhile and started off to get letters, said he would come back immediately—

Warre/   Then he will return about five minutes before dinner—but if *he* has been up an hour and a half it must be half past eleven because you know Horncastle, when *he* has the band called for rehearsal at half past 9 he gets up at a quarter to ten—

N.B. This last assertion Tony indignantly denies.

Warre, upon getting up, found it *was* half past eleven—and the letters did not come before dinner. [75^v] Pocahontas[274] anxious to have Smith go home with her—but he said he [had] to attend to some business in the Box Office—so I attended to it. [75(2)]

[Performance: *Cinderella,* St. Louis Theatre.]

FRIDAY MARCH 28th ST LOUIS

A cold morning.

Much indignation felt here against Ward Beecher[275] & Prof. Silliman[276] in consequence of their speeches at a Kansas meeting in New Haven, to provide Sharps' rifle's to a Company who are about emigrating.[277] Henry Ward

274. Pocahontas (ca. 1595–1617) was a Native American woman; her name in the Powhatan language meant "little wanton." In the records of the Jamestown settlers, she is recorded as having some sort of relationship with Captain John Smith (1580–1631); he claimed that she saved his life on two occasions, but considerable doubt has been thrown on the truth of these stories. Toward the end of her life, Pocahontas became a celebrity in London. The story was well known and circulated in many versions. For one modern account (among many), see Allen, *Pocahontas.* Pocahontas is possibly a nickname for Susan Pyne, perhaps inspired by the surnames of the original Captain John Smith and Le Grand Smith in the Pyne and Harrison Company.

275. Henry Ward Beecher (1813–1887), the brother of Harriet Beecher Stowe, was a liberal Congregationalist and reformer, and a famous and skillful orator. Beecher campaigned against the extension of slavery through the Kansas-Nebraska Act, and his reaction was typical of the New England clergy's response to the violence that followed. See Clark, *Henry Ward Beecher,* 120–23.

276. Benjamin Silliman Jr. (1779–1864), from 1804, a professor at Yale. By then emeritus and a public figure, he and Beecher pledged money, at the meeting mentioned by Reiff, for twenty-five rifles to be sent to the New Haven colony in Kansas. Silliman records his vilification but remarks, "I care not what they say about me. I feel that I did right." See Fulton and Thomson, *Benjamin Silliman, 1779–1864,* 258–60.

277. A reference to the meeting held shortly before in North Church, New Haven, at which

Beecher goes the whole hog for shooting down the border ruffians; says that a Sharp's rifle is a better thing to take to Kansas than a bible. And this is a Minister of God? If Beecher were to come here, I believe he would (even if he escaped with life) be *tarr'd & feathered*.

Saurkraut is for sale in the markets here. Every morning, market women in front of the door, wake me with their jargon supposed to be German, but I am sure that my royal Papa would be almost as much nonplussed as I am, to attempt to understand them.

Horncastle says I am the Man of Letters. Father wrote to Chatel (supposing I had gone) about a letter which he (Father) saw advertised in a German paper for me—after considerable trouble, Ghor got it for me. [75(2)ᵛ] About 4 pm. stopped in at Thos. Harris's first, Ezhl's[278] brother, a very strong family likeness.

Had quite a talk about Mary Coles, &c.[279]

Wrote a letter to Ezhl. [76]

[Performance: *Cinderella*,[280] St. Louis Theatre.]

SATURDAY MARCH 29ᵗʰ   ST LOUIS

The "Omaha" from Council Bluffs, Lexington, Kansas, &c., arrived last night with a cargo of hemp, &c.—ought to have a letter by her.[281]

Smith and I had quite a long conversation. Among other things he told me he was a member of the Covent Garden Theatrical Fund, which will probably now be divided.[282] He invited me to go with him to see some birds

---

Beecher addressed the colonists. The response from the *Liberator* newspaper was similar to Reiff's (Clark, *Henry Ward Beecher*, 123).

278. See note 197 for "Ezhl."

279. "Mary Coles" not further identified; the context suggests she is a New York acquaintance.

280. The program included a "Grand characteristic Pas de Deux, by Mons. Monplaiser and Madame Olocco." This night appears also to have been Louisa Pyne's benefit (*St. Louis Globe-Democrat*, 28 March 1856).

281. The *Omaha* was a new vessel built at Louisville, Kentucky, assuming a correct identification by Lytle and Holdcamper. The cities of Council Bluffs, Iowa, and Omaha, Nebraska, are on opposite sides of the Missouri River, and the steamer would have passed through Kansas City, Missouri, and Lexington, Missouri, to reach St. Louis.

282. The Covent Garden Theatrical Fund was established in 1765 by Thomas Hull and incorporated by Royal Charter in 1776. For a brief account of its history and purpose, see Worrall, *Celebrity, Performance, Reception*, 43–46.

(stuffed); went to a place over Campbell's Minstrel Room,[283] where, among many other curiosities, saw the fossil remains of a monstrous sort of an alligator (or sea serpent). It is 96 feet long; it was found imbedded in the earth somewhere in Alabama. Saw a sloth (stuffed) which the exhibitor told us is very wrongfully named, and also remarked that Buffon is mistaken in regard to it.[284] They climb from tree to tree with astonishing rapidity; this one was about two-foot high, their face resembles the human face as much—if not more—than a monkey's. He showed us specimen of birds (skin), many of which I've seen at Diamond Island Bend and in other places. Swan concluded an engagement with Bateman.[285]

Received a letter from Father & one from Arch. [77]

[Performance: *Cinderella,* and closed with Act II of *La Sonnambula,* St. Louis Theatre.]

SUNDAY MARCH 30th   ST LOUIS

A cold, cloudy blustering day; wrote Ezhl.[286]

At the Cathedral: in the morning they preach French, and in the evening, English. It is a very low building of a sort of French gray-coloured stone, has fine windows on each side, a clock on the steeple, and a small chime of bells.

At about 6 o'clock, a most extraordinary [occurrence] took place. During a heavy snow storm, it thunder'd (very long peals) accompanied with vivid lightning. The effect it had upon the falling snow was very remarkable in-

283. Campbell's Minstrels were a blackface troupe that originated in a group brought together in June 1847 by John Campbell, who owned a New York restaurant on the corner of Bayard Street and the Bowery, and were celebrated in print with song sheets such as "Melodies of the Celebrated Campbells Minstrels"; see White, "Negro Minstrelsy"; Bean, Hatch, and McNamara, eds., *Inside the Minstrel Mask,* 43–63; and Slout, ed., *Burnt Cork and Tambourines.*

284. "It was found imbedded in the earth": "it was found in the ea imbedded in the earth" in Reiff. Georges-Louis Leclerc, Comte de Buffon (1707–1788), the author of the 44-volume encyclopedia *Historie Naturelle* (1749–1788) describing the natural world; an English version of some of the material was produced by William Smellie in 1781 in eight volumes.

285. Hezekiah Linthicum Bateman (1812–1875) was an English-born actor and manager who, by 1855, was manager of the St. Louis Theatre. In 1859 he moved to New York, and in 1871 he returned to London, where he managed the Lyceum Theatre. Swan's engagement was presumably for the next season in St. Louis. The company appears to have participated in a benefit for Bateman on 31 March. See Gayle T. Harris, "Hezekiah Linthicum Bateman," *ODNB,* IV, 302–4.

286. See note 197 for "Ezhl."

deed; I shall long remember it. The papers next day spoke of it being a most extraordinary affair.

Had a *"blow out"*; Horncastle, myself, Adkins, &c, principally for Wallis—Johny Whytal brought Bateman with him, not knowing that Wallis would be present. Bateman, who would have stayed until morning, only remained an hour. Of course, nearly all of us were toasted, I, as the "Young American Conductor" with the [77ᵛ] usual flattery common on these occasions. Chatel got very drunk. [78]

MONDAY MARCH 31ˢᵗ   ST LOUIS

A beautiful day.

With Mr Harrison, visited the [town].

Went to the same place as on Saturday to see the extraordinary, antediluvian, fossil remains of the *"Zeuglodon Macrospondylus,"* 96 feet long, found in Alabama.[287] Many very interesting things of natural history; a peculiar sort of black bird with a sort of plume over its head called the Umbrella Bird,[288] several magnificent eagles, owls, &c., &c.

Was in the "Varieties Theatre" on —— St; [it] is very pretty, in the shape of a horse shoe, a very badly painted curtain (no perspective), two tiers above the parterre or first tier & parquette,[289] the boxes with the usual open ribbed fronts so common to all Western and Southern [theaters]—in fact, the South Western & Southern, because they are not so in either Pittsburgh or Cincinnati.[290] [79]

287. The zeuglodon (Genus Basilosaurus) was a meat-eating member of the whale family, estimated it to be over forty-five million years old (Eocene period) and averaging from fifty-five to seventy feet long with a tail up to forty feet in length. First found in Clarke County around 1833, the zeuglodon has been the state fossil of Alabama since 1984. For an early account, see Buckley, "On the Zeuglodon Remains of Alabama"; and for further discussion of its identity, see the *Proceedings of the Academy of Natural Sciences of Philadelphia*, 4 (1848–49), 4–6.

288. The Cephalopterus, a bird usually found in the rainforests of South America and Central America. It is not clear which of the three species Reiff saw.

289. In American theater usage, "parterre" refers to the area on the ground floor beneath the galleries, while "parquette" (used erroneously for "parquet") refers to the forward area of the ground floor nearest the orchestra (*OED*, XI, 251, 264).

290. The opulent Varieties Theatre, which stood on Market Street, was opened by Joseph M. Field on 10 May 1852. It was said to have resembled Paris's Barthelems Theatre and had an adjustable floor to enable balls to be held there, events which were more affordable and popular than the plays. The building Reiff saw went through a number of iterations, including a

[Performance: *The Crown Diamonds*,[291] St. Louis Theatre.]

TUESDAY APRIL 1st   ST LOUIS TO INDIANAPOLIS

Left Pension Français at half past 8. Went up to (about opposite the Virginia Hotel) Walnut St. took the ferry to Illinois Town on the Island. Illinois Town can scarcely be seen from St. Louis as the island intervenes. The island has a levee (raised) on the west side; it is connected to the main land by roads, earth bridges.

A terrific wind blowing when we arrived on the island. An Adams Express took mine & Horncastle's trunks to the station—and would not take a dime for it.[292] It is about a mile. There are two R.R. stations here. We took the most easterly one,—the Ohio & Mississippi Road & started at 25 mins to 10; [in] 11–15 mins, we are on a very large prairie.

At 12, I got out of cars on a rolling prairie; the earth here is very rich. We are going exactly due east.

At quarter past 12, the prairie around us is on fire, to the south for several miles burning right down to the track. Though the cars passed rapidly, yet the heat struck us as if the windows had been open. The wind is very high and the fires look beautiful; it is set on fire purposely to clear the land for planting purposes. They plough around the fences to prevent them taking fire.[293] At half past 12, passed more prairie fires. [79ᵛ]

Arrived at Sandoval[294] at 1.3 mins. Stopped 20 mins to dinner. Pocahontas[295] & Smith do not agree—so she & sister shared their ale, chicken sandwiches, cake, &c. with Horncastle and me; we made a much better dinner

---

spell under Benjamin DeBar as DeBar's Opera House. See Scharf, *History of Saint Louis City and County*, I, 979–81.

291. Benefit: Bateman (*St. Louis Globe-Democrat*, 29 March 1856).

292. The Adams Express Company, founded by Alvin Adams in 1839; originally a northern company, it was by the 1850s shipping by stagecoach and rail to St. Louis, and it became deeply involved in the South (Stimson, *History of the Express Companies*, 88–136).

293. "They plough around the fences to prevent them taking fire": from 78v, with symbol to indicate insertion.

294. "Sandoval": "Sandovah" in Reiff. Sandoval, Illinois, was laid out by the Illinois Railroad Company, founded in 1854 (Brinkerhoff, *Brinkerhoff's History of Marion County, Illinois*, 185–87).

295. "Pocahontas": "Pochohantas" in Reiff.

than Figaro no 7—who dined at the station.[296] Susan told us Louisa's[297] engagement with Smith (for two years) is up in October. [80]

Sandoval consists of about 9 houses, it is situated on a prairie at the junction of this and the railroad from Cairo. While here, I saw the Cairo train coming up; of course, it can be seen a long distance on this prairie.

1.55 mins—passed to the south. About a mile distant, a very large fire.

2.10 mins—(in the woods) passed a cluster of very primitive looking log huts; the children and women about them were dressed in the rudest, rustic, wild, manner possible. A pretty stream of water over which is a bridge; at this place renders the scene exceedingly picturesque.

2.30—passed some three miles [of] prairie which has been burned; leaves a black loam.

5.40—crossed the Wabash River which is about the 5th of a mile wide here; at present it is very high. This is the boundary between Illinois & Indiana—Vincennes is on the east bank[298]—an old French town. Vincennes was settled by the French in 1735 and with the exception of Kaskaskia,[299] is the oldest settled place in the West;[300] containing about 3000 inhabitants, nothing very remarkable to be seen, except a bevy of pretty girls on the bridge to whom Strettoni waved his handkerchief and blew kisses to; and thereby nearly fell off the cars. [80ᵛ]

The ladies' ale bottle having given out, I set out to get it refill'd. The conductor, with whom I had made friends, told me where to go, and said (we stopp'd here for supper) he would wait *five minutes* for me if I should be late. So off I started feeling quite confident of having the U.S. Mail wait until I could get some ale. Went down a street a quarter of a mile and found a coffee house. Popped in and got a pint of ale for which the cheating Dutchman (St

---

296. This enigmatic note suggests that all is not well within the troupe. Pocahontas (Susan Pyne?) seems not to be getting on with manager Le Grand Smith, for all that she was keen that he accompany her home on 27 March. The falling out meant that the sisters—Louisa and Susan—ate with Horncastle and Reiff, while Smith ("Figaro no 7"), who dined at the station, was the worse off, either for food or company. In Smith's absence, Susan lets out that Louisa's contract with Smith comes up later in the year.

297. "Louisa": "Louise" in Reiff.

298. Vincennes, Iowa.

299. Kaskaskia, Illinois.

300. "Vincennes . . . in the West": inserted from 79v, using Reiff's symbol.

Louis Dutch)[301] charged me fifteen cents; he knew I was on the train. Returned, then went down to the river to the right of the bridge (north), where is a clump of trees under which Gen. Harrison[302] concluded a treaty of peace with the Indians. It was signed in the large house in front of the trees which is now a tavern called the Harrison House.[303] I went in; it's an old-fashioned country house, large fire places, &c. The treaty was, I *think,* with Logan, an Indian chief;[304] I have seen a picture of it somewhere, for I [81] recognised the place immediately.

Half a mile from here we changed cars and took the Evansville & Crawfordville Line to Terre Haute, going along the Wabash for a short distance, almost due north. Arrived at Terre Haute about nine; the wind blowing very heavily. Some miles in the distance we saw a very large fire. Terre Haute is on a prairie—its streets are wide—could see but little of the place as it was very dark and when I walked out, I crossed over several tracks and heard locomotive whistles in all directions and it commenced to rain.[305] Changed cars here, no depot. From here to Indianapolis, we had a car to ourselves, nearly. Some words occurred between Harrison & Susan, she gave him fits. Arrived at Indianapolis—at twelve—where we heard *something* had happened

301. Reiff's German ancestry suggests he was using the term in the sense of "Dutchtown," the early nineteenth-century German neighborhood of St. Louis derived from the word "Deutsch" (*OED*, IV, 1140).

302. William Henry Harrison (1773–1841), the ninth president of the United States, originally gained national fame for leading forces against the Indians at the 1811 Battle of Tippecanoe and as a general in the War of 1812, which was essentially settled by Harrison's major victory at the Battle of the Thames in 1813 (K. R. Constantine Gutzman, "William Henry Harrison," *ANB*, X, 223–26).

303. Probably Grouseland, the house built in Vincennes to the design of William Lindsay in 1804 for William Harrison while he was governor of the Indiana Territory. The house had passed from the family in 1840 (K. R. Constantine Gutzman, "William Henry Harrison," *ANB*, X, 223–26).

304. Reiff seems to have conflated two different events. Captain Logan (ca. 1774–after 25 November 1812) was a scout during the War of 1812, serving under Harrison. The Treaty of Grouseland, signed at the house on 21 August 1805, was negotiated by Harrison (as governor of the Indiana Territory) with Native American leaders for lands in southern Indiana, northeast Indiana, and northwestern Ohio.

305. Terre Haute, Indiana, is on the Wabash River; the name is derived from the French for "high land." Terre Haute dates its establishment from the construction in 1811 of Fort Harrison during an expedition led by William Henry Harrison (McCormick, *Terre Haute*).

to the other train, so we fail'd to make the connection,[306] and took the Terre Haute and Richmond Railroad[307]—passing Wood's Mill[308] (8 miles), Highland[309] (12), Brazil[310] (16), Reel's Mill[311] (25), Fillmore[312] (40), Coatsville[313] (44), Crittenden[314] (46), Morristown[315] (48), Pecksburg[316] (50), Claysville[317] (52), (and some other places), and, lastly, Indianapolis (73).[318] [82] We went over the street from the depot to the American House,[319] where the Ps and Strettoni managed to get rooms, but H—— & I could not. It was as dark as pitch and sprinkling. We started off, I with my travelling bag, leaving my trunk in the depot. We walked along at random but finally found the principal Hotel (Bate's House)[320] in the place, where we were soon domiciled

306. "From here to Indianapolis . . . the connection": text inserted from the foot of the page as indicated in the manuscript.

307. The Terre Haute and Richmond Railroad was founded in 1852 by Chauncey Rose and was later to become the Terre Haute and Indianapolis Railroad (McCormick, *Terre Haute,* 36–37). The figures given for the distances listed here and on 2 April suggest that Reiff copied them from one of the numerous railway or travelers' guides of a sort similar to Appleton's *Southern and Western Travellers' Guide* published in New York. For some discussion of these, see Mackintosh, *Selling the Sights,* especially "Describing the Terraqueous Globe," 23–53.

308. Wood's Mill, Illinois.

309. Highland, Indiana.

310. Brazil, Indiana.

311. Probably Reelsville, Indiana.

312. Fillmore, Indiana.

313. Coatsville, Indiana.

314. Probably Crittenden Creek, Indiana.

315. Morristown, Indiana.

316. Pecksburg, Indiana.

317. Claysville, Indiana.

318. See Robinson, *Railroad and Steamboat Sketches between New York and Kansas,* 15–18, for an account of the same journey.

319. The American House, not otherwise recorded, is listed in *A. C. Howard's Directory for the City of Indianapolis* as being sited opposite the Union Station.

320. Bates's House ("Bate's" in Reiff), a four-storied brick structure with a corner lantern, was started in 1852 by the public figure and banker Hervey Bates (1795–1876). A grand and luxurious hotel, it later gained notoriety when Abraham Lincoln spoke from a balcony on the way to his inauguration in 1861, making one of his first statements on the preservation of the Union. It was demolished in 1901. See Bodenhamer and Barrows, *The Encyclopedia of Indianapolis,* 311; and Kennedy, *Architecture, Men, Women and Money in America, 1600–1860,* 445–52.

in room No 68 where there were two very comfortable beds. About 1 o'clock, I met Smith & Wife in the hall. It now rained very fast. Turned in very tired & sleepy at exactly 2.00 am by the town clock.

WEDNESDAY APRIL 2ⁿᵈ   INDIANAPOLIS

Arose at half past seven. Went out. The principal street is Washington Street, it is as wide as 14ᵗʰ street, N.Y., and runs east and west. Bate's House is on the corner of this and another street.[321] A large wooden house was being moved in Washington Street.

Odd Fellows Hall on the corner of Washington & Meridian Sts is a very good-looking building with a cupola on the top.[322] It seems to be the principal concert room, &c., &c. It is a new building and is to be dedicated on the first of May.[323]

The Capitol is situated in a large park on Washington Street;[324] it is a "conglomerated" piece of architecture[325] has large columns in front (a la Hall of Records, but much larger).[326] The dome on the top resembles the one on the Capitol at Washington. The buildings seem to be of plaster. [82ᵛ] Went in upstairs to the Senate Chamber which, like in most American Capitols, was open to everyone. The gas had been left turned on at the President's desk, and the room was filled with it. I turned it off before I could examine the room: which I did effectually—in true Yankee fashion—opening

321. Bates's House stood at the corner of Washington and Illinois streets.

322. The 1855–56 Odd Fellows Hall was planned by the German architect Francis Costigan (1810–1865) and finished off with a dome by Diedrich August Bohlen (fl. from 1855–d. 1890). See Scherrer, "Francis Costigan, Architect, 1810–1865," 30–33.

323. "Odd Fellows Hall . . . on the first of May": text inserted from the page opposite, 81v.

324. This was Indiana's third capitol building, and the second since Indianapolis became the state capital in 1822. Completed in 1835, the design was by Ithiel Town (1784–1844) and Alexander Jackson Davis (1803–1892). In the Greek Revival style—it was thought to look like the Parthenon, but with the Renaissance dome Reiff describes—it gradually fell into disfavor and disrepair and was demolished in 1877. For the early history, see "Capitol of Indiana," 323.

325. What Reiff means by "conglomerated" is unclear. The one unusual aspect of the building was that it was constructed using blue limestone, a feature which may have led to Reiff's comment that it "seemed to be made of plaster."

326. Reiff is referring to the early New York Hall of Records in City Hall Park. This was originally built in 1757 as a jail and remodeled in the Neoclassical style in the 1830s. See Hall, "A Brief History of City Hall Park, New York," 389–93.

desks, books, &c. The place was horribly dusty, chairs over turned, desks broken, &c.

The Chamber is about 30 ft deep and 60 broad, with columns (16 in number), eight on each side, four in a row, the other four a few feet behind, leaving the absolute Chamber square (being no galleries; the places beyond the columns are for the public.). A pretty dome over the room. The other chamber was locked up, but I got in the Supreme Court Room which is on the first floor, of oblong shape. [83]

At breakfast Davidge sat opposite to us;[327] he was much surprised to see Horncastle, & I was introduced to him when he, Horncastle, Harrison, & myself took a walk through the town; everything is new, the streets are laid out very wide.

We call'd to see the ladies. I returned to the hotel, where I hastily wrote home a letter telling them I was all safe, &c. I was cut short suddenly by the cry "Passengers for the cars"; was obliged to see Mrs Smith to the cars. The Depot is one of the finest I've ever seen, very high.[328]

Started at 10.30, a cloudy, but warm, spring morning. [84]

INDIANAPOLIS TO LOUISVILLE[329]

We go due south on the Jeffersonville Railway.[330] Almost immediately, made friends with the conductor, Woodland.

Southport (6 miles), a small village in the middle of the woods.[331] Green-

327. The English comedian William Pleater Davidge (1814–1888), who had an early career at Drury Lane, and arrived to work at the Old Broadway Theatre in August 1850. He had appeared with the company in New York, when spoken parts were required; see Gänzl, *Victorian Vocalists*. In 1855, he left the theater and undertook a tour through the country, where Reiff appears to have encountered him; see his own account of his time in the American theater in Davidge, *Footlight Flashes*, especially 124–31. They obviously remained good friends; Reiff was one of the participants in Davidge's seventy-third-birthday benefit at the Brooklyn Academy of Music. See report in the *New York Times*, 16 April 1887.

328. The Indianapolis Union Station opened in 1853 at 39 Jackson Place and was the world's first Union Station. Hetherington, *Indianapolis Union Station*, 3–10.

329. A heading by Reiff, who adds: "(108 miles)."

330. The Jeffersonville Railroad was the name given to the old Ohio and Indianapolis Railroad in 1849; it ultimately became the Jeffersonville, Madison and Indianapolis Railroad (Sulzer, *Ghost Railroads of Indiana*, 75–83).

331. Southport, Indiana.

wood (10 miles)[332] to Franklin (20 miles),[333] a dense forest—of beach (or beech), poplars, and some sycamores. Occasionally, a few acres are cleared, and some few common log huts or cabins meet the view. Passed immense quantities of wood, some of which had been cut and some had fallen, enough to supply New York for at least two years, in fact, so much that, if I was to state my actual belief,[334] it would be thought a stupendous exaggeration. It seems quite sinful that so much beautiful wood should be wasted— but wastefulness and prodigality is common to the Southern and Western people.

Passed thousands of cut wood piled (this, of course, is to be used), also some immense timber which is made into boards. Some of these logs are from five to six (perhaps seven) ft in diameter. There are quite a number of steam sawmills along the line of the road.

No hills; level land, but no prairies.

Endirsburg—(30 miles)[335] is a small place of some 300 population; looks very muddy just now. [84ᵛ]

Taylorsville—35 miles[336]

Columbus—42[337]

Walesboro—46[338]

Waynesville—47[339]

Bannersville—48[340]

Jonesville—52[341] (Some of the best land in the state is about here)

Rockford—57[342]

Seymour—59[343]

Farmington—62[344]

[85]

---

332. Greenwood, Indiana.

333. Franklin, Indiana.

334. "Belief": "believe" in Reiff.

335. Endirsburg (Edinburgh?), Indiana.

336. Taylorsville, Indiana.

337. Columbus, Indiana.

338. Walesboro, Indiana.

339. Waynesville, Indiana.

340. Bannersville (not extant), Indiana.

341. Jonesville, Indiana.

342. Rockford, Indiana.

343. Seymour, Indiana.

344. Probably New Farmington, Indiana, laid out in 1852.

At quarter past twelve, passed a large sycamore forest about three quarters of a mile to the east. Arrived at Waynesville at half past 12; a very small place. At Rockford (57 miles) some small hills, the first I've seen today.

Was in the baggage car some time, 20 mins. At Seymour is a sawmill. The Cincinnati & St Louis Railroad crosses our track here from northeast to southwest; we are now going exactly southeast. Vienna (82)[345] contains about 30 houses and is a very miserable looking place.

Arrived at Jeffersonville[346] at half past 3pm. [86]

In Louisville, the streets are somewhat as follows. The levee running east & west; then Main St (principal business St); then Market St (with three markets: Speed [Market], Fleet Market, Kentucky Market, all sorts of common stores, on market days, the streets are lined with farmer wagons, stands, &c.); then Jefferson St (wide as 14th St, N.Y.), a promenading street for the Louisville belles; then Green St, the theatre is on this street; then Walnut; then Chestnut; then Broadway, a new and very wide street wider than Canal St, N.Y. This street contains many beautiful residences with door yards, a la Fifth Avenue. Beyond this, there is not much of anything in the shape of a city. The streets running across are 1st, 2nd, &c.[347]

Put up at Merchants Hotel (my name was published among the arrivals as Mr Graiff, N.O.!). Went to Fauld's Music Store,[348] then to the school[349] where Matt Ward shot Butler.[350] I examined it thoroughly; it stands back from the street about twenty-five feet, the room is about 50 by 25 commonly but respectably furnished. The pilot of the "Baltimore"[351] told me that for Matt Ward's trial, the venue was moved to a small country place and the jury

345. Vienna, Indiana.

346. Jeffersonville, Indiana.

347. "In Louisville, the streets are somewhat. . . . The streets running across are 1st, 2nd, &c.": inserted from 85v.

348. The store on West Main Street was owned by David P. Faulds (d. 1903), a significant music publisher, who was active until 1882. Louisville held an important place in the history of music publication generally; see Kleber, *The Encyclopedia of Louisville*, 641–42. Faulds was probably the promoter, and also acted as the ticket agent for the troupe's visit (*Louisville Daily Courier*, 1 April 1856).

349. "School": "shoal" in Reiff.

350. Matt F. Ward shot the principal of Louisville High School, William H. G. Butler, on 2 November 1853, which resulted in a notorious trial that almost led to mob violence in Louisville. See also note 352.

351. The *Baltimore*, a side-wheeler wooden-hull packet launched in 1853 at Wheeling, Virginia, traveled mainly Louisville–St. Louis and Louisville–New Orleans. When Reiff encountered the pilot, the boat was still owned by the Wheeling Louisville Union Packet Line; how-

(who were mostly poor men and friends of Ward's) each received a $1000 to bring in a favourable verdict.[352]

Mozart Hall will hold about 1500 persons;[353] it is on the corner of Jefferson and another of which I have forgotten the name.[354]

Beautiful, pleasant, weather. Took a walk down by the Falls;[355] has very little appearance of a "falls." There is a canal here through which boats go to avoid the falls.[356] [87]

[Performance: concert, selections from *La Sonnambula*,[357] Mozart Hall.]

THURSDAY APRIL 3ʳᵈ   LOUISVILLE

Call'd upon the Miss P——. Took a walk, and after concert, went to the the-

---

ever, she was sold by public auction in June 1856 and was snagged and lost above St. Louis in 1859.

352. Ward was acquitted by a jury that was widely believed to have been "bought" by his wealthy father, Robert J. Ward. There is no doubt that the move of the trial to Elizabethtown played a role in his acquittal. In 1854, the year of the trial, $1,000 was the equivalent of some $25,000 today (Inflation Calculator). See McClure, *Two Centuries in Elizabethtown & Hardin County, Kentucky*, 241–42.

353. According to the *Courier* of 15 February 1851, Mozart Hall was built by John F. Hedlin, to the design of amateur architect George C. Davies. See also Weisert, *Mozart Hall*.

354. The address of Mozart Hall was 117 Fourth Street. It was built in 1851 and was opened with a concert by Jenny Lind. See Casto, *Actors, Audiences, and Historic Theaters of Kentucky*.

355. The Ohio Falls at Louisville is the only natural obstacle on the Ohio River, from Pittsburgh to the Gulf of Mexico.

356. The Louisville and Portland Canal was a two-mile-long canal that bypassed the Ohio Falls. As early as 1783, efforts were made to build the canal; it finally opened in 1830 and was operated by the Louisville and Portland Canal Company until 1874. A much-enlarged version of the canal still operates. See George H. Yater, "Louisville and Portland Canal," *The Kentucky Encyclopedia*, ed. Kleber, 580–81.

357. The program was: Part 1: Glee ("Here in a Cool Grot," 1779, Earl of Mornington) Louisa Pyne, Susan Pyne, Harrison, and Stretton; Aria ("The Last Man," Calcott) Stretton; Scotch Ballad ("Hunting Tower") Susan Pyne; Ballad ("We May be Happy Yet," *Daughter of St Mark*, Balfe) Harrison; Aria ("Skylark," Benedict) Louisa Pyne; Buffo Song ("Ye Tormentors," *Cinderella*, Rossini) Horncastle; Glee ("Down on Shannon's Banks," trad., arranged for the troupe by E. M. Levy) Louisa Pyne, Susan Pyne, Harrison, and Stretton. Part 2: Selections from Vincenzo Bellini's *La Sonnambula* "in full character costume": Cavatina ("Sounds so joyful") Susan Pyne as Liso; Grand Scene ("All is lost"—"Still so gently o'er me stealing") Harrison as Elvino; Recitative and Cavatina ("Dearest Companions"—"Oh love for thee") Louisa Pyne as Amina; Aria

atre, the Denin girls are playing there.[358] Mrs Gibbs, the promptor's wife, some others on the stage, and all the orchestra glad to see me.[359]

Took a cider with the dancing Englishman.[360]

[Performance: concert, selections from *The Crown Diamonds,*[361] Mozart Hall.]

FRIDAY APRIL 4th   LOUISVILLE TO CINCINNATI

Turned out at half past 4 am. Omnibus, after taking us to all the hotels, finally got over the ferry to Jeffersonville. Cars started at 6.25 mins, the same road we came upon on Wednesday 2nd. At 7.15 we stopped for breakfast. I did not breakfast, but managed to enjoy myself in another manner. This is a beautiful spot—two or three houses and a few cabins—entirely surrounded by magnificent woods.[362] On arriving at Seymour, we changed cars and took the Ohio and Mississippi Railroad (it is not complete either from St Louis or Cincinnati). We had previously been going north, now due east. From

("As I now vow"—"Maid, those bright eyes") Stretton as Count Rodolpho; Aria and Rondo Finale ("Ah! Yes for thee"—"Ah! Do not maiggio[?]") Louisa Pyne as Amina; Comic Song ("Lord Lovel") Horncastle (in character). See *Louisville Daily Courier,* 1 April 1856.

358. Susan (1835–1875; at one time Mrs. Woodward, and three other marriages) and Kate (1837–1907; Mrs. Fox, later Mrs. John Wilson) Denin. The sisters were born in Philadelphia and were child actors, under the guidance of their stepfather, the actor John Winans. See obituaries, *New York Times,* 7 December 1875 and 6 February 1907. They were reported on 18 May 1852 as being "both beautiful and magnificently formed women," with Kate having "a most beautiful foot and ankle." See *The Journal of J. Warner Erwin, 1839–1854,* ed. Home. They became notorious after an incident in 1854, when Susan, separated from Mr. Woodward, put herself "under the protection of Mr Bingham"; Bingham was subsequently shot by Woodward at Aspinwall (now Colón) on the Isthmus of Panama, on the return journey from San Francisco to New York. See *New York Times,* 26 June 1854.

359. "Gibbs" not further identified.

360. "Dancing Englishman" not further identified.

361. The program was: Part 1: Concert in One Act. Part 2: Selections from Daniel Auber's *The Crown Diamonds* "in costume": Don Henrique de Sandoval: Harrison; Rebolledo: Stretton; Diana: Susan Pyne; Catarina: Louisa Pyne. Louisa Pyne will introduce Rode's celebrated air and variations (somewhat implausibly) "costumed in the full coronation robes of Queen Victoria" (*Louisville Daily Courier,* 3 April 1856). The air by Pierre Rode (1774–1830) was the Variations in G major, a violin solo that was "vocalized" by Catalani, Malibran, Viardot, and others.

362. "This is a beautiful spot.... magnificent woods": text inserted from 86v as indicated by a dal segno sign in the manuscript. "By magnificent woods": "by a magnificent woods" in Reiff.

Seymour to the Ohio River, about 85 to 90 miles is almost entirely a forest. Broken country but not very high hills. The railroad has only been through here a short time, yet villages are springing up all along. The first one we came to will serve as a sample. In the midst of the forest was about two acres cleared, that is to say, the trees cut down, for the stumps still remained in the ground and the general debris had not been taken away. A store was erected and three houses all entirely new; not a particle of paint, no fences, nothing, in fact, yet this may [88] be the commencement of a large town.

Stretton remarked that in 25 years, I might be giving a concert here. The railroad builders, in making the road, have cut down an immense quantity of the largest trees which lie rotting; it seems quite shocking. Horncastle says he cannot bear to look at it (the prodigal waste of wood), it seems too bad. Occasionally, we pass some cabins.

We struck the Ohio at a place called Aurora, about 27 miles from Cincinnati, at a little past one. We cross a stream here, and while we were on the bridge, one of our brakes broke, and we had to stop to repair. We were not over the water, but just previous to getting to it, but at a considerable distance from the earth. From here to Cincinnati, we run along the river's bank with a canal on our left. The scenery the whole distance is superb; hills, the river winding around the hills, the grass first springing up, the cattle, horses, sheep, &c.; made the whole view quite enchanting. Stretton said (we were at the back of the last car) "it was the finest thing of the kind he had seen in America"!

We (at North Bend) passed General Harrison's grave, which is on the side of a hill; a plain small (seemingly) almost straight slab of marble.[363]

Passed many vineyards; there are, of course, here many Germans. [88(2)]

CINCINNATI

Arrived at the Woodruff House, Cincinnati at 2 pm.[364] I was expected; while eating my dinner, the girls all came rushing in—"Tony's arrived" had

363. The William Henry Harrison Tomb State Memorial was built in 1841 to serve as a permanent place of sepulcher for Harrison and his wife. When Reiff saw the memorial, only the tomb was present; the plain obelisk of Bedford limestone, which rises sixty feet above the tomb, was added later by the state of Ohio.

364. The Woodruff House (later known as the Koch House) was a newly erected edifice when Charles Cist described it in 1851. It had "a west front on Hammond Street, as well as its principal front on Sycamore Street. . . . It is five stories high, exclusive of the basement, and

spread through the house—and the welcome I got will not soon be forgotten. India[365] has grown some, Jenny looks as good as ever—and little Laura is still more of an enchanting *"little floozies"* girl.[366]

They said I was wonderfully altered; had grown so fat. Blackguarded my *tie* and *whiskers*; wished me to throw the former *away* and shave off the *latter*, both of which I declined doing.

Figure 10. *Burnet House, Hôtel Burnet, Cincinnati, Ohio.* Reiff and the company gave a concert at the Burnet House on 4 April; Reiff records visiting William Harrison's room, where he opened mail from New York.

---

measures, from the side-walk to the top in front, seventy feet. The building contains rooms, equal to one hundred and thirty of the size usual in hotels. This house is located in the most populous and business portion of the city, a short distance from the Ohio river, at the centre of the public landing, and convenient to the railroad depots, Post-office and Canal, and within one square of Main Street. The roof of the building affords a pleasant promenade, as well as a fine view of the river and surrounding country." See Cist, *Sketches and Statistics of Cincinnati in 1851,* 166.

365. "India": "Indiana" in Reiff, but later referred to as "India." The family here not further identified.

366. While now generally held to be a slang term for a woman of disreputable character, sometimes offering sexual favors, Reiff's employment of "floozies" here rather suggests more one with a knowing flirtatiousness (*OED,* V, 1079).

Got my old room (87), and found in a drawer a wrapper of a newspaper which Father had sent me more than three months ago. Received a letter from Father telling me that Uncle John had arrived home, but that the letter containing the particulars was at Baltimore. Strange that in this very room three months ago, I read a letter from Father telling me that Uncle John was in Antwerp and now (while talking to Jenny as I was before) I receive this news.[367]

[Performance: concert, Burnet House.][368]

SATURDAY APRIL 5ᵗʰ   CINCINNATI

Got the Baltimore letter from Brough (and one from Gould—a good one);[369] read it while in Harrison's room 66 at the Burnett House.[370] I was much affected and shall be impatient to see him. Father's letter also tells me about Lackner of Manheim, PA[371] wishing me to go there (heard through Eickhorn).[372] Also got my salary. Nothing to do tonight; all this combined makes this one of the happiest days of my life and the weather is most charming. I went over to Covington, Kentucky where are some very nice houses; from thence to the Licking River which separates this town from Newport.

A suspension bridge spans the river; the bridge is 550 ft between the towers—the river about 375.[373] [89]

367. "Received a letter. . . . I receive this news." Text inserted from 88(1)v as indicated in the manuscript.

368. On this occasion, the Burnet House's "Large Dining Hall [was] fitted up for the occasion with a stage, &c., as a handsome concert saloon by kind permission of A. B. Coleman, Esq." The concert was billed as a "farewell concert," which—given they had just arrived—is perhaps a reference also to their earlier visit. The program is virtually a repeat of that given in Louisville on 2 April (*Cincinnati Enquirer,* 4 April 1856).

369. Possibly the Philadelphia music publisher James E. Gould; apart from family, Reiff's correspondence seems to have been mostly professional, and on this trip, was at least twice with music publishers.

370. Built by Abraham Coleman, the Burnet House, on the corner Third and Vine streets, was designed by Isaiah Rogers, and opened in 1850. Dubbed "the finest hotel in the world" by the *Illustrated London News,* it played an important role in the city's history and was the site of the 1864 meeting between Generals Ulysses S. Grant and William T. Sherman. It was closed and demolished in 1926. See Lindow and Miller, "Queen City History," 16–17.

371. "Lackner," possibly "Lachner"; probably a concert promoter, not further identified.

372. "Eickhorn" is almost certainly German cellist L. Eichhorn, who performed in New York during the 1850s; see Lawrence, *Strong on Music II,* 253, and elsewhere.

373. Built in 1854, the suspension bridge replaced one that had collapsed under the weight of eighteen cattle and two men earlier that year; see *New York Times,* 18 January 1854.

The view from the bridge is most beautiful, the Ohio & Licking Rivers backed by hills covered with trees and grass; make a fine scene. Newport does not contain any fine houses as does Covington. There are two Catholic Churches in Newport, one a German Church.[374] There is a U.S. Barracks.[375] I popped in and examined the bedsteads, &c., as there was nothing very bad about it; I shall let it *remain. Magnanimous!* Tony! 11 pm; wrote to Uncle John & Father.

At night, saw Hackett play Falstaff in *Henry the IV.*[376] There had a tete-à-tete with the girls—India got me some nice cake to eat—and I retired at twelve quite a happy man; who wouldn't be under the circumstances?

SUNDAY APRIL 6th   CINCINNATI

A charming day; seems more like Sunday than any day I have experienced in some time. Stretton and I took a long walk over the canal (we went out on Sycamore St) to Mount Auburn;[377] then walked about a mile or so, the

374. There were, in fact, three Catholic churches in Newport. The first, Corpus Christi in the lower part of the town, had by 1853 outgrown the sizable Catholic population, and two new parishes were created. Corpus Christi built itself a new church, consecrated on 24 December 1854; St. Stephen's, in the upper part of the town, was a two-story combination church, school, and rectory, of which the cornerstone was laid in the autumn of 1854; and the Immaculate Conception Parish, the first parish in Newport for English-speaking Catholics, was dedicated on Sunday, 23 December 1855, in honor of the Immaculate Conception, a dogma solemnly defined on 8 December 1854. Reiff could have seen any two of these three churches. See Ryan, *History of the Diocese of Covington, Kentucky,* for a discussion of these parishes.

375. At the junction of the Ohio and Licking rivers, the Newport Barracks were built by James Taylor, the founder of Newport, on land he offered the War Department. Jacob Albright was appointed the first commanding officer of the Newport Barracks on 6 March 1806. The site was vulnerable to flooding, and in 1849–50 was hit by the cholera epidemic that swept Cincinnati. When Reiff visited them, the barracks were a depot of the Eastern Department of the Recruiting Service. They were finally given up in 1895. See Louis R. Thomas, "Newport Barracks," *The Kentucky Encyclopedia,* ed. Kleber, 680.

376. James Henry Hackett (1800–1871), an American actor and manager, known for his encouragement of drama. He first played Falstaff in Shakespeare's *Henry IV, Part 1* in 1828; it remained one of his most popular roles (Francis Hodge, "James Henry Hackett," *ABD,* IX, 768–70).

377. Mount Auburn—named after the then-new Mount Auburn Cemetery in Cambridge, Massachusetts—was for many years Cincinnati's only suburb; it was annexed to the city in 1849. Charles Dickens commented: "I was quite charmed with the appearance of the town, and its adjoining suburb of Mount Auburn: from which the city, lying in an amphitheatre of hills, forms a picture of remarkable beauty, and is seen to great advantage" (Dickens, *American Notes,* 29).

view is most magnificent. Cincinnati is on the northwest bank of the river. From here you can overlook the entire city and see a pretty turning in the river below the town—it turns to the west—the river is not over a quarter of a mile wide at this place and very crooked, something like this:

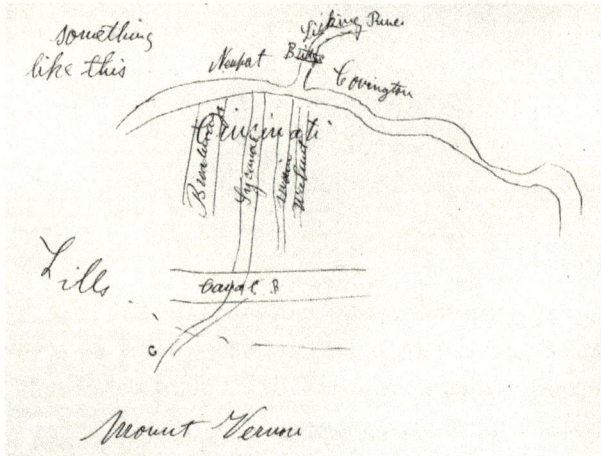

A Spencer House.[378]
B Canal, locally termed the Rhine.[379]
C From here a most magnificent view is had; all persons visiting Cincinnati should go up this for the pretty views.[380]

The people here call the canal the "Rhine" and the town on the other (the north) side "Germany" (that is before you ascend the hill). [89ᵛ] I begin to feel anxious to get home; think strongly of going to Europe.

At night (a beautiful) evening, I went with the girls to a Presbyterian Church on Broadway near Fourth St; heard a pretty good sermon, subject "Why do the wicked live?"[381] [90]

---

378. Built in 1853 and demolished in 1935, the landmark Spencer House stood at 321 East Sixth Street (*Cincinnati: A Guide to the Queen City and Its Neighbors*, 43).

379. The largely German neighborhood of Cincinnati known as "Over-the-Rhine" was reached by a bridge over the Miami and Erie Canal, "jocosely called the Rhine." See Pulszky and Pulszky, *White, Red, Black*, I, 297.

380. "Cincinnati is on the northwest bank . . . the pretty views": text inserted from 88(2)v as indicated in the manuscript.

381. The First Presbyterian Church, between Main and Walnut streets, built in 1853 with a spire said to be ten feet taller than Trinity Church, New York (Kenny, *Illustrated Cincinnati*, 105).

MONDAY APRIL 7th   CINCINNATI

Beautiful warm day. Was roused by Atherton knocking at my door at 6 am.
The "Silver Wave" had arrived;[382] Warre and Ghor woke me an hour later. Bid
everyone goodbye; kissed the *girls* and shook hands with the men. Made a
call to the "Silver Wave," and shortly after was writing in my state room N*o*
5 (starboard side) on steamer "Pittsburgh," a side wheeler.[383]

It is election day here, everything very quiet. The "Silver Wave" left while
we were dining; our dinner was pretty good.

Heard that the "Baltimore" is almost smashed to pieces by the sway she
struck. I am in the same room with Horncastle. The cabin is something similar to the "Baltimore's," only has more gilt about it. We have spring mattress
beds. Today is almost too warm to be comfortable. [92][384]

CINCINNATI TO WHEELING

Left Cincinnati at 10 mins to 6. Just above the city proper is a very high
range of hills; the scenery is lovely. The city—or rather an extension of it
called Fulton—extended along the bank for a long way. The hills are beautiful.

Ought to be lucky this month (according to Md) for I saw the new moon
over my right shoulder, a charming evening.

Read some of Maury's Wind and Tide work.[385]

TUESDAY APRIL 8th   PORTSMOUTH TO POMEROY

Clear but somewhat chilly. Out at 6:30, we are just passing the "Silver Wave."

382. The *Silver Wave* was a paddle-wheeler built in Glasgow, Pennsylvania, in 1855.

383. The *Pittsburgh*, nicknamed the Black Dragon, was a side-wheeler wooden-hull packet.
Launched in 1851 at Shousetown and dismantled in 1857, she worked the Pittsburgh-Cincinnati
run for the Pittsburgh and Cincinnati Packet Line.

384. Page 91 omitted in the MS numbering.

385. Either Matthew Fontaine Maury, *Lieut. Maury's Investigations of the Winds and Currents of the Sea* (1851), or his *Physical Geography of the Sea* (1855); the latter, being new and
ultimately more famous, may well be the one Reiff was reading. Maury (1806–1873) was a
multitalented oceanographer who made important contributions to charting winds and ocean
currents. He was keen to harness the observations of mariners, carefully noted, and then
ignored. He was the first superintendent of the US Naval Observatory from 1842 to 1861. See
Norman J. W. Thrower, "Matthew Fontaine Maury," *ANB*, XIV, 743.

We are now in the Scioto Valley the hills on either side with a few syca-mores; occasionally, pretty farm houses, &c., give us some beautiful views. At half past 7 we arrived at Portsmouth, Ohio, which is on the northeast bank of the Scioto River, which river comes in from the north. Portsmouth is the County seat of Scioto Co.; its present population is 6000; it is a large manufacturing place; I was ashore for a few moments. [93] This is the ter-minus of the Ohio Canal.[386] The place has a smoky appearance; there are many tall chimneys here. It is situated on a plateau of land surrounded by hills which are about a mile & a half back of the town. The flat strip of land extends along the river for about seven miles.

At every turn in the river, the scenery is most beautiful, and at every change, it seems to the beholder to grow more enchanting until one is quite lost in admiration.

From Portsmouth up to Wheelersburgh[387] (20 miles) the scenery is par-ticularly handsome; the latter place is prettily situated at a turn in the river.

Hanging Rock—six miles above—derives its name from a cliff of rocks about four hundred feet high which projects over the rear of the town. A house was pointed out to me in which lives a lady who several years [ago] lost her husband, who had (previous to dying) requested that she should not marry while his body was above ground. According to the husband's directions, he was buried *above* ground! His corpse remained undisturbed for three years, when one day (to the surprise of the neighbours) the body was interred in the earth; of course almost immediately after the widow married.[388]

At 11–20 mins arrived at Ironton, Lawrence Co., Ohio. The town was commenced in June 1849. 2000 persons are employed here; it is a large man-ufacturing place; all the houses look new and are, with scarcely an exception, brick. Hanging Rock is easily seen from here; it is four miles below.

Five miles above Ironton is (on the Kentucky shore) the town of Ashland; 18 months old, it is the biggest "infant" I've ever seen. It is said to have 1900 inhabitants. [94] The houses are nearly all of brick; a new and large hotel

386. The Ohio and Erie Canal was constructed in the 1820s and early 1830s under the su-pervision of the engineer James Geddes (1763–1838) and carried freight traffic from 1827 to 1861, when it was superseded by rail freight. See Woods, *The Ohio & Erie Canal*, 14–15.

387. "Wheelersburgh": "Greenupsburgh" in Reiff.

388. "A house was pointed out to me . . . after the widow married": text inserted from 92v as indicated in the manuscript.

is just about being finished.[389] Nine miles above, is the mouth of the "Big Sandy" a *small* river; it is the boundary between Kentucky and Virginia.[390] We arrived here just at dinner time, 12–30 mins.

Twelve miles above (at 2.00.pm) we arrived at Guyandotte, an old Indian place. It is at the mouth of a river of the same name—the Ohio is at present writing, fearfully muddy, and this stream (the Guyandotte) coming in here is as clear as an eastern rivulet. I went ashore (first time I've trod Virginia soil) and got a drink of water from the Guyandotte.

It is very warm.

Went into the Pilot House where I remained until tea time, scarcely passing a town, but many log huts and some farm houses.

Gallipolis, 38 miles above Guyandotte, is the next place worthy of being called a town; it is prettily situated.

Pomeroy we passed at night, but judging from the stores (all open and lit up at 9 pm) it seems to be a lively place; it is the county seat of Meigs Co., Ohio. It was first settled in 1816 and the coal mines opened in 1832. It is situated on a narrow strip of land running along the river for a "*smart*" distance—most of the houses are of brick. [94ᵛ]

Our passengers are mostly a rough looking set—Western old men—they reckon, mighty smart, thar and bar—to an awful extent. A particularly good waiter (Negro) attends us at table. Darkie perceived we were "Gemmen" immediately. Stretton's dignified moustache, Horncastle's portly form, and my impudent manner—combined with the fact that we are more fastidious and give more trouble than any one else—established the *fact* that we *were the people!* [95(1)]

WEDNESDAY APRIL 9ᵗʰ   MARIETTA TO WHEELING

A chilly morning but hot at 1 pm; saw a beautiful sunrise. We stopped at Marietta, the county seat of Washington Co., Ohio at half past 6. It is situated

389. The hotel was the Ashland Hotel, later the Aldine Hotel, commissioned by the Kentucky Iron and Coal Manufacturing Company on 24 July 1854 from plans by L. R. Bush and Company, when the town, formerly Poage Settlement, was established. It was not completed until early 1857. See Wolfford, *A History of Ashland, Kentucky,* 58.

390. The Big Sandy River, a tributary of the Ohio, derives its name from its extensive sandbars; for its entire length, it forms the border between Kentucky and Virginia. See Carol Crowe-Carraco, "Big Sandy River," *The Kentucky Encyclopedia,* ed. Kleber, 76–77.

at a bend in the Ohio, and at the mouth of the Muskingum River, a beautiful stream; there are many falls on this river. At Harmar—opposite Marietta—we took on board considerable freight; Harmar has 1200 inhabitants. Marietta is called after Maria Antionette of Austria.[391] It is noted for many historical events, especially concerning the Indians.[392] Marietta is built on a low level plot of ground and is frequently overflown by the Ohio.

The scenery seemed to grow more and more enchanting, but was especially so at a place where there are two pretty islands called Grape & Batten Islands. The beauty of this spot is far beyond my humble powers to express. The islands are low, covered with trees, and country surrounding us is lofty hills.

The next interesting point is "Big Grave Creek" at Elizabeth Town; a short distance up the creek is a large Indian Mound, said to be the largest in the United States.[393] It is between thirty and forty rods in circumference at the base and about seventy-five [95(2)] feet in height. Its sides are partially covered with large trees; there is an Observatory on the top.

We arrived at Wheeling, Va., at a little past four. It has a fine levee and a good-looking hotel stands on the river street called Sprigg's House.[394] The

391. The first permanent settlement here was established on 7 April 1788, on the arrival of General Israel Putnam (1718–1790) and a group of men from the Ohio Company of Associates. They named the town after Austrian-born Marie Antoinette (1755–1793), Queen of France, who had supported America in the War of Independence. See Summers, *History of Marietta*, 10–23.

392. Reiff is referring to the signing of the 1785 Treaty of Fort Harmar, the settlement across the river, which brought some solution of controversies in trade and boundaries with several Native American nations, and to the 1795 Treaty of Greenville that allowed the new residents to move beyond the forts and into the countryside. See Hayden, *The Senate and Treaties*, 1–16, 37–38.

393. The Great Mound is now at the center of Mound Cemetery, and is part of a mound complex known as the Marietta Earthworks. Reiff was incorrect; the mound and other similar earthworks have been regarded since the nineteenth century as the product of a prehistoric society now called the Mound Builders, which predated the American Indian tribes. See Lynott, *Hopewell Ceremonial Landscapes of Ohio*, 154–56.

394. Sprigg's House, named after Zachariah Sprigg, was on the site of the present Windsor Hotel, and started life as Gooding's Inn, named after its builder, Jacob Gooding. It was the earliest brick building erected in Wheeling: "The building was but two stories high, but it covered a large area of ground. On either side of the old house with its long pillared porch were two wings which were but one story each." See Blanche Steenrod, "Potpourri," *Wheeling News Register*, 1938; Cranmer, *History of Wheeling City*, 143.

depot of the B&O Railroad is on the levee.[395] The town seems to stand on a plot of ground something similar to Cincinnati, but the hills in the rear are not so high. The suspension bridge is the most notable thing about the place and that looks ungraceful from the fact of its being lower on one side (opposite Wheeling) than it is on the other;[396] [it is a] wire suspension bridge and was built at a cost of nearly $200,000.[397]

Horncastle and I were much chagrined to find that we would have to cross the mountains at night, or wait 24 hours which we could not do. It was very warm, I was very angry, Horncastle ditto, Stretton sorry (he remained behind), the streets very dusty, and the train about to start. I purchased my ticket got a seat (in last car—last seat) but never thought of my trunk! which had, however, been put aboard; after we started I got into the baggage car, where the man was enquiring for the owner of my trunk. Having satisfied him that it was mine, he gave me the check. [96]

WHEELING TO BALTIMORE

Via Baltimore & Ohio Railroad (fare $8.50 cents). Left Wheeling at half past 4 pm. Ran along the river to big *mound*, when we struck off among the hills; the scenery was wild and rude in the extreme. We keep along in the valleys, the hills surrounding us—being from four to five hundred ft in height—we follow (generally) a stream which, of course, runs through the lowest part of a valley, the road in consequence is very crooked. One of the most singular things is losing sight of the sun; sometimes it will seem two hours high and in *two* minutes afterwards, it has disappeared behind the hills, then again it is directly in front of us, and probably in five minutes, it is popping in from the back windows of the cars.

395. "B&O Railroad": the Baltimore & Ohio Railroad. The line to Wheeling received permission from the Virginia legislature under the 1847 act, and was completed on New Year's Eve, 1852 (Stover, *The History of the Baltimore and Ohio Railroad*, 66–73).

396. The Wheeling Suspension Bridge was the largest suspension bridge in the world when it opened in 1849, and the first bridge to span the Ohio River; it remains the oldest long-span suspension bridge still in regular use for vehicular traffic. Built to the design of Charles Ellet Jr. (1810–1862), the cables were laid out in the main street of Wheeling during construction. The bridge Reiff saw was the product of a reconstruction by Ellet after a storm in 1854. See Gene Lewis, *Charles Ellet, Jr.*, 110–11ff.

397. "It is a wire . . . $200,000": text taken from 95(1)v as indicated in the manuscript. Reiff's sentence for insertion is "Wire Suspension bridge across the Ohio at Wheeling built at a cost of nearly $200,000," but unlike his other inserts, this one does not connect up to the text.

Rude cabins are met with, built in all sorts of extraordinary places, on the steep sides of a hill, on the banks of stream, or in a hollow. The very children belonging to these cabins seem to partake of the wildness of their homes; and no wonder, for they are completely shut out from the world. Wherever possible seems to be a field cultivated (to a certain extent).

The locomotives are somewhat different from any I've ever seen. They burn coal, a sort of a carriage top is fixed up to almost the top of the pipe; the place where the fire is made seems very low, the Engineer is over the boiler. [97] The hills we are whizzing apast and around (at thirty miles an hour) are mostly covered with large trees—when looking at these hills, our train seems like a small serpent crawling around it. We stopped at one place where are some machine shops belonging to the road. I went into one of the shops; they were repairing a locomotive, and as I perceived the men understood their business, why, I left them without volunteering my aid.

We stopped at Fairmont, Marion Co., Va on the Monongahela River[398] for supper—but I preferred looking at the suspension bridge at this place![399] The river has a slight falls at this place, and is altogether a very pretty place. I was nearly left here; the cars started while I was purchasing some cakes. I ran after it, but some boys who were in my way seemed to hinder me on purpose. I pushed one, but he scarcely moved. When I, getting angry, gave him another blow, which *nearly* cost him his life, for, had I shoved him a little stronger he would have gone[400] under the cars. Of course, this all happened in a second or so. I was quite faint with excitement *when* I did get on board, but was quite revived when Horny pulled out his whiskey bottle; either the sight of the bottle or the taste of its *contents,* recovered me. I have not decided which it *was.* [98] Fairmont is 77 miles from Wheeling. From a short distance beyond this, we ran along side of a very pretty river (*very* small) called Tygart's Valley River,[401] at Grafton;[402] 100 miles is the junction of the N.W. Virginia Railroad.[403]

398. "Monongahela": "Mouongahela" in Reiff.

399. The "Great Iron Bridge" was built in 1852, and connected Fairmont and Palatine, Virginia (now West Virginia); it was finally replaced in 1908 (Miller and Maxwell, *West Virginia and Its People,* III, 1072).

400. "Would have gone under": "would have went under" in Reiff.

401. The Tygart Valley River is a principal tributary of the Monongahela River; it was settled by Europeans when David Tygart and Robert Files (1715–1753) separately moved there in 1753. See Maxwell, *The History of Barbour County,* 180–81.

402. Grafton, Virginia (now West Virginia).

403. Opened on 1 May 1857, the "Northwestern Virginia Railroad" was the operating name

We have passed through several tunnels. Between Newburg[h] (113)[404] and Tunnelton (119 miles)[405] we went through Kingwood Tunnel which is nearly a mile long; it seems to be supported (from the sides) with timber, it is very high.[406] In the middle is a house! Several men were here with lanterns as there are in *all* the tunnels; on this road there are *ten* (so I counted) from here (Wheeling) to Baltimore.

Figure 11. *View of Eastern End of the Great "Kingwood Tunnel."* Built between 1849 and 1852, the Kingwood Tunnel carried the Baltimore and Ohio Railroad through from Baltimore to Wheeling. Reiff recorded that the tunnel was "nearly a mile long; it seems to be supported (from the sides) with timber, it is very high. In the middle is a house!" Reiff"s encounter with the tunnel was typical of the company's rail journeys; most lines were new, and features such as the tunnel were novelties.

We are now twisting about and *ascending* the Alleghany Mountains.[407] The ascent is easily perceived from my seat, the end of the last car. It is moonlight; on the north side of the mountains, we frequently see[408] large

of the Parkersburg Branch of the Baltimore and Ohio Railroad. Reiff must be referring to a new but as yet unused junction (*Poor's Manual of Railroads*, 347).

404. Newburg, Virginia (now West Virginia).

405. Tunnelton, Virginia (now West Virginia).

406. Built between 1849 and 1852, the Kingwood Tunnel, near Tunnelton, West Virginia, completed the Baltimore and Ohio Railroad's construction across what is now West Virginia to Wheeling. Replaced in 1912, it was sealed in 1962. See also William Smith, *The Book of the Great Railway Celebrations*, 161–62, and plate opposite 163.

407. "Alleghany": also spelled "Allegheny" and "Allegany" in Reiff.

408. "Frequently see large": "frequently seen large" in Reiff.

patches of snow, though it is so warm that Horncastle and I have our windows open. We twist and go about like a vessel tacking; at between one and two o'clock, we are at the top of the mountain at *Altamont*[409]—156 miles, we are 2,700 ft above Baltimore. Here is plenty of snow; at the risk of getting flung off, I was on the back platform looking down the deep valleys. [99]

It is a beautiful and magnificent sight; on the top there is not so much forest and occasionally some cabins, but ascending the mountains the trees are very large. There is considerable snow on the top.

At Cumberland, is the station Bedford Spring; at half past five, the sun rose most beautifully.

We are now running along the Potomac River; the face of the country is large hills, rivulets, much rock and stone, and, frequently, farms. Looks more eastern, no cabins, though I did see two or three sycamores.

Harper's Ferry, 298 miles, is prettily situated in a sort of valley—it seems compactly built and looks remarkably neat.[410] The hilly country is very beautiful here. A canal runs along here.[411] We are running in valleys though not so high ones as we passed through last night.

Upon arriving at Washington Junction—called the Relay House[412]—many people got out and a beautiful scene is here presented rolling hills, cedars, &c.[413]

Arrived at Baltimore at half-past past 10, a clear, windy warm morning. [100]

---

409. "Altamont": "Altamount" in Reiff. Altamont, Maryland.

410. Harpers Ferry is located at the juncture of Maryland, Virginia, and what became West Virginia in 1861. A 1734 patent gave Robert Harper (1718–1782) the land; he founded a ferry across the Potomac in 1761, and the town was established in 1763. When Reiff visited, the town was an industrial center, one that would be destroyed in the Civil War. See Barry, *The Annals of Harper's Ferry*, 22–28.

411. The Chesapeake and Ohio Canal, which ran along the Potomac River from Washington, DC, to Cumberland, Maryland, was begun in 1828, and operated from 1831 to 1924. It reached Harpers Ferry in 1833. See Ward, *The Early Development of the Chesapeake and Ohio Canal Project*, 101–10.

412. "Call'd the Relay House": text inserted from 98v as indicated in the manuscript.

413. Relay House—along with the town of Relay—was the original staging post for the horses that drew the first B&O trains from Baltimore to Ellicott Mills, Howard Company. The buildings, illustrated in *Harper's Weekly* for April 1853, show train sheds and the white Relay House hotel. The junction would become crucial in the Civil War. See Federal Writers' Project, *Maryland*, 308.

Thursday April 10th   **Baltimore**

Horncastle said I looked like a sweep; riding most of the night on the back platform over the mountains, it's not to be much wondered at. Was absolutely begrimed with dirt, I don't recollect of my face ever being as dirty as it is this morning.[414]

After cleaning, I went to the Holliday[415] where I was immediately carried *nons volens*[416] next door next door to whiskey; it was repeated upon Sandy getting hold of me, and oysters were not left untasted.

Rehearsal with Mrs Chapman.[417]

At night went to the Holliday to see Forrest play Virginius.[418] What I saw of it, he does exceedingly well. I escaped from Jameson, &c., and got to bed actually at half past 12, and this in Baltimore, too. Letters from home & Zkl.[419]

Friday April 11th   **Baltimore to Washington**

After attending to Mrs C—, went to theatre, then to Shaw's, where Atherton was sick.[420] Went to Theatre. Wrote answers to my letters in great haste.

Left Baltimore for Washington at 3 pm. Nothing particular happened on the road which occupied 2 hours—Bladensburg, however, is rather a pretty place to the left of the railroad.[421] The remainder of the way is through poor and very unexciting country. [101]

414. "Was absolutely begrimed . . . it is this morning": text inserted from 99v as indicated in the manuscript. The preceding sentence, "I had been on the rear platform of the last car nearly the whole night," merely repeats the information in the earlier part of this one and has been excised.

415. Built in 1813 as the Baltimore Theatre to replace the 1793 wooden structure, it was known to the populace by a variety of names, including Old Drury. It was finally destroyed by fire in 1873 (Bordman and Hischak, *The Oxford Companion to American Theatre*, 314).

416. "*Nons volens*" seems to be a version of "nolens volens," meaning "willing or not" (*OED*, X, 467).

417. Possibly Mrs. Anne B. Chapman; see *Woods' Baltimore Directory for 1856-57.*

418. The actor Edwin Forrest (1806–1872), one of whose major roles was the title role in James Sheridan Knowles's 1820 tragedy, *Virginius.* See Bruce Cornache, "Edwin Forrest," *ODNB*, XX, 378–80.

419. See note 197.

420. Shaw's not further identified, but possibly a hotel or boardinghouse.

421. Bladensburg, now a residential suburb of Washington, DC, was originally called Garrison's Landing, but was renamed in honor of Thomas Bladen, governor of Maryland, 1742–47. The site of the defeat of US troops by General Robert Ross who went on to burn Washington, it was chartered in 1742 and incorporated in 1854 (Hellmann, *Historical Gazetteer of the United States*, 472).

Went to the National Theatre[422] where I received two letters, one from Father, the other from Uncle John. Walked up Pennsylvania Avenue to the President's House—& could not get in—sat in one of the iron settees in the grounds, and read my letters; most magnificent day. Then went to see the Washington Monument—which has stopped for want of funds[423]—France can build monuments to her Napoleon, England to Nelson—yet there is not patriotism enough in America to build a monument to our Pater Patriae, Washington. Yet for *true* greatness, how immensurably superior is he to either of these great characters. A beautiful piece of what seems granite but with a brown polish, was sent from Bremen, it has this inscription:

> Washington
> Dem grossen—guten—und gerechten—
> (here a key and some other Symbolic Sign)
> Das befreundete
> Bremen[424]

Stones from China, Indian tribes, Turkey, and from many of the States, are in a shed.

At night, was to Browns Hotel, a large white building.[425] [102]

SATURDAY APRIL 12th   WASHINGTON

The most dusty day I ever experienced.

Visited the Patent Office, a most stupendous and beautiful building.[426] The curiosities most wonderful and interesting, especially the Declaration

422. The National Theatre on Pennsylvania Avenue was opened in 1835; the building Reiff experienced was replaced in 1845 after a major fire and reopened with performances by Jenny Lind (Bordman and Hischak, *The Oxford Companion to American Theatre*, 453).

423. Reiff had seen a block of marble on 22 February in Lafayette Square in New Orleans apparently intended for the Washington Monument (see note 237). At the time of Reiff's visit, it stood at 154 feet. Work had largely stopped from 1854 amid general dissatisfaction with the project and from want of funds and was not resumed until 1880 (Emery, *The Washington Monument*, 4).

424. "To (or "For") Washington, the great, good, and just. From Bremen in friendship."

425. The Brown's Hotel that Reiff knew was the product of extensive alterations (including the addition of a white marble facade) by the architect John Haviland (1792–1852). On Pennsylvania Avenue and known originally as the Davis Hotel, it had been bought by Jesse B. Brown in 1820 and renamed Brown's Indian Queen Hotel. It became Brown's Marble Hotel when it reopened in 1851 after Haviland's refit (Carrier, *Washington D.C.*, 47).

426. A major Greek Revival building, the Patent Office was started in 1831 to the design of Robert Mills (1781–1855), and after his dismissal in 1851, under the supervision of Thomas

Figure 12. *Washington Monument at 154 feet!* Reiff, who on 22 February 1856 had seen in New Orleans a block of marble intended for the Washington Monument, now saw the actual edifice, which stood only 154 feet. Work had stopped in 1854 amid general dissatisfaction with the project and from want of funds. Reiff commented, "France can build monuments to her Napoleon, England to Nelson—yet there is not patriotism enough in America to build a monument to our *Pater Patriae,* Washington."

of Independence, of which the signatures are fast fading.[427] What a misfortune. Washington's coat with large brass buttons, his buckskin waistcoat and breeches,[428] together with his camp chest,[429] writing desk,[430] &c. Affected me very much to see from what common tin plates our great Washington eat

Ustick Walter (1804–1887). It took thirty-one years to complete. The building served as a kind of national repository until the construction of other institutions such as the National Archives. See Reiff, *Washington Architecture,* 38–39.

427. The Declaration of Independence was transferred in 1841 to the then-new Patent Office, where it and George Washington's commission as commander in chief were mounted and displayed together. They hung there for thirty-five years, "accelerating the deterioration of the ink and parchment of the Declaration," a situation Reiff astutely observed. After a number of homes, it was transferred to the National Archives in 1952. See America's Founding Documents.

428. The uniform was worn by George Washington from 1789 until his death in 1799; it was transferred to the Patent Office from the Columbian Institute in 1841, and to the Smithsonian Institution in 1883. It can be seen in a number of life portraits from Washington's later years, including the 1789 watercolor by John Ramage.

429. George Washington's "Camp Chest" is, in fact, a canteen, with pots, plates, and platters made of tin-plated sheet iron. Sold at auction after Washington's death, it passed to Colonel Henry Maynadier, who presented it to the federal government; it was transferred from the Patent Office to the Smithsonian Institution in 1883.

430. These were possibly Washington's desk and armchair, which were purchased during

from; and his common writing desk and sword is enough to affect the heart of anyone who loves America and America's proudest boast: Geo. Washington! How better could I spend the anniversary of Harry Clay's birth?[431]

In the afternoon, Stretton, Geo, and I went to the Smithsonian Institute, a peculiar Norman style of architecture.[432] It contains a library of 22,000 vols, a picture gallery, mostly Indian, a room of chemical machines, a lecture room and a large hall upon entering with pillars (two rows) running through the centre to entire length.

Geo. and I took a bath. At night, went to market, &c. [103]

SUNDAY APRIL 13th   WASHINGTON

Rain'd last night and laid the dust.

Went to the Episcopal Church with Geo and Horncastle.[433] Heard a very fair sermon, the text was "Today thou shalt be with me in Paradise."[434]

Wrote letters all the afternoon; to St. Louis, N.Y., Cincinnati, and Buffalo.

After supper, George and I walked out to Georgetown, across a canal

---

his presidency, probably from Thomas Burling, a New York cabinetmaker. When Washington retired, he took them to Mount Vernon (they therefore escaped the fate of the rest of the president's furniture, which was burned with the White House in 1814) and bequeathed them to James Craik, his physician. They were returned to Mount Vernon about twenty-five years ago. See Decatur, "Flashback: George Washington's Furniture," and Van Cott, "Thomas Burling of New York City," 32–50.

431. "How better . . . birth?": text inserted from 101v as indicated in the manuscript.

432. Completed in 1855, the Smithsonian Institution was designed by architect James Renwick (1818–1895) and constructed of red sandstone from Seneca Creek, Maryland, in the Norman style; the building in the form Reiff knew was damaged by a fire in 1865, which destroyed the upper story of the main block and the north and south towers (Reiff, *Washington Architecture*, 89ff).

433. Reiff is referring to St. John's Episcopal Church in Lafayette Square. The church in its original form was designed by Benjamin Henry Latrobe (1764–1820) and was complete by the end of 1816 (Hamlin, *Benjamin Henry Latrobe*, 462–63). Latrobe described the church as "a smart thing enough, at which the natives stare exceedingly, because it does not resemble a barn, but has the form of a Cross and is covered with a dome": Latrobe to Henry S. B. Latrobe, 8 November 1815, in Van Horne, *The Correspondence and Miscellaneous Papers of Benjamin Henry Latrobe*, III: 1811–1820, 702.

434. A quotation drawn from St. Luke's gospel, 23:43: "And Jesus said unto him, Verily I say unto thee, Today shalt thou be with me in paradise." Assuming the rector was preaching, Reiff heard a sermon by Rev. Dr. Smith Pyne, rector 1845–64 (Grimmett, *St. John's Church*, 153–54).

(bridge).[435] Its streets are very wide, the place is more compactly built than Washington; we walked through the city to the other end of it.

Previous to arriving at the Georgetown Bridge, we passed through a pretty park called the circle at the head of a very beautiful avenue.[436]

We returned by passing the White House, of which the back is towards Pen[a] Avenue. I think it is a very good building, quite sufficiently fine for a President of the U.S. Pennsylvania Avenue runs nearly east & west, at [103[v]] the east end stands the Capitol and the other (one mile's distant) the White House.

Georgetown is on the Potomac, but a canal (the Alexandria) runs between the town and the river.[437] George & I sitting on a pile of timber (it is a beautiful moonlight night) had a long talk about things in general, and about the probability of our being at our homes in a little more than four weeks. [104]

MONDAY APRIL 14th   WASHINGTON

Received a number of letters. Visited (with George) Congress.[438] The Senate chamber was very crowded when we came in. Stephen A. Douglas of Illinois[439] was speaking against the reception of a petition from Gen. Lane

435. This was the aqueduct bridge, started in 1833 and demolished in 1923, which took the Alexandria Canal over the Potomac River, and allowed boats from the Chesapeake and Ohio Canal to cross the river and continue on down to Alexandria's seaport. See note 437 on the Alexandria Canal, and Kapsch, *Canals,* I, 238.

436. Reiff appears to be referring to Washington Circle, the junction of Twenty-Third Street, K Street, New Hampshire Avenue, and Pennsylvania Avenue; it became Washington's first traffic circle when the area was enclosed and landscaped in 1856. See Bednar, *L'Enfant's Legacy,* 185–192.

437. The charter to build the Alexandria Canal that connected the city of Alexandria to Georgetown was granted by Congress to the Alexandria Canal Company in 1830. The charter included an aqueduct bridge—see note 435—and the system was finished by 1843 (Kapsch, *Canals,* I, 238).

438. Reiff went to visit the first session of the Thirty-Fourth US Congress, which ran from 3 December 1855 to 18 August 1856; the Congress ran until 3 March 1857.

439. Stephen A. Douglas (1813–1861) was a US senator who represented Illinois and held office from 1847 to 1861. He had been largely responsible for the Compromise of 1850, which seemed to settle the slavery question, but also reopened the issue by promoting the Kansas-Nebraska Act of 1853. In the period Reiff saw him in action, he was regarded as a major figure in the house. See Robert W. Johannsen, "Stephen Arnold Douglas," *ANB,* VI, 805–8.

concerning Kansas.[440] Douglas looks like a very vain man; he was replied to by a senator (about 55) from either Ohio or Iowa;[441] [I later ascertained it was] Wade of Ohio.[442]

In the House of Representatives, someone was speaking upon a bill concerning the "Better prevention of fire in the District of Columbia." None of the members seemed to be paying attention to him; in fact, there was so much speaking and walking about, that it was almost impossible to hear the honourable member—he was replied to by a tall member from New York.

We soon retreated from the gallery, for it [was] most filled with a dirty set of fellows (Irishmen in the majority) that the odour was anything but pleasant. Nearly all of them had their feet on the seats, their hats on, and were talking—Ugh! There should be an official here to make the people behave themselves. [105]

[Performance: *La Sonnambula*,[443] National Theatre.]

TUESDAY APRIL 15th   WASHINGTON

Was in the Patent Office for a long time. Saw the autographs of Napoleon, Alexander the 1st of Russia, Louis 16th of France, Louis 18th of ditto, George IV when Prince Regent, Louis Philippe, Ferdinand of Spain, the Emperor of Brazil, &c.[444] [and also] the original Declaration of Independence.

[Performance: *The Crown Diamonds*, National Theatre.]

---

440. James Henry Lane (1814–1866) was elected to Congress in 1852 and subsequently voted for the Kansas-Nebraska bill, which repealed the Missouri Compromise. In 1855, he moved to Kansas, and in response to his party's uncompromising attitude on slavery as it affected the state, joined the Free Soil Party. In June of that year he assisted in organizing the "National Democracy," one of the cardinal principles of which was that the citizens of other states should "let Kansas alone." See Mark A. Plummer, "James Henry Lane," *ANB*, XIII, 121–23.

441. This was Benjamin Wade (1800–1878), an Ohio lawyer, who after an early political career as a Whig, joined the Republican Party, and was elected to the Senate in 1851. He opposed the Kansas-Nebraska Act and was a radical Republican, a group in the party from 1854 to 1877 which opposed slavery and, after the Civil War, supported civil rights and suffrage for the just-freed slaves. See Hans L. Trefousse, "Benjamin Wade," *ANB*, XXII, 431–32.

442. "Wade of Ohio": text inserted from 103v as indicated in the manuscript.

443. The troupe's arrival was advertised with the publication clippings and reviews of Pyne, Harrison, and Streeton (*Evening Star*, 14 April 1856). Miss Fannie Morant took the part of Liza at short notice (*Evening Star*, 15 April 1856).

444. Napoléon Bonaparte, Emperor of France (1769–1821); Alexander I of Russia (1777–

WEDNESDAY APRIL 16th   WASHINGTON

Visited the Capitol; the proper front is facing the east, but the city has been built mostly in the other direction. Westerly, the President's House is a mile, at the head of Pennsylvania Avenue. Facing the northwest, the Treasury is contiguous.

Heard Mr Jones of Iowa read a very long, uninteresting, speech.[445] Sam Houston was whittling, he called for the pages to bring him pieces of wood; he is certainly an original.[446]

Senator Butler of South Carolina is one of the finest and most venerable looking men in the Senate; his hair perfectly white and very long.[447] Hale (of New Hampshire) is a thick set sort of man, stiff hair, and somewhat jolly countenance.[448] [106]

[Performance: *Maritana,* National Theatre.]

THURSDAY APRIL 17th   WASHINGTON

I—— P—— arrived today; said she I was [. . .].[449]

Visited the Senate; a bill for giving 166 acres to soldiers, &c., &c. who

1825); Louis XVI of France (1754–93); Louis XVIII of France (1755–1824); Louis Philippe I of France (1773–1850); George IV of England (the Prince Regent, 1762–1830); Ferdinand VII of Spain (1784–1833); and Dom Pedro II, Emperor of Brazil, "The Magnanimous" (1825–1891).

445. George Wallace Jones (1804–1896), an attorney and judge, served in the Senate from 1848 to 1859; he supported the Kansas-Nebraska Act of 1854. See James A. Rawley, "George Wallace Jones," *ANB,* XII, 195–96.

446. Sam Houston (1793–1863), a key figure in the history of Texas and after whom Houston is named, was elected to the Senate in 1845, serving from 1846 to 1859. He was in office during the Mexican-American War and, throughout his term, presciently opposed the growing polarization of the North and South, supporting the Compromise of 1850 and opposing the Kansas-Nebraska Act of 1854. See Randolph B. Campbell, "Sam Houston," *ANB,* XI, 279–81.

447. Andrew Pickens Butler (1796–1857), one of the authors of the Kansas-Nebraska Act, served as senator of South Carolina from 1846 to 1857. Butler was well known for his rhetorical skills, and surviving photographs attest to Reiff's description of his white head of hair. See Orville Vernon Burton, "Andrew Pickens Butler," *ANB,* IV, 88–90.

448. John Parker Hale (1806–1873) served in Congress as a Democrat from 1843 to 1845, and as an independent senator for New Hampshire from 1847 to 1853, and again as a member of the Free Soil Party and then the Republican Party, from 1855 to 1865. He was a leading and outspoken opponent of slavery. See Donald P. Cole, "John Parker Hale," *ANB,* IX, 826–28.

449. "I—— P——," obviously a woman, but not further identified.

have been in the service of the US, was under consideration. Bell (Tenessee),[450] and Judge Collamer[451] (of Vermont) offered amendments which were negatived.

Heard the following Senators speak—Butler (of South Carolina), Bell (of Tennessee), Collamer (of Vermont), Foot (of Vermont),[452] Pugh (Ohio, a young man rather dandified, did not like him),[453] Stuart (Michigan, a plain looking man, fair talents seemingly),[454] Mason (Virginia),[455] Brown (of Miss.),[456] Crittenden (of Kentucky, a small man with hair mainly white, spoke very well).[457]

450. John Bell (1796–1869), known as "the Great Apostate," served Tennessee from 1827 until 1841 in the House of Representatives, and in the Senate from 1847 until 1859. He also served as Speaker of the House from 1834 to 1835 and was only one of two southern senators to vote against the Kansas-Nebraska Act. See Daniel W. Crofts, "John Bell," ANB, II, 509–11.

451. Jacob Collamer (1791–1865), a barrister and an associate justice of the supreme court of Vermont, was elected to the House of Representatives in 1842 and to the Senate in 1855 as a conservative, antislavery Republican (Biographical Directory of the American Congress, 845).

452. Solomon Foot (1802–1866) was elected as a Whig congressman in 1843 and as a senator in 1850. He was opposed to the Kansas-Nebraska Act. After the formation of the new Republican Party, he was reelected as a Republican senator in 1856 and served until his death in 1866. See Frederick J. Blue, "Solomon Foot," ANB, VIII, 188–89.

453. George Ellis Pugh (1822–1876), a Democratic senator from Ohio, was a lawyer and solider who served a single term from 1855 to 1861 and who supported a policy of nonintervention in the matter of slavery in the territories; his subsequent bids for office were unsuccessful. See Thomas W. Kremm, "George Ellis Pugh," ANB, XVII, 921–22.

454. Charles Edward Stuart (1810–1887) was a lawyer who became a Democratic senator in 1853 and served until 1859 (Biographical Directory of the American Congress, 1901).

455. "Mason": "Masau" in Reiff. James Murray Mason (1798–1871) was a Democratic senator elected in 1848, 1850, and 1856 who worked for maintaining the Union; he drafted the Fugitive Slave Law in 1850, which required that all runaway slaves be returned to their owners. He subsequently changed tack, refusing to support a Union that did not integrate southern values and leadership, and was prepared to succeed. See Charles M. Hubbard, "James Murray Mason," ANB, XIV, 650–51.

456. Albert Gallatin Brown (1813–1880) was a widely loved former governor of Mississippi, a great supporter of education, both at grade-school and university level, and a supporter of the expansion of slavery. He served as US senator for Mississippi from 1854 to 1861. See William L. Barney, "Albert Gallatin Brown," ANB, III, 651–52.

457. "Crittenden": "Cruttenden" in Reiff. John Jordan Crittenden (1787–1863) was a politician active for many years in Kentucky politics, and was appointed attorney general in 1850 by President Millard Fillmore. His priority throughout the 1850s was the preservation of the Union, and he was reelected to the Senate after his term as attorney general, where he not only

I was disappointed with Senator Seward's appearance, he seems small and insignificant; walked about with his hands in his pocket.[458] Slidell is an old man; had always thought to the contrary.[459] Sumner of Massachusetts is a tall, fine looking, man about 35,[460] Wilson of Massachusetts is a thick, fat Yankee (and seems to feel his dignity!).[461]

Saw Greenough's statue of Washington.[462] [107]

In the evening, the President visited the Opera. Whether it is my prejudice of the man or not, I cannot say but that I was much disappointed with his looks; he has a long thin nose, dark hair, a somewhat sallow complexion, small forehead, and altogether a very unprepossessing appearance.[463]

---

sought out moderates who might support him but formed the Constitutional Union Party in 1860. He was the author of the Crittenden Compromise, which attempted to address the concerns of the southern states but was rejected by Congress. See Thomas E. Stephens, "John Jordan Crittenden," *ANB*, V, 740–42.

458. William Henry Seward Sr. (1801–1872) was a senator from New York from 1849 to 1861. He was vigorously opposed to the spread of slavery in the years prior to the Civil War and was a major figure in the formative years of the Republican Party. See Daniel W. Crofts, "William Henry Seward," *ANB*, XIX, 676–81.

459. John Slidell (1793–1871), a lawyer and businessman, was a senator for Louisiana from 1853 to 1861, and a supporter of the South in the years before the Civil War. See Carolyn E. De Latte, "John Slidell," *ANB*, XX, 87–89.

460. "Sumner": "Summers" in Reiff. Reiff must be referring to Charles Sumner (1811–1874), an academic lawyer who was the leader of the antislavery forces in Massachusetts. He denounced the Kansas-Nebraska Act the month after Reiff saw him and was beaten on the floor of the Senate for his views; he was unable to attend the House for the next three years. See Pierce, *Memoirs and Letters of Charles Sumner*, II, 461–524; Palmer, *The Selected Letters of Charles Sumner*, I, 457–538; and Frederick J. Blue, "Charles Sumner," *ANB*, XXI, 137–39.

461. Opposed to slavery, Henry Wilson (1812–1875), later vice president, was a senator from Massachusetts elected by the Know Nothings in 1855. He became one of the organizers of the new Republican Party. See Richard H. Abbott, "Henry Wilson," *ANB*, XXIII, 579–81.

462. The American sculptor Horatio Greenough (1805–1852) modeled his *Enthroned Washington* on the great statue *Zeus Olympios*. Commissioned by Congress for display in the Capitol rotunda, the statue of the half-naked Washington became a subject of much controversy when it arrived in 1841, and in 1843 it was relocated to the East Lawn of the Capitol, where Reiff must have seen it. See the letter of 28 January 1834 from Greenough to Edward Livingston describing his intentions in Wright, ed., *Letters of Horatio Greenough American Sculptor*, 173–74, and also Wright, *Horatio Greenough, the First American Sculptor*, 118–59.

463. This was Franklin Pierce (1804–1869), president 1853–57. Reiff's description certainly agrees with Pierce's image in the 1858 portrait by George Alexander Healy (1813–1894) that hangs in the White House. Reiff's dislike of Pierce was based on his reputation as a "dough

A heavy shower during the day.

[Performance: *The Daughter of the Regiment*,[464] National Theatre.]

FRIDAY APRIL 18th   WASHINGTON

A beautiful day. Visited the Congressional burying ground—with I——
P——. The ground is southeast from the Capitol; the tombs of the Congressmen are all of the same shape   the top is round.[465]

Among others is Henry Clay's (his remains are in Kentucky),[466] Calhoun,[467]
&c. It is a rather pretty ground, is on the bank of the Potomac, the east
branch.

At supper, old Adkins[468] said to me that the Americans were all jaw, were
hogs, and blackguards,[469] and made particular mention of New Yorkers.
Many words passed; I said to him, among other things, that he got his living
in New York, and ought to be ashamed to speak so of the place; he said it

---

face, a northerner with Southern principles"; he was a supporter of the Kansas-Nebraska Act
and was seen as "truckling to the South," and his popularity was at a low point. See Larry Gara,
"Franklin Pierce," *ANB*, XVII, 495.

464. The opera will be performed "with all the original music. . . . After the Opera, the
National Anthem of Hail Columbia will be sung" (*Evening Star*, 17 April 1856). "President
Pierce and lady, with Mr. Sidney and several members of the Cabinet were present" (*Evening
Star*, 18 April 1856).

465. The Congressional Cemetery, originally established by private citizens in 1807, was
later made over to Christ Church on Capitol Hill and named the Washington Parish Burial
Ground. The first section was on E Street between Eighteenth and Nineteenth streets Southeast but had expanded three times by the period of Reiff's visit. The "tombs" (cenotaphs) on
which Reiff comments were the design of Benjamin Latrobe (1760–1820). See Johnson and
Johnson, *In the Shadow of the United States Capitol*, chaps. 1 and 2.

466. Henry Clay's burial site is in the 1849 Lexington Cemetery, where the remains of Clay
and his wife, Lucretia, are contained in two marble sarcophagi in a vaulted chamber, over
which stands a limestone Corinthian column topped by a statue of Clay. See Milward, *A History of the Lexington Cemetery*, 40–55.

467. John C. Calhoun (1782–1850), the seventh vice president of the United States. See John
Niven, "John C. Calhoun," *ANB*, IV, 213–16.

468. "Old Adkins": see note 182.

469. "Upon my saying that he who": succeeding phrase deleted by Reiff; it looks as though
he was going to write "he who cast the first stone."

was a lie.[470] But I stop'd by telling him that, in the presence of ladies, I should not pursue the subject farther but that [at] a proper place I would resume the quarrel. [108] I continued my supper, during the time he was looking at me as at a fiend. When I arose, he did so (we were sitting opposite to each other), he came up to me in a very threatening manner and demanded that I should take back what I said. My reply was a decided negative, possibly harshly expressed. He then raised his hand to strike, but I caught his arm; we struggled for a moment nearly overturning the dishes, when Mrs O'Bryan threw herself between us. Some caught hold of him, and others of me; we were then parted. I was perfectly livid with passion; several told me that I was quite as white as whitewash. Mrs O. B—— pitched into Adkins (with words) at a fearful rate, saying that he repeatedly insulted her boarders and herself by so continually speaking ill of Americans. I said "If I have used any ungentlemanly expression" while in the heat of passion, I ask the pardon of the ladies for so far forgetting myself. Mrs. O'Bryan took my part in every possible way, as did everyone.

It was supposed that Adkins would meet me outside, and Stretton came to my room and insisted upon going with me and advised not to seek him. Before going, a young lady caught hold of me and said I had promised to take her to the theatre (she thought that if a lady was with me [109] it would prevent the possibility of a row) but I told her that I would *not* see her to the theatre, but the girls bid fair to have hung on to me until Stretton had promised he would see that I did not get in any difficulty.

Sat up very late with dear Joe, and slept very little; Adkins sat in the next room purposely to annoy us.[471]

[Performance: *The Bohemian Girl*, National Theatre.]

SATURDAY APRIL 19th   WASHINGTON

Dined with Gerhardt (Violaist) and Musgriff. Gerhardt keeps a sort of Lager Beer[472] Garden near the Capitol—then went to wenches, and Withers's.

---

470. "I said to him . . . he said it was a lie": this sentence appears isolated on 107v but clearly belongs in this paragraph.

471. "Dear Joe" is clearly Joseph Stretton; they seem to have spent the evening in what appears to have been Mrs. O'Bryan's double parlor, with Adkins listening in.

472. "Beer": "bier" in Reiff.

Copied the song of the Fairy Queen from *Cinderella*.[473]

Strange to say that it was originally supposed that the city would have been built east of the Capitol, but it has been built almost entirely to the west of it. It seems to the east of the Capitol was bought up by speculators who asked more for the land than it was worth in consequence of which people bought on the west side. [110]

[Performance: *The Barber of Seville*,[474] National Theatre.]

SUNDAY APRIL 20th   WASHINGTON TO RICHMOND

Left Washington on the steamboat "Baltimore" for Aquia Creek.[475] The Potomac is very broad, hilly, the boat is a small, low pressure, one pipe, steamer. It was a cold chilly morning and raining. Nothing specially occurred until we passed Mount Vernon—we did not pass on that side of the river—the tomb seems of a brown colour—and very near the house—the place is on a small hill—and is quite surrounded with trees.

Alexandria seems an old fashioned sort of place with narrow streets.

Arrived at Aquia Creek at a quarter to ten. Took the cars. Passed through a very pretty county, the trees begin to leaf, the wheat is springing up, grass ditto, and everything looks pleasant. Went through but few towns. Proctor, Kenible, Warre, and Horncastle got horribly drunk;[476] Ghor & I were obliged to almost carry Horncastle to the Broad St. House,[477] by which means my baggage was locked up, and I could not get it until next morning.

473. This appears to have been the song "Delightful hours of rapture," the finale from Act II, unless a solo number for the Fairy Queen had been added to the text; see Lacy, *Cinderella; or, The Fairy and Little Glass Slipper*, 25.

474. Benefit: Pyne (*Evening Star*, 19 April 1856).

475. Aquia Creek is a tributary of the tidal segment of the Potomac River in northern Virginia, and later a Civil War battle site. See Salmon, *The Official Virginia Civil War Battlefield Guide*, 9–12.

476. "Proctor" and "Kenible" are not otherwise mentioned by Reiff but may have been two of the musicians employed on the tour.

477. The Broad Street House seems to be the hotel in which at least Horncastle stayed; Reiff mentions no hotel for himself, although this remark implies that he may have also been staying there. It stood a block away from, and on the opposite side to, the Richmond Theatre, at Broad and Ninth. See Map of the City of Richmond, engraved by M. Ellyson, and included in Ellyson, *The Richmond Directory and Business Advertiser*.

Called upon Sally Partington.[478] Found her riding horseback in her yard; looks rather thin. Met Kitty in the street who scarcely knew me, said I had grown so fat.[479] [111]

Figure 13. *Richmond, from the Hill above the Waterworks.* The view of Richmond by George Cooke takes a vantage point above the Kanawha Canal and the James River, and encompasses Jefferson's state capitol, which Reiff visited on 21 April 1856.

MONDAY APRIL 21ˢᵗ   RICHMOND

Snowing all day; seems as if we had come north instead of south. No going out; this the most unpleasant day we've had since leaving Providence, R.I.

478. Sally (or Sallie) Partington (1834–1907) was a British-born actress who, as a young girl, emigrated with her family to New York City, and then moved to Richmond. She and her three sisters Jennie (later Barnes), Katie, and Mary played at the Richmond Theatre for many years, and she gained some notoriety by performing during the Civil War and by continuing to believe that John Wilkes Booth was never captured. See "Sallie Partington: A Favorite of Theatregoers during Civil War Era," *Richmond Times-Dispatch,* 4 August 1935.

479. The "Kitty" Reiff met was possibly Katie Partington, as he seems to have encountered her as he left Sally Partington's house; see note 478.

Took a walk around the State House.[480] The State House stands on a very high piece of ground in a fine park overlooking the James River.[481] The building would be very fair but seemed to be in a very dilapidated condition. On the steps on the N.W. side are two bronze[482] statues cast in Munich of Jefferson, and Patrick Henry. They are to be put on the lower part of a magnificent pedestal near the State House (in the park) for which, as the principal figure, an equestrian statue of Washington is now being made in Munich (Germany); it is expected to be finished by the 4th of July.[483]

The Capitol faces the southwest and the park runs downhill to the street below; in fact, after leaving, the next street to Broad, the city slopes towards the river. The James River here runs from the northwest to southeast, just below the city it turns suddenly to the south, southeast. There are many mills (principally flour) worked by water power which is got from many miles above here; runs into a canal down into the city, the canal here, of course, being much higher than the river: between the two, the mills are.

[111ᵛ] Today upon leaving my room, I had left my pocket book containing between $30 and $40 in it. I returned about two hours after but did not miss it. The darkie (who attends to me) as I was going out, said "Massa, you forgot sumthin." "No, I haven't," said I, but [he] wanted me to go up to my room

480. "Took a walk around the State House": this piece of text appears separately at the top of page 111 in Reiff.

481. The Virginia State Capitol was completed to a design that was the result of a collaboration between Thomas Jefferson and the architect Charles-Louis Clérisseau (1721–1820) between 1785 and 1789, and although not completed, was first used in 1792. The building's model, the Maison Carrée, was illustrated in Clérisseau's *Antiquités de la France,* and held special significance for Jefferson, who thought it a Republican period building. This was the building Reiff saw, one for which Albert Lybrock completed measured drawings in 1858. It was extensively rebuilt after a major collapse in 1870. See Fiske Kimball, *The Capitol of Virginia,* especially page 61 for Lybrock's plans.

482. "Bronze": "brown" in Reiff?

483. Reiff is describing the Washington Monument, for which the state had raised funds since 1799. The foundation stone had finally been laid in 1850 in the presence of President Zachary Taylor. The design was by the American sculptor Thomas Gibson Crawford (1814–1857), and the statues Reiff saw were modeled in Rome. As well as the central equestrian statue (which arrived in 1857) and those of Jefferson and Henry mentioned by Reiff, there were later sculptures of Andrew Lewis (1720–1781), John Marshall (1755–1835), Thomas Nelson (1738–1789), and George Mason (1725–1792) by Randolph Rogers. See Dimmick, "A Catalogue of the Portrait Busts and Ideal Works of Thomas Crawford," especially 718.

so bad, that I finally did. He showed me my pocket book, not a dime[484] had been taken. If this had been North, would the servant have returned it? Of course not. And yet this slave, who is a perfect stranger to me, does so. In fact, now when I go out of the room if he happens to be here, he always very respectfully asks "Massa have you not forgot anything?" [112]

[Performance: Opera postponed, Harrison ill,[485] Richmond Theatre.][486]

TUESDAY APRIL 22nd   RICHMOND

Beautiful day, wonderful change in the weather. Took a walk with the "Old Lady" and Massachusetts, visited a tobacco factory; saw them pressing it into plugs, dipping it into liquorice & some wenchies were packing it. Darkies[487] were at work here, some of the darkies were singing something of the "suseaunal style:"[488]

as they did on the "Swan," &c.[489] They harmonized the tunes remarkably well. From there onto the Petersburg and Richmond R. R. bridge at the foot of 8th street. The bridge is very high and the view from here is perfectly beautiful.[490] The country can be seen for a long distance, it's very panoramic. Manchester, on the opposite side of the river lies below this bridge (south,

484. "Dime": "cent" scored out.

485. *Richmond Dispatch,* 22 April 1856.

486. The theater at Richmond—"The New Richmond Theatre"—at Broad (then "H") and Seventh streets, is listed on Moses Ellyson's 1856 Map of the City of Richmond (included in H. K. Ellyson's *Richmond Directory and Business Advertiser*), where it appears as the Marshall Theatre. It had opened in 1819, replacing the 1810 theater of the same name that had burned on 26 December 1811. See Shockley, *The Richmond Stage,* 360–82.

487. "Darkies": this word is indecipherable, but could also be "wenches," or even "welshies."

488. "Suseaunal": could also be "suseawnal."

489. On 16 January, Reiff commented that he had gone "into the Engineer's Room and saw a number of slaves dance and sing as they do on the plantations."

490. The bridge mentioned by Reiff was a truss bridge that carried the Richmond and Petersburg Railroad across the James River; it opened in 1838, was destroyed by the Confederate Army prior to the fall of Richmond, was rebuilt, and then closed in 1882. See Griggs, "James River Bridge at Richmond, Virginia," 12–14.

southeast), is a very pretty village.[491] The river runs over stones which can be seen here and there about, of course there is no navigation here. In the middle is a long, low, island, a bridge below here runs to the island there's another across from the island to the main shore opposite the city. To the right of the bridge is (about a half mile distant) a nail factory, next to it on the left (south east) is a saw mill above a flour mill (very large), the principal part of the city is on a high hill. The leaves are just out, the grass is green and the beautiful river makes the *coup d'oeil* from this [113] bridge most beautiful.[492] I think it is the handsomest situated city I've seen yet upon my travels.

In the afternoon, Geo. and I walked on Broad Street, which runs from the northwest to the southeast. We went up the road which crosses a valley, a sort of creek. (The city used to be only on this side but is now growing on the other). The street runs to 28th St on the opposite side of the creek, where it suddenly ends and immediately beyond, farms commence; the view is magnificent. The city seems very smoky, as the bituminous coal is also burnt here. Saw some very pretty young slaves; it must be acknowledged that a pretty Negro may sound strange to Northern ears, but such is nevertheless the fact, though in the North I never saw a pretty Negro child; here it is very common.

There are more slaves here than in any place I've yet seen. I had a talk with one—a boy of about 12 years—he seemed very happy and was well dressed (they are all comfortably dressed); he run of errand and waited on the table. The slaves in this house are very civil and attentive; I shall always dislike Northern servants after this.

Main St is the principal business street here, running parallel with the river. On the lower part of [114] the city the streets are nearly all laid out at right angles. The Exchange Hotel (for lots of travellers it is *the* hotel); under it is the Post Office.[493] The neighbourhood was the State House Park, is very pretty; there are many trees in the city.

491. Manchester, incorporated in 1769 on the south bank of the James, was an independent city, an active port, and an entry point to the United States for slave ships during the eighteenth century. It became part of Richmond in 1910. See Weisiger, *Old Manchester & Its Environs.*

492. Reiff seems to mean the glancing view from the bridge, "at the stroke of an eye." See also note 490.

493. The Exchange Hotel stood on the southeast corner of Franklin and Fourteenth streets; built to the Greek Revival design of Isaiah Rogers (1800–1869), it opened in 1841, closed in 1896, and was demolished in 1900–1901. As Reiff's remark suggests, the building contained

Received a letter from Father, announcing R. L. Steven's death.[494]
[Performance: *La Sonnambula,* Richmond Theatre.]

WEDNESDAY APRIL 23rd   RICHMOND

Raining all day. Cold—sitting by fires.
[Performance: *The Crown Diamonds,* Richmond Theatre.]

THURSDAY APRIL 24th   RICHMOND

A very warm day. Geo & I walked out to a cemetery, but were nearly kill'd with the heat and lazyness. I feel so horribly home sick—as I fear there is a probability of my being in N.Y. for but so short a time, that I can scarcely enjoy anything.

This cemetery is northwest of the city;[495] from here we walked down to the canal & river—we laid down for some time on a bridge which crosses the canal; the view is lovely. About a quarter of a mile above is a dam, an artificial one made to divert the water into a sort of canal or basin (which is lower that the canal & higher than the river below) for the purpose of watering the city. The water is pumped up into a reservoir (beyond the cemetery) by water power. The works look something like Fairmount (on a small scale), is call'd the City Water Works; we went to the water fall and sat at the bottom of it.[496] [114^v]

The river is studded with islands but can scarcely be call'd much of a river

---

other businesses; apart from the post office, there was also a reading room, baths, & stores. See Moses Ellyson's Map of the City of Richmond, 1856 (in H. K. Ellyson's *Richmond Directory and Business Advertiser*), and Greg Kimball, *American City, Southern Place,* 42–43.

494. "Received . . . R. L. Steven's death": inserted from 113v in Reiff. Robert Livingston Stevens (1787–1856) was an inventor and shipbuilder, who in 1807 with his father designed the first steamship, the *Phoenix,* which successfully navigated the ocean, and was commissioned by the US government to build the first ironclad warship. See Isles, *Leading American Inventors,* 3–39.

495. This is probably the Hollywood Cemetery that sold its first gravesite in 1848, and opened in 1850, a garden cemetery designed to be informal and tranquil. See Greg Kimball, *American City, Southern Place,* 55–57.

496. Reiff is referring to the results of the development of the James River and the Kanawha Canal, which provided a man-made turning basin, and a canal with access to the town's mills. The 1850s saw the construction of the Tidewater Connection Locks—five granite locks which dropped the canal sixty-nine feet, plus a Great Ship Lock, which connected the canal basin

here, for I think one could—on foot—by jumping from one stone to another, cross it. Our view from the bridge gave us the city to the southeast, the river; the Petersburgh railroad bridge, Manchester, &c., and in the W.N.W., the beautiful undulating country, winding river, falls, canal, &c.; the rushing waters sound charmingly. Going home (along the canal) we saw a fall of water from the canal towards the river of about 40 ft, rushing down amid the rocks giving us a beautiful prospect. [115]

[Performance: *The Bohemian Girl,* Richmond Theatre.]

FRIDAY APRIL 25th   RICHMOND

Received a very pleasant letter from Brow of Providence[497] and one from Washington, particularly pleasant. Visited the State House, the Senate Chamber; saw the Statue of Washington taken from life in 1788.[498]

In the afternoon, we crossed over a bridge—south-southeast of the Petersburgh—call'd Mayo's Bridge (1 cent toll) to Manchester.[499] Geo Atherton, with his usual magnanimity, paid my toll over the bridge; shall not forget his kindness. Manchester is [a] contemptible looking place. From here walked to the Petersburgh Bridge—a railroad runs from Manchester under the road (through an arch) of the P. & Richmond road. From the bridge, we view the scene—so charming—until a train of cars passed over the bridge. Geo got so nervous as to stoop down behind one of the large tubs—which are placed about every 25 ft apart—filled with [water] to put on fire, in case

---

to the James River below Richmond. See also Greg Kimball, *American City, Southern Place,* 16–17, and the *Report of the Committee on the James River Improvements.* Reiff appears to be referencing the Fairmount Waterworks in Philadelphia; of a grand classical design by Frederick Graff (1775–1847), they were built between 1812 and 1872.

497. Presumably Providence, Rhode Island; Brow seems not to have been among those he encountered in the theater.

498. The marble, life-size statue by French sculptor Jean-Antoine Houdon (1785–1788) was commissioned in June 1784 by the General Assembly, who ordered a statue to be made "of the finest marble and best workmanship." Houdon visited Mount Vernon in 1785 to make a plaster cast of Washington; it was finished in 1788 and shipped to America in 1796. See Poulet, *Jean-Antoine Houdon,* 263–68. It was regarded as an accurate likeness: "That is the man, himself," Lafayette said, "I can almost realize he is going to move."

499. Mayo Bridge, also now known as Richmond's Fourteenth Street Bridge, was finished in 1788 at the instigation of John Mayo (1769–1818); the bridge has been much rebuilt, and the current structure was opened in 1913. See Dabney, *Richmond,* 45.

of necessity. It seems that schooners come into a canal to get up to the city, it looks so from where I was. We could from the bridge see the fall from the canal (mentioned yesterday). [115ᵛ] Grace, Franklin, and N. Western part of Maine, together with a portion of the streets that cross it—are the aristocratic streets. Cary St is a sort of Front St., N.Y., once Broad st—the Bowery.[500] The wards here are not numbered, but are call'd Jefferson, Madison, Monroe.

I received a very pleasant letter from Siss Carrie.

Shote here means Roast Pig. Tote—to carry. [116]

[Performance: *Maritana,* Richmond Theatre.]

SATURDAY APRIL 26ᵗʰ   RICHMOND

Geo and I walked out back of the city—north easterly—over some hills. At the end of 3rd St. is a cemetery, rather pretty.[501] It is an older one than the one we saw the other day. Passed through it—the trees are mostly pine & cedars. After passing some hills (which resemble slightly the environs back of St. Louis) we came to a road which reminded me of the road at Grandfather's place in Jersey.[502] At about three quarter of mile up, we came to a very pretty pine woods—short scrubby sort of pine. We sat down here for some time; the stillness of the country is quite delightful to me. Returned by another road which crosses a little purling stream. [117]

[Performance: *The Daughter of the Regiment,*[503] Richmond Theatre.]

SUNDAY APRIL 27ᵗʰ   RICHMOND

Very warm.

500. Reiff is referring to Broad Street in the Bowery district of New York, a commercial street in lower Manhattan which in 1676 replaced an earlier canal (Moscow, *The Street Book*). Cary Street was a similarly commercial street probably named after Colonel Archibald Cary (1721–1787), who lived on the Ampthill Plantation in Chesterfield.

501. This is the Shockoe Hill Cemetery, opened in 1820 and with its first burial in 1822. Enlarged in 1833 and 1850, it was the city's first publicly owned burial ground. See Stoddard and Thomas, *Richmond Cemeteries,* chap. 5.

502. Reiff's mother was Sarah Dobbs, "of the family connected with Dobb's Ferry"; see "Descendants of the Philharmonic Founders," 3. It is not clear precisely where his grandfather was living.

503. Benefit: Louisa Pyne (*Richmond Dispatch,* 26 April 1856).

We started off early and walked up along the canal (north westerly) pass-ing the city water works, falls, &c., that we visited on Wednesday. Today we walked between three and four miles up the canal, along which the scenery is beautiful. The river is near the canal; the odour from the trees in blossom and the sweet briars, &c., gave a most delicious fragrance to the atmosphere. I enjoyed the stroll beyond description. The canal twists about, continually varying the scene; it passes almost entirely through woodland. The river is on our left; a small steamboat call'd the "Calypso," about 30 ft long and 8 wide with a pipe looking like a *stove pipe* passed up the river; she is an excursion boat and the smallest specimen of craft of the kind I ever beheld.

We passed some time at the waterfall mentioned on Wednesday (the 40 ft fall).

In the afternoon we went to an African Church (white preacher) on the corner of Broad St.[504] I stuck George in a pew with three wenches sat outside of him; he could not get out. The choir sang very well, but the *congregational* singing was extremely ludicrous; I could not help laughing. [118]

MONDAY APRIL 28th   RICHMOND

Very warm. We walked up Broad St. to 28th St (end of the city) then to-wards the river. On a hill here the James River can be seen for some miles, as it turns southerly. The river is quite narrow here, even more so than at Cincinnati, is the Ohio. We went down to the "shipping," consisting of half a dozen[505] schooners, two steamships, and two steamboats. We went on board the "Jamestown," [a] packet steamer between here and New York; she is a very good vessel built in N.Y., engines at Morgan's Iron Works, 1853.[506] From thence on board of the steamer (propeller) "City of Richmond," a poor look-

504. The African Baptist Church of Richmond was founded in 1841 by the black members of Richmond's First Baptist Church. The church had always had a mixed congregation, but both sides were uncomfortable with the situation and promoted the split, with the now black congregation adding the word "African" to the title. The original church building of 1802 was sold to the new black congregation and was the one that Reiff knew. For an account of these circumstances, see Kimball, *American City, Southern Place,* 28–29ff.

505. "Dozen": "don" in Reiff.

506. The *Jamestown* was blown out to sea as far as Cape Hatteras in the great storm of Sep-tember 1857 and was seized at City Point, sixty miles below Richmond, during the Civil War in 1861. She was sunk to obstruct the James River at Drewry's Bluff in 1862.

ing affair made in Philadelphia.[507] I went even down down in the firemans' hold as there was fire in the boilers; I soon retreated from there as it was horribly hot.

The steamboat "Curtis Peck" (formerly of N.Y.) we next boarded,[508] and lastly, the "Belvidere," a peculiar looking steamboat, the forward deck entirely enclosed.[509] She runs to Baltimore, and is a freight boat. The canal in which the schooners run commences at about the foot of 27th St.; it is very convenient as the vessels go to the very warehouses. We also saw (just off Broad St), a church in which Patrick Henry made some famed speech.[510]

Returning, we witnessed a funny scene, in seeing some little girls sliding down a hole at least 20 ft high. [118ᵛ]

Last night—or rather this morning—at 2 am, I was awoke by a terrific cry of "murder" and heard a tremendous struggle, just on the floor below. I was so nervous that I jumped out of bed—got hold of my pants upside down—tried to get them on—finally did—rushed out of my room, where I found the boarders tumbling out of their rooms in all sorts of "costumes"; Kunkel, Stretton, Floy'd, &c. The agent of the hotel was whipping a slave, who had neglected to shut the house up; the darkie yelled most fearfully, but was hurt but very little. Some of the boarders were not as *much* dressed as I was, but were not aware that two girls were looking through a blind window at us.[511] [119]

During the afternoon, saw the Firemans' Parade; there are seven companies here, dressed like New York firemen; No 7 played best.[512]

507. The *City of Richmond* was built in Philadelphia in 1851.

508. As a Confederate steamer, the *Curtis Peck*, built in New York in 1851, was (like the *Jamestown*, note 506) sunk to obstruct the James River in Chesterfield County, in the Battle of Drewry's Bluff in 1862.

509. The *Belvidere* was a paddlewheeler built in Baltimore in 1851.

510. This is a rather off-hand reference for Reiff, who seems on other occasions in the diary to be so aware of (even at times reverential toward) history. The speech—which is known by its closing phrase, "Give me liberty, or give me death!"—was given by Patrick Henry (1736–1799) on 23 March 1775 at St. John's Church. In the runup to the American War of Independence, Virginia's delegates met at St. John's to consider putting Virginia into "a posture of defense"; Henry addressed them, and the vote was a narrow victory in support of the resolution. See Thad Tate, "Patrick Henry," *ABD*, X, 615–18.

511. "Blind window": Reiff appears to mean either a window with a blind down around which they were peeping, or a window with one-way glass.

512. The context here suggests that the "Parade" involved a (possibly brass) band.

Met S.P.[513] in the crowd, while walking with Smith & Pocahontas—she invited No 7 to the Opera; they came, of course.

[Performance: *Crown Diamonds,* Richmond Theatre.][514]

TUESDAY APRIL 29th   RICHMOND

Very hot. Rehearsed concert. [120]

[Performance: concert, Metropolitan Hall.][515]

WEDNESDAY APRIL 30th   RICHMOND TO WASHINGTON

Left Richmond at 6:30 am from Broad Street depot;[516] got to Slash Cottage at 7 minutes to ten.[517] Stopped for breakfast. Slash Cottage is on a level piece of ground, there are several houses here about a quarter of a mile from each side of the rail road is woods the road here runs exactly due north, as it does nearly the entire distance. There are not many houses along the route, the general face of the country is now amost beautiful green. Considerable wheat seems to have been sown. Also saw a species of sycamore, a sort of quasi sycamore and buttonball tree. Much of the soil has that red appearance like is found in Baltimore, and between the latter place and Washington. The scenery is generally uninteresting, excepting when the cars crossed the Rap-

513. "S.P.": Sally Partington; see note 478.

514. A "Farewell Opera Night," with the opera by request (*Richmond Dispatch,* 28 April 1856).

515. The Metropolitan Hall, which stood on the northwest corner of Fourteenth and Franklin streets, was built in 1828 as the First Presbyterian Church, and became the Metropolitan Hall in 1853 with investment from Robert A. Mayo; it was a three-story brick building with a towered entrance. It was demolished in 1882 (Dabney, *Richmond,* 144).

516. The Richmond, Fredericksburg and Potomac Railroad ran down the middle of Broad Street, terminating on the same block as the Broad Street Hotel; see note 477. See Map of the City of Richmond, engraved by M. Ellyson, included in H. K. Ellyson's *Richmond Directory and Business Advertiser.*

517. The site of mineral springs, the resort of Slash Cottage was named after damp, lowland forest that may have been cut down and logged. Already popular, it was developed by Edwin Robinson and the Richmond, Fredericksburg and Potomac Railroad Company in the 1850s, and by 1854, a contemporary lithograph shows the town laid out with a hotel, ballroom, bathhouses, bowling alley, bar, and a gas house for lighting the buildings and grounds. The name was changed to Ashland in 1855, but the actual cottage or hotel retained its original name. See Hellmann, *Historical Gazetteer of the United States,* 1134–45.

pahannock River. And just there the view is quite lovely. Woods, hills, and well-tilled fields lie beneath the traveller in a beautiful panorama.

We arrived at Aquia Creek at a quarter to ten, am. The creek runs into the north. There is quite a long wharf here. Took the steamboat "Baltimore" (described 20th April) for Washington. The river is (I think) wider than the Mississippi, nothing of particular interest occurred until we came to Fort Washington on the right hand bank of [the creek].[518] [121]

[Went to the Capitol.] Hale and Clay of Alabama had a difficulty.[519] Clay wants Hale to fight him, but the latter will not. Clay called him every thing *small* he could; said Hale sheltered behind petticoats. Hale replied making fun of it, Clay replied in still more bitter terms; was considerable symptoms of a row. Heard Wade, Douglas, Weller of California,[520] Cass,[521] Jones of Iowa, Stuart of Michigan. Cass said that Benjamin's speech was a truly patriotic speech, &c., &c.[522] He seems to think that there is a danger of a dissolution of the Union. Seward replied to him chiefly on points of law.[523] [122]

[Performance: *The Crown Diamonds*, National Theatre.]

518. This point in the diary is the center of a folded group of pages, and a fold consisting of at least two sides (and possibly four) is missing.

519. See note 448 for Hale. Clement Claiborne Clay (1816–1882) was a lawyer and was elected to the lower house of the Alabama legislature in 1842 and 1844–1845, then to the U.S. Senate in 1853 and again in 1857. He was an enthusiastic supporter of states' rights and opposed most public expenditure—except aid to southern railroads (Michael Chesson, "Clement Claiborne Clay," *ANB*, V, 20–21).

520. "Weller": "Welles" in Reiff. Reiff was referring to John Brown Weller (1812–1875), who was a Democratic senator from California from 1852 to 1858. He was first a Democratic senator from Ohio from 1838 to 1845, and after a colorful interlude which included service as a lieutenant colonel in the Mexican-American War and a member of the commission to establish the boundary line between California and Mexico, he became the fifth governor of California, from 1858 to 1860. See Robert J. Chandler, "John Brown Weller," *ANB*, XXIII, 2–4.

521. Lewis Cass (1782–1866), an American military officer, was a longtime politician, whose career embraced roles as diverse as governor of the Michigan Territory, minister to France (he later wrote *France, Its King, Court and Government*), and secretary of war (under Andrew Jackson). His support for the doctrine of popular sovereignty (which would have passed the power to decide on slavery to a territory level) split the Democrats and caused many of the party to join the Free Soilers. When Reiff saw him speak, he was a Michigan senator, an office he held from 1849 to 1857. See Klunder, *Lewis Cass and the Politics of Moderation*, 266–67.

522. See Hans L. Trefousse, "Benjamin Wade," *ANB*, XXII, 431–32.

523. "He seems to think . . . chiefly on points of law": inserted from higher on the page.

THURSDAY MAY 1ˢᵗ WASHINGTON

[Performance: *Cinderella*, National Theatre.]

FRIDAY MAY 2ⁿᵈ WASHINGTON

[Performance: *Cinderella*, National Theatre.]

SATURDAY MAY 3ʳᵈ WASHINGTON

Went with Loomis (a friend of A's) and Atherton to Mr G. W. Custis's place.[524] Took a boat had a fellow to row us over. Passed a small island in the middle of the river. Landed at the Arlington Springs; a small floor is laid on the shore a little ways up the bank by the spring it has a roof over it and is used by picnic parties. A place is fixed for an orchestra. It was told me that he often comes down with his fiddle and joins the parties; one of the musicians who plays with me told me old Custis generally comes into the orchestra on these picnics. The spring comes from under a large old oak; it is excellent water, took a drink from a gourd (a sort of pumpkin or squash). We then walked up a small road or lane up the hill, passing a barn and some slave cabins. The road was very muddy. We took a short way by going partly through the woods up the hill; the house is between three quarters and half a mile from the springs.

The house overlooks the city (opposite) Georgetown above, and the Potomac River below. The house is of brick covered with cement with immense large columns in front. The entry is exactly in the centre. The colour of the exterior of the mansion is a sort of yellow the front looks a *little* like the Tombs, N.Y.[525] On the south side of the portico some of the [123] windows

524. Arlington House near Jamestown is built on a high hill above the Potomac opposite the Mall. It was started in 1802 by George Washington Parke Custis (1781–1857), the step-grandson (and adopted son) of George Washington, and was intended to be his living memorial. On Custis's death, the house passed to his son-in-law, Robert E. Lee, and was confiscated during the Civil War on strategic grounds. After the war, sixteen thousand war dead were buried around the house, to begin what is now Arlington National Cemetery; the house survives as the Robert E. Lee Memorial. See Nelligan, *Custis-Lee Mansion,* for a history of the house.

525. "The Tombs" was the nickname for the Halls of Justice, the New York law courts, police building, and prison constructed between 1835 and 1840 to the design of John Haviland (1792–1852). The complex took up the square bounded by Centre, Elm, Franklin, and Leonard streets, and after years of wrangling was replaced in 1902. The central portico has—as

had not even a sash in the lower part. A board was painted black with streaks to represent a sash! The same in the rear of the house. It is almost completely surrounded by trees, except just in front.

Upon entering the large hall, the first thing that attracts attention is the pictures. There is one of Washington when a small boy, and one also of his wife when a child. There are many portraits of some antique looking old fellows. The darkie (who showed us about) told us they were some of the descendants of Washington. And also representations of the battles of Trenton and Princeton;[526] they were all oil paintings.[527] In the parlour (the first door on the left) is a portrait of Gen. Lee—whose grand-daughter has somehow intermarried with the Custis family.[528] There were portraits of many different persons and when (or have been) fine looking people, that is supposing the pictures to be good likenesses. The room was very well furnished; a six octave Nuns & Clark piano[529] and a violin graced the parlour; this last

---

Reiff emphasizes—only a little in common with that of Arlington House. See Sutton, *The New York Tombs: Its Secrets and Its Mysteries*, 48–52; as the subtitle of Sutton's 1874 work suggests, the place was of some contemporary fascination. See also Munro, *The New York Tombs*, for a modern account.

526. On 26 December 1776, Washington's troops crossed the Delaware River and attacked the unsuspecting Hessian garrison at Trenton, forcing it to surrender. On 3 January 1777, they again crossed the Delaware, outmaneuvering the force sent to crush Washington, and attacking and defeating the enemy at Princeton. See Samuel Smith, *The Battle of Trenton/The Battle of Princeton*, for a modern account of these events.

527. Writing of these pictures in 1860, Custis's daughter, Mary Lee, wrote: "One of the principal amusements of Mr. Custis's later years, was painting revolutionary battle-scenes in which Washington participated. Upon these he worked with the greatest enthusiasm. Considering the circumstances under which they were produced—painted without being first composed or drawn in outline, by an entirely self-taught hand more than threescore and ten years old—they are remarkable. In general conception and grouping, they are spirited and original. He was not disposed to devote the time and labor requisite to their careful execution, and therefore, as works of art merely, they have but little merit. Their chief value lies in their truthfulness to history in the delineation of events, incidents, and costumes. They are all at Arlington, six in number, namely, battles of Trenton, Princeton, Germantown, and Monmouth, Washington at Yorktown, and the Surrender at Yorktown"; see Custis, *Reminiscences and Private Recollections of Washington*, 68.

528. See note 524.

529. Nuns & Clark, established in 1823 in New York and active from 1836 to 1860, was a firm known for the excellence of both the action of the instruments, and the cabinet work of their cases. See Libin, "Nuns & Clark," III, 398.

I tried. When I attempted to tune the violin, the darkie [said] "Look out, dar—you'll break'em strings." Atherton told him I played a little, and therefore, he allowed me to handle it. I played Yankee Doodle;[530] it is the old Custis's fiddle.[531] From here, we went into another room to the left; a small dark narrow sort of room; crossed it and entered another room which is the end of the building this side. Neither of these last two are finished;[532] no plaster. [123ᵛ] In this room are some unfinished paintings of the old Custis; he thinks himself one of the greatest painters of the age and is an enthusiast of music, the violin in particular. [124] In this latter room is an old pianoforte that formerly belonged to Washington. It is in the shape of a grand. Has two banks of keys each of five octaves F to F' upper F.

London maker Longwood & ——, a name I forget.[533] I played Yankee Doodle[534] & Washington's March[535] on it, Atherton played "Hail Columbia!";[536] most of the notes would not sound, and all of them very indiffer-

530. The text of "Yankee Doodle," Roud Folk Song Index 4501, accessed online, 30 March 2010, dates back to the Seven Years' War, although today the song is most often played in a patriotic context in the United States.

531. "When I attempted. . . . it is the old Custis's fiddle": Text inserted from 122v as indicated by Reiff with a dal segno sign in the manuscript.

532. "Neither of these last two are finished": "Neither of these last two are not finished" in Reiff.

533. Depending on the date of the instrument, the firm Reiff could not remember was, from 1767, Longman, Lukey & Co; from 1773, Longman, Lukey & Co; from 1776, Longman & Broderip; and from 1797, Longman, Clementi & Company. It may also have been from the firm of Longman's son, Longman & Heron, from 1802 until about 1816 (Peter Williams, "Longman," II, 537–38).

534. See note 530.

535. "Washington's March" (or "The President's March") was composed by Philip Phile (ca. 1734–1793) to honor George Washington, and was used in April 1789 on the Trenton, New Jersey, leg of his journey from Mount Vernon to his inauguration in New York City. The tune was published in 1793. See Fuld, "Patriotic Music," III, 485.

536. The anthem "Hail, Columbia," was composed in 1789 by Philip Phile (ca. 1734–1793) for the inauguration of George Washington; the lyrics by Joseph Hopkinson (1770–1842) were added in 1798, and until 1931 (when it was officially replaced by "The Star-Spangled Banner") it was considered to be the US national anthem. See Fuld, "Patriotic Music," III, 485.

ently. Had the old gentleman been home we would not have had the chance to touch the instrument. And an old sort of valise trunk on the top (it was leather covered) was the letters G.W. done with brass tacks. We had the impudence to absolutely examine some of the papers.

Custis is painting a picture of the Battle of Trenton here in this room; it is almost entirely finished.

This is the room in which there are no sashes in the lower part of the window, but simply black-painted board. Even the parlour has only been finished about a year; the place, (gardens, &c.), very pretty.

When returning in the small boat we got considerable of a drenching by a shower of rain. On the islands in the river we saw fishermen hauling in a net; rowed up to it, they catch shad-herring,[537] &c., &c.

After landing, we visited the Observatory, which stands on a hill in [a] pretty park. The building is of brick, two wings. On the main building is [124ᵛ] a large cupola in which is the main telescope. The first room we were shown to there were two very large telescopes made in Munich. Each telescope stands on its own foundation separate from the building.[538]

A large ball (about 2 and half ft in diameter) is hoisted on the top of the cupola; it drops at precisely 12 noon.[539] We were shown into a room where the *time* is kept, by chronometers, &c. There is one particularly large clock, the chronometers are in a large case. Each chronometer is in a small case by itself about six inches square; they are all made in New York, or London. [124(2)] Saw Lieutenant Maury:[540] he is a man about forty-five to fifty years of age, slightly bald, grey hair, has a fine, large forehead. He is a Man of men, and in any other country but ours, he would be highly honoured.

The front of the building faces the north.

In the afternoon, visited the Navy Yard nothing very particular there, except the new steam war vessel "Minnesota" which has only been launched a

537. The shad-herring is a clupeoid fish, native of America. It is similar to the shad in habits and appearance, but smaller and less sought after as food.

538. The observatory was established in 1830 as the Depot of Charts and Instruments, and became a national observatory in 1842, with a primary aim to care for the Navy's navigational equipment. When Reiff visited it, it was located at Foggy Bottom near the Lincoln Memorial. See Weber, *The Naval Observatory*, 1–16.

539. The timeball was created by the inventor Charles Goodyear (1800–1860), to the specification of the observatory's director, Matthew Maury; it went into service in 1845. See Dick, *Sky and Ocean Joined*, 85.

540. See note 385.

few days. Her engines were tried yesterday for the first time she was moored fast off the dock. She is one of the largest of the six. Has only the main part of her masts and bowsprit as yet.[541] I walked out on the latter. [124(2)ᵛ]

[Performance: *Cinderella*, National Theatre.]

SUNDAY MAY 4ᵗʰ   WASHINGTON TO BALTIMORE

Fine day. Wrote letters all day nearly. Took a walk near the President's House. There is to be built another White House and the avenue (Pennsylvania) which runs to the south of the house will be closed up and the grounds

541. The USS *Minnesota* was a wooden steam frigate launched in 1855. The ship served for two years before being decommissioned, and was commissioned again at the outbreak of the Civil War. She served until the end of the century, being sold in 1901 and finally burned at Eastport, Maine. See *Dictionary of American Naval Fighting Ships*, IV (1969), 372–74.

of the house will extend to the river, including the Washington Monument.

The City Hall is (on D St, I think) near the depot (for Baltimore) it is a seeming sort of brown stone, possibly may be plaster, for I did not have time to examine it closely.[542] [126] Left Washington at half past 4 and arrived at Baltimore[543] at 6. We stopped at a private sort of house in Holliday Street, one boarder besides Geo and I.[544] In the evening called in Mulberry Street where I spent the evening ———. Slightly cool.

MONDAY MAY 5th   BALTIMORE

Took a short walk, wrote letters.
  [Performance: *Cinderella*, Holliday Street Theatre.]

TUESDAY MAY 6th   BALTIMORE

  Cool. Went to a cemetery about two miles from the theatre, almost due north.[545] Many very nice monuments, the grounds are nothing like as fine as Greenwoods.[546] Are evidently a number of Catholics buried here from the [cross inserted here]'s. The grounds have been open sixteen years.
  [Performance: *Cinderella*, Holliday Street Theatre.]

WEDNESDAY MAY 7th   BALTIMORE

Rainy; cold, cheerless, day. [127]
  [Performance: *Cinderella*, Holliday Street Theatre.]

542. Old City Hall, built between 1820 and 1850, was Washington City's first public building. Housing a court of law, it is a large Greek Revival building built to the design of the architect George Hadfield (1763–1826). See Reiff, *Washington Architecture*, 42–43. Reiff noted that the building was not made of stone, but of stucco. The current limestone facade was added when the building was renovated between 1916 and 1919.

543. "Arrived at Baltimore." Reiff gives "arrived at Washington," which must be an error.

544. "Sort of house in Holliday Street, one boarder besides Geo and I": "sort of house one boarder besides Geo and I in Holiday Street" in Reiff.

545. Reiff is visiting Green Mount Cemetery, incorporated in 1837, and already architecturally and historically distinguished. It is one of the earliest garden cemeteries, and was established as the result of the inspiration of Samuel Walker, a Baltimore tobacco merchant who had visited Cambridge's 1831 Mount Auburn Cemetery three years before. See Gobright, *The Monumental City or Baltimore Guidebook*, 63.

546. Green-Wood Cemetery in Brooklyn, New York, another early rural cemetery, founded in 1838. See Cothran and Danylchak, *Grave Landscapes*.

THURSDAY MAY 8th   BALTIMORE

Geo & I called up in Mulberry St., where he got a warm reception, and I a rather cool one. Rain.

[Performance: *The Crown Diamonds,* Holliday Street Theatre.]

FRIDAY MAY 9th   BALTIMORE

Took a walk, went down Baltimore St., east exactly. The Potomac River comes in from the southeast and runs to the south of Fort McHenry.[547] A small branch extending to Light St. comes up north of the fort. It forms the principal harbour and is well protected by the fort. The strip of land upon which the fort is built is about a mile and a half in length and at the point, not once a quarter of a mile in width, but becomes wider as it extends up towards the city and Light St. The fort lies low.[548] [127^v]

We went to the end of the city limits in this direction, east. The absolute city ends very abruptly—from closely packed, built, squares, it immediately comes to post and rail fences. We (just inside the limits) visited a Methodist and a Catholic burying ground. In the former, a lady's corpse had just been buried. Speaking to the Sexton he expatiated upon the fact that she had a most beautiful grave, no water could get in, &c., &c. I replied "that it was no doubt very nice for her." George nearly *busted.* [128]

Upon our return, we went into the Maryland Institute, a large hall for giving concerts, &c.[549] It is over the market. The room is *very* long and narrow. When concerts are given they have a partition which can be put up leaving only about two thirds of the room. The gallery is small and supported by slim iron braces not looking strong. The building is on Baltimore Street.

The Post Office is on the corner of Gray and Baltimore Streets; it is a very

547. The star-shaped Fort McHenry was built at Locust Point on Baltimore Harbor overlooking the Chesapeake Bay in 1798. Constructed to the design of Jean Foncin, it was named after the Scots immigrant James McHenry (1753–1816), who was appointed secretary of war by President Washington in 1796, serving until 1800. See Hancock, *Fort McHenry,* 5.

548. Page 126v contains Reiff's map.

549. The Maryland Institute for the Promotion of Mechanical Arts Hall (also known as the Centre Market Building or the Great Mechanics' Hall) was located on Baltimore Street and Centre Market Space. Designed by William H. Reasin (ca. 1820–1867), it was built in 1852 to replace a building lost elsewhere in the 1835 fire; it was itself destroyed in the Great Fire of Baltimore in 1904. See Lane, *Architecture of the Old South: Maryland,* 232 and 242n131.

good building, has a beautiful dome over the rotunda. The Custom House is in the same building.[550]

[Performance: *The Crown Diamonds,* Holliday Street Theatre.]

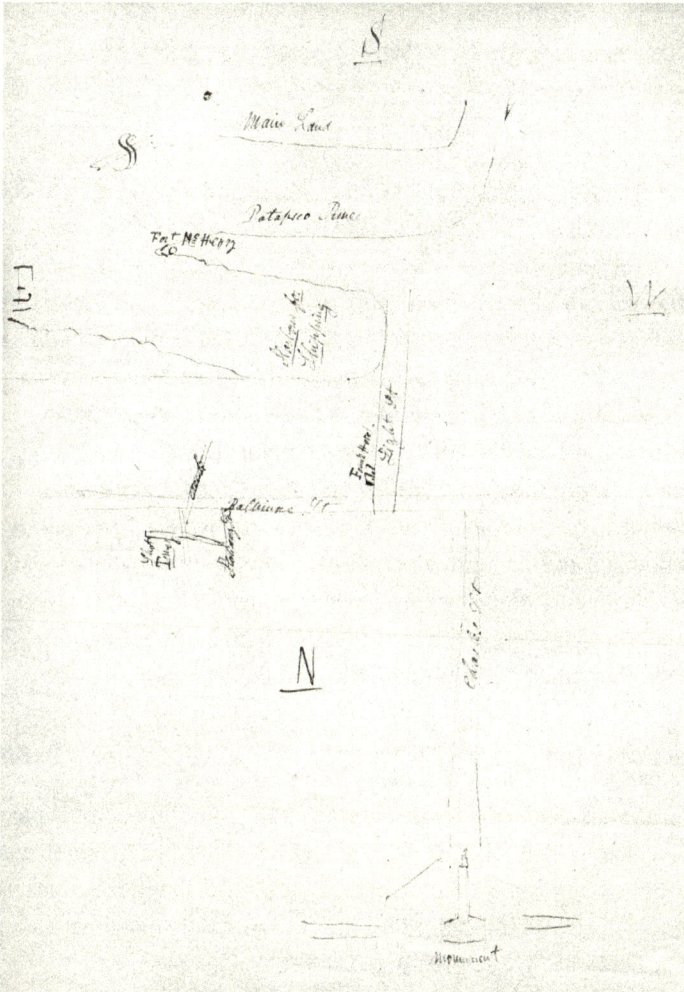

550. This building was the Merchants' Exchange Building or the Baltimore Exchange, rented from about 1820 to house the Customs Service. Its design was the work of Maximilian Godefroy (1765–1840) and Benjamin Latrobe (1764–1820), but disagreements between the two men during construction led to a parting of their professional careers (Hamlin, *Benjamin Henry Latrobe,* 486–97). The building Reiff saw was replaced with the present building, completed in 1903.

SATURDAY MAY 10th   BALTIMORE

Went out of town up Baltimore Street (west) up past Mr Wynant's clebrated house. Got upon a high hill and looked back upon the city. [129]
[Performance, matinee: *Cinderella,* Holliday Street Theatre.]
[Performance: *Guy Mannering,* Holliday Street Theatre.]

SUNDAY MAY 11th   BALTIMORE

A clear beautiful day. Am quite bilious, do not feel very well. Geo & I went to Grace Church corner of Park and Monument, a brown, freestone church, the most fashionable church in the city.[551] Got good seat directly in front, near the chancel. Three stained windows at back.

A young minister read the service. Rev. M. Coxe[552] preached the sermon took his text from Psalms, preached very fair sermon, but not practical. The singing was fair, Organist good. Wrote home (No 22) since St Louis.

Geo and I walked up Baltimore St, very hot. Then went to ——'s, stayed to tea, then sat on the stoop. N.B. People here (in the beginning of the evening) sit on their stoops and converse from one house to another. It would seem shocking in our refined NY. Took a long walk with ———. We went down Mulberry, Saratoga, up and down Charles, Baltimore, across the creek to Ferout, up again, Pearl, &c., &c. [130] Went to a fire in Baltimore St, near the creek. Remained there until a little past 12.[553]

MONDAY MAY 12th   BALTIMORE

A Company of Firemen no 20 "Good Will" from Philadelphia paid some Company here a visit. The "Good Will" [visitors] dressed in white over coats with capes, cream coloured hats, same shape as ordinary dress hats, though not quite so high.[554] The Baltimore fireman generally have these same hats of various colours, one company red, another white, &c., &c.

551. Grace Church was founded in 1850, and its building constructed in 1852. Built to the design of the firm of Niernsee and Neilson, it is considered to be a copy of John Notman's St. Mark's Church in Philadelphia (Lane, *Architecture of the Old South: Maryland,* 201). The brown stone Reiff observed was Connecticut brownstone (this was one of the first Gothic Revival churches in the South to use it), and the windows he noted were imported from Hardman of Birmingham, England.

552. "Rev. M. Coxe" not further identified.

553. "Went to a fire in Baltimore St, near the creek": inserted from 129v.

554. The companies of Philadelphia had the previous year been reorganized under a 25 Jan-

Mr Buchanan visited the opera having arrived at seven [o'clock].[555] He is a fine-looking old fellow, white head, thin hair. He was received with tremendous cheers. Between the acts, I played (all standing) Hail Columbia[556] and Yankee Doodle;[557] the cheers were almost deafening. The old fellow got up and bowed, but would not speak

I had left my night key, all the hotels were full. Found a man going in next door to our house; he got me into his house I scaled the brick wall and then tried to wake Geo. I pitched dirt and stones in the window. . . . [131]

[Performance: *Maritana*,[558] Holliday Street Theatre.]

TUESDAY MAY 13th   BALTIMORE

Very unwell. Laid down the entire afternoon.

Today going to Brough's room at Barnum's[559] finding him out (i.e. *not in*) I tried the door which was open; popped in (a la Paul Pry) went to the table where I saw a list of the salaries as follows:

| Stretton | $75.00 | Horncastle | 40.00 |
| Brough | 44.00 | Chorus | 15.00 (per man)[560] |

[Performance: *The Daughter of the Regiment*, Holliday Street Theatre.]

---

uary 1855 ordinance: "The Select and Common Councils of the City of Philadelphia do ordain, That the Fire Department shall consist of such regularly organized Engine, Hose and Hook and Ladder Companies, within the limits of the City of Philadelphia." "Company 20" was either a Hose, Hook and Ladder company, whose number was not to exceed 30 members, or an engine company, whose number was not to exceed 50. See *Journal of the Common Council, of the city of Philadelphia*, 436–42.

555. A politician and diplomatist, James Buchanan Jr. (1791–1868) would be nominated as the Democratic presidential candidate in June 1856 and win the US presidential election in November. See William E. Gienapp, "James Buchanan," *ANB*, III, 835–39.

556. See note 536.

557. See note 530.

558. The invitation for Buchanan's visit was issued by John T. Ford, the theater's manager; he offered the president and his party private boxes, and they were "saluted and welcomed by the singing of the national anthem Hail Columbia, by the whole of the Pyne and Harrison troupe and the performance of the various national airs by the orchestra under the direction of Professor A. Rief, jr." (*Baltimore Sun*, 12 May 1856).

559. Barnum's Hotel was begun in 1825, by David Barnum, and opened toward the end of 1826. Famed as a bastion of luxury, it was in the hands of Andrew McLaughlin when Brough stayed there. See Scharf and Westcott, *The History of Philadelphia*, I, 515.

560. The text of the second paragraph inserted from 130v as indicated by Reiff with a dal segno sign in the manuscript.

WEDNESDAY MAY 14th   BALTIMORE

Received a letter from Harry Watkins in answer to mine stating that he had heard nothing from Border and could not account why; that he feared something very serious has happened, &c., &c.[561] I feel dreadfully worried—it's so strange.

Took a dose of medicine. [131[v]]

Baltimore is a very social city; hence it is bad for amusements in the way of theatres, &c. Many persons own a small house (of which there are a great number), and live in them themselves; it is unusual to see a number of families in one house. In the evening the occupants go out on their stoops, sidewalks, &c., the children play about and the whole thing has a very pretty effect; people even talk to each other across the street.

One of the peculiarities of the city is the high stones at some of the cross ways; they are very good for *pedestrians* in wet weather, but awkward for *equestrians* at any time.[562] [132]

[Performance: *The Bohemian Girl*,[563] Holliday Street Theatre.]

THURSDAY MAY 15th   BALTIMORE

Very unwell. Received a letter from Father stating that he is unwell with the same illness: biliousness. Answered him with eight pages. Gerhardt (viola) from Washington called in to see me; he is a most clever, nice fellow. My tongue is as white as chalk, I have been growing thinner since I came East of the Allegheny Mountains. I wish I had had a daguerreotype portrait of myself taken at Mobile, New Orleans, or Memphis so our folks would have seen how fat I'd grown.

Gosden stopped at the theatre; he scarcely knew me, seemed astonished I wasn't a little boy.[564] Felt like Dominie Sampson did when he asked "where

561. The actor and manager Harry Watkins (1825–1894). See Thomas Brown, *History of the American Stage*, 380. "Border" not further identified.

562. The stones noted by Reiff were the subject of comment by various authors: "Ah, what a delight after a storm to stand perilously upon these high stones and look down into the turbulent stream dashing away to the Falls, and gurgling so enchantingly as it dashed" (Stockett, *Baltimore*, 136).

563. Benefit: William Harrison (*Baltimore Sun*, 14 May 1856).

564. J. Gosden, who had clearly known Reiff since he was a small boy, was a flautist, probably with the orchestra of the Park Theatre; it can be assumed that Reiff Sr., a bassoonist, was

is the little infant and exclaiming Prodigious!"[565] Of course, we didn't talk about Father and the Park Theatre.[566]

[Performance: *The Crown Diamonds*, Holliday Street Theatre.]

FRIDAY MAY 16ᵗʰ   BALTIMORE

Still very unwell. A very short rehearsal of *Maritana*.

Had my breakfast in my room yesterday and today. Miss Emily, our landlady, is the Principal of the High School in this city; she is a perfect, precise, affable, Old Maid. She is a superior woman both as regards scholastic abilities and general good sense. No subject can be mentioned but she is posted up on it.[567] Her father is an invalid and very old. The other two occupants of the house are a Mr and Mrs Husban (I forgot they have two or three small children). He (Mr H) is a very austere & opinionated, silly sort of a man, a Pennsylvanian by birth and architect by profession. He is continuously advancing some wonderful news or *facts* (?) which Miss Emily [133] completely upsets with her superior knowledge and awkward truths. She does it such an unassuming and quiet manner withal that it is quite refreshing. I cannot help feel a great admiration for her. Mrs H is a light complexion—reddish (I mean auburn) coloured hair. She is very enthusiastic, quite an antipode of her husband. She has been married for fifteen years (but does not look as if she was over thirty), has not been to the theatre since she was married! Her

---

also a member of the band. The reference, then, appears to be to the collapse of all the New York theaters—the Park, the National, and the Bowery—at the start of 1841, which threw all the band members out of work. Gosden is recorded playing the flute at one of the replacement promenade concerts in 1841, and again with the then-new New York Philharmonic Society in 1842; Reiff Sr. was a founding member. See Lawrence, *Strong on Music II*, 131, 170.

565. This is a garbled reference to Walter Scott's *Guy Mannering; or, The Astrologer,* which Reiff knew through Daniel Terry's musical play version in repertory on this tour. In the novel, Dominie Abel Sampson had the habit of crying "Prodigious, Prodigious, Prodigious" on any occasion of surprise. Harry Bertram was kidnapped as a child, and when his identity is revealed some twenty years later, Mr. Sampson (in the opera), exclaims, "I must behold the infant," while Miss Lucy (who Reiff appears to have mistakenly called "Lavinia") is called on to embrace her long-lost brother. See Scott, *Guy Mannering,* II, chap. 28, and Terry, *Guy Mannering; or the Gipsy's prophecy,* 67.

566. The last paragraph of text inserted from 131v as indicated in Reiff.

567. "Posted up on it": Reiff means that she has been kept "posted," meaning "kept up to date," but no contemporary use of the phrase has come to light.

husband in fact seems a cold lump of ice, while she is all vivacity; he seems to care about nothing except reading the N.Y. Herald.[568] He built the church in 4th St Cincinnati with the high steeple, the one that stands back with a house on one side of the front, partly hiding it.[569]

I gave them tickets for the opera tonight, Miss Emily was much pleased and Mrs H was almost crazy with delight, said she could scarcely restrain herself from jumping on the stage and kissing Miss Pyne; she wants to go to the opera every night.

During the afternoon, I was pleased and surprised by Nanny's (old servant woman) coming upstairs and telling me that two ladies wanted to see me. I was down in the parlor in a quarter of a second where the two ladies said they had orders to capture me and [134] convey me up town where I was to teach them, one the Fairy Queen, and the other Clorinda in *Cinderella*. Mrs Jefferson (one of the ladies) met Mr Ford just outside the door,[570] and I was left in charge of the other young lady. I however did not find my captivity very disagreeable, *viz* the fact that after having rode some distance in a stage, Mr Ford and Mrs Jefferson got in, and when we got out, he insisted on paying for us all, which I in an excess of good nature, allowed him to do. Was introduced to Leghorn, a jolly, short, light complexioned man. Had a good talk about Father, gave him our direction;[571] said he would write to him. Ford talking to me in a way that leaves me but little doubt but that I can come here next season.[572] After singing for about two hours, supper was announced and not until I had (reluctantly, *of course*) done ample justice to that, was I permitted to escape.

568. The *New York Herald* was a penny-press newspaper established in 1835, whose founder, James Gordon Bennett (1795–1872), was a pioneer in aspects of tabloid newspaper journalism. It merged with the more serious *New York Tribune* in 1924 to form the *New York Herald Tribune*, which ceased publication in 1966.

569. St. Paul's Methodist Church was built in 1853 (Hench, *History of St. Paul's Methodist Church*, 2). It was billed as having a spire ten feet higher than the spire of Trinity Church, New York.

570. John Thompson Ford (1829–1894) had assumed control of the Holliday Street Theatre, Baltimore, in 1854, and was in charge until 1879. He was also an opera promoter, building Baltimore's Grand Opera House in 1871. See William Stephenson, "John Ford," *ANB*, VIII, 242–43.

571. "Gave him our direction": Reiff gave him the family's New York address.

572. "Was introduced to Leghorn . . . here next season" inserted from 133v, where it otherwise falls in the middle of "the two ladies said they had orders to capture me and [. . .] carry me up town where I was to teach them."

Miss Emily has some supper for me. I supplied Gosden with tickets tonight at the opera.

[Performance: *Maritana*, Holliday Street Theatre.]

SATURDAY MAY 17th   BALTIMORE

Still unwell. Received a letter from Amb.[573] Geo says I was very morose in the orchestra this morning. Was up town in the afternoon and stayed to supper. [134ᵛ] St Alphonsus is a brick building sanded over; looks like sandstone, it is a German Catholic Church and is a very fine building.[574] The inside is something like St Patrick's, N.Y., but with those peculiar "confession closets" common to Catholic churches.[575] [135]

[Performance: *The Barber of Seville* and Act II of *La Sonnambula*,[576] Holliday Street Theatre.]

SUNDAY MAY 18th   BALTIMORE

Today is six months since I have seen father and mother; it was then Sunday, a cold day. Now it is very warm. I last saw them in the Jersey City Depot.[577] Will I see them next Sunday this time? I hope so. I have laid out all sorts of plans for where I am going and what I shall do the first days I am home.

573. "Amb." Ambrose; see note 194.

574. "Alphonsus": "Adolphus" in Reiff. St. Alphonsus Church, "the German Cathedral," was built at Saratoga Street and Park Avenue in 1845 to the design of Robert Cary Long (1810–1849), and belongs, in style, to the South German Gothic and English Perpendicular. See Stanton, *The Gothic Revival and American Church Architecture*, 225–38.

575. Reiff is referring to what is now known as St. Patrick's Old Cathedral, which was begun in 1809, and finished to a design by Joseph-François Mangin (1764–after 1818). It was dedicated in 1815, but the interior to which Reiff refers was destroyed by a fire in 1866. The building was superseded by the present cathedral, which was finally completed in 1878 (Diamonstein-Spielvogel, *The Landmarks of New York*, 57).

576. Benefit: Louisa Pyne (*Baltimore Sun*, 17 May 1856).

577. Jersey City Depot was the colloquial name for the Pennsylvania railroad station located on Exchange Place in Paulus Hook on the Hudson River side of Jersey City. It was the main terminus for railway companies servicing New York from 1834 until the construction of the river tunnels, which allowed the building of New York's Penn Station in 1910. It was linked to Manhattan by a ferry service that began in 1812. See John Cunningham, *Railroading in New Jersey*, 12–13.

Gosden called in to see me. I spent the evening up town, took a long walk with —— down Saratoga to Charles and through Baltimore over the bridge to Canal Street then up again to Eutaw Street, &c., a very long walk. When we passed St Augustine's Church, Atherton had just been put out because he would not kneel.[578] The evening is perfectly beautiful, full moon. I never experienced a more charming evening.

MONDAY MAY 19th   BALTIMORE TO WASHINGTON

Left Baltimore for Washington at a quarter past nine. Had the felicity to escort Miss ——er[579] all the way. That the young lady was well attended to, it need only be said she had the gallant conductor of the P. & H. C—— for her escort.[580]

We arrived at 11 all right and not tired. Very warm. [136]

WASHINGTON

The Avenue is thronged with ladies dressed in the most superb manner. In the afternoon, I visited the Young Man's Christian Library Association; it is free to young gentlemen, they have branches of it in different cities, in Quebec, at 22 Great James Street.[581] The evening was very warm; a beautiful moonlight night. The Smithsonian looked particularly romantic.

[Performance: *The Bohemian Girl*, National Theatre.]

TUESDAY MAY 20th   WASHINGTON

Very warm: 128 degrees in the sun today, thermometer 88 degrees in the shade.

Very unwell; was obliged to lie down most of the afternoon. The people on the stage are all very clever to me. The doorkeeper of our theatre (old

578. There appears to be no relevant "St. Augustine's" Church in early Baltimore on the route that Reiff mentions; this is possibly his second mistaken reference to St. Alphonsus Church; see note 574.

579. "Miss ——er" possibly "I—— P——"; see note 449.

580. "The P. & H. C——." The Pyne & Harrison Opera Company.

581. Reiff is incorrect; the YMCA at 22 St. James Street was, in fact, in Montreal, the first to be founded in North America. The YMCA in Washington was formed in 1852. See Hopkins, *History of the Y.M.C.A. in North America*, 15–53.

James) is quite an original, fancies that everything depends upon him. I generally ask him "Is everything all right"; his usual reply is "Everyone is here Mr Reiff, except the drummer, but I'll send him down the moment he arrives, don't you worry yourself," &c., &c. Possibly it may be at least half a hour before the time. He thinks me a remarkably clever fellow.

During the latter part of the afternoon, Geo and I went up to the President's Grounds which are magnificent. A little incident occurred showing the simplicity of our democratic institutions. Several children were running around the inner part of the fountain. A man (who had charge of the grounds) came and stopped them. When one little girl (commonly dressed) said "I reckon we can play here, Mrs Pierce said we might."[582] The younger ones had seen her on the veranda and had asked her if they could play there. It would be rather more difficult to "get at" the wife of the head of some of the smallest despotic governments.[583] [136ᵛ] The grounds are the most beautiful park I've ever seen. In front of the White House (two hundred feet (about) south) are four hills; whether they are artificial or natural puzzled the "Committee."[584] Saw a singular tree, the Linden Tree, the blossom shoots out from the under part of the leaf, quite singular. We sat in an iron settee for some time; these settees are all about the grounds. [137]

[Performance: *Cinderella*, National Theatre.]

WEDNESDAY MAY 21ˢᵗ   WASHINGTON

[Performance: *Maritana*, National Theatre.]

THURSDAY MAY 22ⁿᵈ   WASHINGTON

[Performance: *Guy Mannering* with *The Waterman*,[585] National Theatre.]

582. Jane Means Appleton (1806–1863), wife, from 19 November 1834, of Franklin Pierce (1804–1869), fourteenth president of the United States, 1853–57. See Larry Gara, "Franklin Pierce," ANB, XVII, 495.

583. "A little incident occurred ... smallest despotic governments." This text inserted from 135v as indicated by Reiff's dal segno sign at the bottom of 136.

584. The "Committee" of Reiff and Atherton.

585. *The Waterman; or, The First of August*, arranged and with a libretto by Charles Dibdin, premiered at London's Little Theatre, Haymarket, on 8 August 1774. Cast: Wilhelmina: Louisa Pyne; Tom Tug: Harrison; Robin: Joseph Jefferson; Mr. Bundle: Mr. Burnet; Mrs. Bundle: Mrs. Germon.

FRIDAY MAY 23rd   WASHINGTON

With —— went down to Mount Vernon. From the foot of seventh street (west)[586] on board steamboat Thomas Collyer,[587] it is very warm have on board a large number of [passengers]. We left at 1/4 past 9 arrived at Mount Vernon at 1/4 to 11. The visitor ascends a partly planked winding path[588] about the twentieth of a mile from the river is the tomb, it faces south, south east, the tomb is of brick about 10 feet high built on a slight hill the elevation running up from the front the chambers (in which [are] the bodies) is about 20 ft wide and 10 or 20 deep, is plastered and whitewashed.[589] The entrance to the vault is guarded by double iron gratings (doors). Over the chamber is a small piece of marble with the following inscription on it:

> Within this enclosure lies
> the mortal remains of
> Gen: George Washington

Washington's body is in a sarcophagus about 7 or 8 ft long and 2 and a half feet wide about four feet from Washington lies his wife the only inscription on her sarcophagus is "Martha, consort of Washington."[590] Washington's sarcophagus was presented by James Struthers, marble worker of Philadelphia in 1837.[591] [138]

586. The Southwest Waterfront at the foot of Seventh Street was an important link for the shipping of freight and passengers, and from the 1790s, travelers could book passages on local ferries and ships bound downriver (Paul Williams, *Southwest Washington*, 39–52).

587. The *Thomas Collyer*, built in 1850 in New York City at seventy-four tons, was the last boat by the famous New York boatbuilder Thomas Collyer and seems to have plied from Washington to Richmond.

588. "The visitor ascends a partly planked winding path": "The visitor ascends (partly planked) a winding path" in Reiff.

589. This tomb was built in 1831, following an attempt to rob Washington's grave (Grizzard, *George Washington: A Biographical Companion*, 791).Washington had stipulated in his will of 1799 that a new grave be built to replace the family crypt, which had already fallen into disrepair (Manca, *George Washington's Eye*, 11).

590. The redoubtable Martha Dandridge Custis Washington (1731–1802) married George Washington as her second husband in January 1759; her fortune, which was greatly to his assistance, was reported at around £23,000. See Forrest McDonald, "George Washington," *ANB*, XXII, 760.

591. Probably John Struthers, who emigrated from Glasgow in 1816, and who became associated with Thomas Wilson, the owner, variously, of an architect's office and a marble yard; his son founded the great Philadelphia marble-working firm of William Struthers and Son. See Scharf and Westcott, *The History of Philadelphia*, III, 2293–94.

On the left of the tomb a place has been dug away as if a house was to be built there the plastering in the chamber of the tomb is falling off, and the bricks of the tomb on top are loose, broken and many of them have fallen off. In the enclosure of the tomb (over the top of the chamber which is an arch) there are growing wild grape vines, briars, and even small trees. I clambered in from the back and got down in the enclosure where I obtained some leaves; the bricks nearly fell over with me. Everything about the tomb is in a dilapidated state, and I verily believe that, if nothing is done to it, that the tomb itself will crumble down in twenty years.

In front of the Tomb (one at each end) are two Tombstones—this form— one to Judge Bushrod Washington a nephew of Washington's[592] and the other—to Bushrod's nephew. In the chambers of the tomb, was a bird's nest on the top of Washington's sarcophagus. In bas-relief is the American bald eagle, arrows, shield of the United States with a sort of drapery around the whole. The sarcophagus is about six inches above the ground; two large trees generally presented in pictures of this spot are not here, there are *no* trees just by the tomb. [139]

Inside the chamber there are pieces of sticky leaves, stones, &c., &c., we went to the right from the Tomb north about 40 yards and came in at the back of the house. The house is two stories, very small windows, wooden, and white-washed (at the back). It is about 80 ft long and 20 deep, possibly 25, an entry way of about 10 to 12 feet runs through the centre (the two rooms on the left, entering from the back) N.N.E. are the only ones to which visitors are admitted. They are about 10 feet deep and about 15 feet wide. The small windows, stucco work on the ceiling, very old fashioned; over the doors are something like this (pediment drawn here) fire places old fashioned, silver chandeliers; in the back rooms are numerous engravings (in old gilt frames) of the Defence of Gibraltar. In the front room is a very old-fashioned sofa (in this room visitors enter their names). On the opposite side of the Hall is (in a small case) the "Key of the Bastille,"[593] presented to Washington by La Fayette. In this Hall is a writing chair of the General's. The

592. Bushrod Washington (1762–1829), the son of George Washington's brother, John Augustine, was a Supreme Court associate justice from 1798. A federalist and nationalist, he inherited Mount Vernon on George's death in 1799. See W. Hamilton Bryson, "Bushrod Washington," *ANB*, XXII, 756–57.

593. The case to which Reiff refers is still displayed in the hall at Mount Vernon; it contains a key to the west door of the French prison of Bastille, sent to Washington in 1790 by the Marquis de Lafayette (Manca, *George Washington's Eye*, 237).

Figure 14. *Mount Vernon in the 1850s.* This stereo-card view shows a decrepit Mount Vernon before its sale to the Mount Vernon Ladies Association, with the piazza roof supported by ship masts; it was replaced in 1860. Reiff commented that the columns were "going to decay as fast as possible for want of paint!"

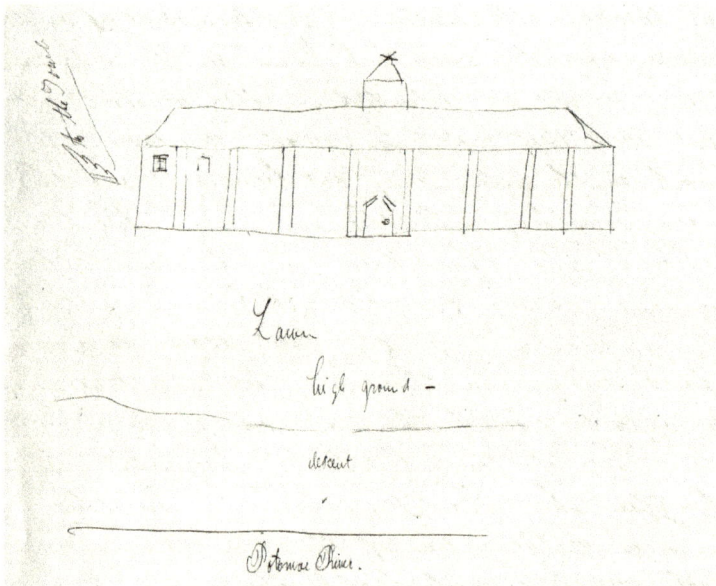

roof (which is nearly flat) extends so as to cover the piazza (which is only one step up from the ground). The piazza is supported by eight wooden pillars which are going to decay as fast as possible for want of paint!

The lawn in front of the house is beautiful running at least 50 ft before the ground descends. [139ᵛ]

[140] On top of the house is a cupola with the points of the compass on it. The house is in a north-west direction from the tomb. The situation of the house is magnificent—connected to the main building by a sort of piazza colonnade (Italian style) are two servants houses standing sideways from the main building. The[re] are several slave cabins one of which I entered and bought a cane or stick.

Off to the right (six or seven rods in the rear) is an enclosed garden; bought a bouquet of flowers. There is a beautiful lawn at the back. Between the tomb and the house is a large brick barn (two thirds roof); everything is going to decay. At the back of the house is a lawn, about 100 ft deep, but it is sadly neglected.

Over one of the doors in the entry way is a large telescope or spy-glass formerly used by the General. In rear of the house are several houses or cabins for the slaves. The windows of the house are very small. [141]

Upon returning, we went a few miles down the river to a place called the White House,—a long white house in which are given balls, parties, &c. On going up the river, we stopped at Fort Washington on the right;[594] we arrived at home at 3 pm.

Miss —— very sick, rushed for a doctor, &c., &c. Talked to Atherton about our homes until 3 am. [142]

[Performance: *The Daughter of the Regiment*,[595] National Theatre.]

SATURDAY MAY 24ᵗʰ   WASHINGTON, BALTIMORE, PHILADELPHIA, NEW YORK

Awoke (by our one-eye'd boy) at half past 4; left the Depot at 6. Feel very unwell and bilious. Arrived at Baltimore at a quarter to 8. At the Camden

594. Fort Washington, the only defensive fort for Washington, DC, was sited in such a way as to have a good canon shot down the Potomac. The building Reiff saw was built in 1824 and remodeled in the 1840s, with the first canon being mounted in 1848 (Block, *The Pelican Guide to Maryland*, 86).

595. This was the last possible performance the company could give; they were "announced at Niblo's Garden in New York on Monday night" with *The Daughter of the Regiment* (*Evening Star*, 23 May 1856).

station,[596] went slowly through the streets in the cars to the President St. Depot;[597] went slowly! Atherton went to Miss Emily's. Left Baltimore at a quarter to 9; Harve de Grace looked perfectly beautiful, it was winter when I passed through here.[598]

Later . . . [599]

We arrived at Philadelphia at 1pm, cars went slowly down Washington St. to the Navy Yard. Then she took us to the foot of Walnut St. Geo and I ran up to Exchange Square where we dined; hastily started at 2 pm.[600] Jersey is very dusty, country generally level—did not stop at the works. From Amboy came on the John Potter[601] to N.Y. by the outside way, arrived at The Battery, New York! At 5 mins to 7 pm; dashed for *Home* like lightning.

Hurrah!

596. Camden Station was originally built by the Baltimore and Ohio Railroad as its main passenger terminal in Baltimore. Started in 1855 to an Italianate design by Niernsee and Neilson, it was completed by 1857 (Lane, *Architecture of the Old South: Maryland*, 201). It remained in use until the 1980s, thereby becoming one of the longest continuously operated terminals in the United States. See Stover, *The History of the Baltimore and Ohio Railroad*, 76–77ff.

597. Opened on 18 February 1850, the President Street Station was the Baltimore terminus of the Philadelphia, Wilmington and Baltimore Railroad. It was linked to the Baltimore and Ohio Railroad's Camden Station by the track that ran up Pratt Street, on which Reiff traveled, connecting PW&B trains arriving from Philadelphia with B&O trains to Washington. See Fisher, *Philadelphia, Wilmington & Baltimore Railroad Company*.

598. Originally Le Havre-de-Grâce, Havre de Grace, a port town in Harford County, Maryland, incorporated in 1785 and named after the French port of Le Havre, inspired General Lafayette's likening of the town to the original. For an account of the early years, see the introduction to Glatfelter, *Havre de Grace in the War of 1812*.

599. "Later": abbreviated as "L" in Reiff.

600. Reiff and Atherton appear to be traveling by the Camden and South Amboy Railway Company, which ran trains between Philadelphia and New York. The last twenty-seven miles were by the steamboat *John Potter*, built in 1847 in Hoboken, New Jersey, with the average journey being four and a half hours. See Hunt, *Merchants' Magazine and Commercial Review*, 764–65.

601. See note 600.

Selected Bibliography

Ahlquist, Karen. *Democracy at the Opera: Music, Theater, and Culture in New York City, 1815-60.* Urbana: University of Illinois Press, 1997.

Allen, Paula Gunn. *Pocahontas: Medicine Woman, Spy, Entrepreneur, Diplomat.* San Francisco: HarperCollins, 2003.

American Military History. Washington, DC: Office of the Chief of Military History, 1969.

American National Biography. Ed. John A. Garratty and Mark C. Carnes. 22 vols. and 2 supplements. New York: Oxford University Press, 1999.

America's Founding Documents. www.archives.gov/exhibits/charters/treasure/declaration_travels.html (accessed 20 July 2020).

Anderson, Robert. *An Artillery Officer in the Mexican War, 1846-47.* New York: G. P. Putnam's, 1911.

Arndt, Karl J. R. "A Bavarian's Journey to New Orleans and Nacogdoches in 1853–1854." *Louisiana Historical Quarterly,* XXIII, no. 2 (1940).

Barry, Joseph. *The Annals of Harper's Ferry: With Sketches of its Founder, and Many Prominent Characters.* Martinsburg, WV: Berkeley Union, 1872.

Bauer, K. Jack. *Zachary Taylor: Soldier, Planter, Statesman of the Old Southwest.* Baton Rouge: Louisiana State University Press, 1985.

Bean, Annemarie, James V. Hatch, and Brooks McNamara, eds. *Inside the Minstrel Mask: Readings in Nineteenth-century Blackface Minstrelsy.* Hanover, NH: University Press of New England, 1996.

Bednar, Michael J. *L'Enfant's Legacy: Public Open Spaces in Washington.* Baltimore: Johns Hopkins University Press, 2006.

Biographical Directory of the American Congress. Alexandria, VA: CQ Staff Directories, 1997.

Block, Victor. *The Pelican Guide to Maryland.* 2nd ed. Gretna, LA: Pelican Publishing, 1998.

Blumhofer, Edith L. *Her Heart Can See: The Life and Hymns of Fanny J. Crosby.* Grand Rapids, MI: Wm. B. Eerdmans Publishing, 2005.

Bodenhamer, David J., and Robert Graham Barrows. *The Encyclopedia of Indianapolis.* Bloomington: Indiana University Press, 1994.

Bogle, Victor M. "The Eclipse versus the A. L. Shotwell; Memorable Contest Almost Forgotten." *Filson Club History Quarterly* 35 (1961), 125–37.

Bordman, Gerald, and Thomas S. Hischak. *The Oxford Companion to American The-atre*. 5th ed. New York: Oxford University Press, 2004.

Brinkerhoff, J. H. G. *Brinkerhoff's History of Marion County, Illinois*. Indianapolis: B. F. Bowen, 1909.

Brown, John Kennedy. *Limbs on the Levee: Steamboat Explosions and the Origins of Federal Public Welfare Regulation, 1817–1852*. Middlebourne, WV: ISS Press, 1989.

Brown, Thomas Allston. *History of the American Stage: Containing Biographical Sketches of Nearly Every Member of the Profession that has Appeared on the American Stage, from 1733 to 1870*. New York: Dick and Fitzgerald, 1870.

Buckley, S. B. "On the Zeuglodon Remains of Alabama." *Sillim. Amer. Journ.* 2nd ser., vol. 2 (1846), 125–31.

Burrows, Edwin G., and Wallace, Mike. *Gotham: A History of New York City to 1898*. New York: Oxford University Press, 1999.

Cable, Mary. *Lost New Orleans*. New York: American Legacy Press, 1980.

Campanella, Richard. *Time and Place in New Orleans: Past Geographies in the Pres-ent Day*. Gretna, LA: Pelican Publishing, 2002.

———. "The Ursuline Nuns' Lost Landmark on the Mississippi River." *Preservation in Print*, December 2015, 14–15.

"Capitol of Indiana." *Family Magazine: Or Monthly Abstract of General Knowledge*. Cincinnati: Eli Taylor, 1837, 323.

Carrier, Thomas J. *Washington D.C.: A Historical Walking Tour*. Charleston, SC: Ar-cadia Publishing, 1999.

Casto, Marilyn. *Actors, Audiences, and Historic Theaters of Kentucky*. Lexington: Uni-versity Press of Kentucky, 2000.

Chambers, Julius. *The Mississippi River and Its Wonderful Valley*. New York: Put-nam's, 1910.

Cincinnati: A Guide to the Queen City and Its Neighbors. Cincinnati, 1943.

Cist, Charles. *Sketches and Statistics of Cincinnati in 1851*. Cincinnati: W. H. Moore, 1851.

Clark, Clifford E., Jr. *Henry Ward Beecher: Spokesman for a Middle-Class America*. Urbana: University of Illinois Press, 1978.

Clérisseau, Charles-Louis. *Antiquités de la France*. Paris: De l'Imprimerie de Philippe-Denys Pierres, 1778.

Costello, Brian J. *Carnival in Louisiana: Celebrating Mardi Gras from the French Quarter to the Red River*. Baton Rouge: Louisiana State University Press, 2017.

Cothran, James R., and Danylchak, Erica. *Grave Landscapes: The Nineteenth-Century Rural Cemetery Movement*. Columbia: University of South Carolina Press, 2018.

Cowan, Walter G. *New Orleans Yesterday and Today: A Guide to the City*. 5th ed. Baton Rouge: Louisiana State University Press, 1983.

Craig, Berry. *Kentucky Confederates: Secession, Civil War, and the Jackson Purchase.* Lexington: University Press of Kentucky, 2014.

Cranmer, Gibson Lamb. *History of Wheeling City, and Ohio County, West Virginia and Representative Citizens.* Chicago: Biographical Publishing Co., 1902.

Creecy, James R. *Scenes in the South, and Other Miscellaneous Pieces.* Washington, DC: Thomas McGill, 1860.

Crescent City Business Directory. New Orleans, 1859–60.

Cunningham, John F. *Railroading in New Jersey.* New Jersey: Associated Railroads of New Jersey, 1951.

Cunningham, Peter. *A Hand-Book of London: Past and Present.* New ed. London: John Murray, 1850.

Custis, George Washington Parke. *Reminiscences and Private Recollections of Washington.* New York: Derby & Jackson, 1860.

Dabney, Virginius. *Richmond: The Story of a City.* Charlottesville: University Press of Virginia, 1976.

Dakin, James H. Diary. Mss 509. Louisiana and Lower Mississippi Valley Collections, LSU Libraries, Baton Rouge.

Daspit, Fred. *Louisiana Architecture, 1840–1860.* Lafayette: Center for Louisiana Studies, University of Louisiana at Lafayette, 2006.

Daughdrill and Walker's General Directory for the City and County of Mobile, for 1856. Mobile, AL: Farrow, Stores and Dennett, 1856.

Davidge, William. *Footlight Flashes.* New York: American News Co., 1866.

Decatur, Stephen. "Flashback: George Washington's Furniture." *American Collector,* February 1941.

"Descendants of the Philharmonic Founders." *Philharmonic Symphony League Bulletin,* IV (1 October 1941–3 April 1942), 3.

Diamonstein-Spielvogel, Barbaralee. *The Landmarks of New York: An Illustrated Record of the City's Historic Buildings.* 5th ed. Albany: State University of New York Press, 2011.

Dick, Steven J. *Sky and Ocean Joined: The US Naval Observatory, 1830–2000.* Cambridge, UK: Cambridge University Press, 2003.

Dickens, Charles. *American Notes for General Circulation.* London: Chapman and Hall, 1842.

Dictionary of American Naval Fighting Ships. 8 vols. Washington, DC: Navy Department, Office of the Chief of Naval Operations, Naval History Division, 1959–81.

Dimmick, Lauretta. "A Catalogue of the Portrait Busts and Ideal Works of Thomas Crawford (1813?–1857), American Sculptor." PhD diss., University of Pittsburgh, 1986.

Ellyson, M. *The Richmond Directory and Business Advertiser.* Richmond, VA: H. K. Ellyson, 1856.

Emery, Ina Capitola. *The Washington Monument.* Washington, DC: Emery, 1909.

Erskine, John. *The Philharmonic-Symphony Society of New York.* New York: Macmillan, 1943.

Erwin, J. Warner. *The Journal of J. Warner Erwin, 1839–1854.* Ed. S. Hamill Home. www.brynmawr.edu/iconog/jwe/jweint.html.

Etiquette at Washington. Baltimore: Murphy and Co., 1857.

Etiquette for Gentlemen. Philadelphia: George S. Appleton, 1851.

Fawcett, John. *The Barber of Seville.* Boston: Eastburn Press, 1856.

Federal Writers' Project. *Maryland: A Guide to the Old Line State.* Oxford, UK: Oxford University Press, 1940.

Find A Grave. www.findagrave.com/memorial/52649873/henry-mandeville (accessed 9 November 2019).

Fisher, Charles E. *Philadelphia, Wilmington & Baltimore Railroad Company.* Boston: Railway and Locomotive Historical Society, 1930.

Follett, Richard. *The Sugar Masters: Planters and Slaves in Louisiana's Cane World, 1820–1860.* Baton Rouge: Louisiana State University Press, 2005.

Frost, Sarah Annie. *The Book of Tableux and Shadow Pantomimes.* New York: Dick and Fitzgerald, 1869.

Fuld, James D. "Patriotic Music." In H. Wiley Hitchcock and Stanley Sadie, eds., *The New Grove Dictionary of American Music.* 4 vols. London: Macmillan, 1986.

Fulton, John F., and Elizabeth H. Thomson. *Benjamin Silliman, 1779–1864: Pathfinder in American Science.* New York: Henry Schuman, 1947.

Gänzl, Kurt. *Victorian Vocalists.* New York: Routledge, 2017.

Gilleland, J. C. *The Ohio and Mississippi Pilot, Consisting of a Set of Charts of Those Rivers.* Pittsburgh: R. Patterson & Lambdin, 1820.

Glatfelter, Heidi L. *Havre de Grace in the War of 1812: Fire on the Chesapeake.* Charleston: History Press, 2013.

Gleeson, David T. *The Irish in the South, 1815–1877.* Chapel Hill: University of North Carolina Press, 2001.

Gobright, John C. *The Monumental City or Baltimore Guidebook.* Baltimore: Gobright and Torsch, 1858.

Gould, Elizabeth Barrett. *From Fort to Port: An Architectural History of Mobile, Alabama, 1711–1918.* Tuscaloosa: University of Alabama Press, 1988.

Gray, Thomas. *On a distant view of Eton College.* 1742.

Greenberg, Kenneth S. *Honour and Slavery: Lies, Duels, Noses, Masks, Dressing as Women, Gifts Strangers, Death, Humanitarianism, Slave Rebellions, The Proslavery Argument, Baseball, Hunting, and Gambling in the Old South.* Princeton, NJ: Princeton University Press, 1996.

Griggs, Frank. "James River Bridge at Richmond, Virginia." *Structure,* April 2014, 12–14.

Grimmett, Richard F. *St. John's Church, Lafayette Square.* Washington, DC: Mill City Press, 2009.

Grizzard, Frank E. *George Washington: A Biographical Companion.* Santa Barbara, CA: ABC-CLIO, 2002.

The Grove Dictionary of American Music. 2nd ed. Ed. Charles Hiroshi Garrett. 8 vols. Oxford, UK: Oxford University Press, 2013.

Grove Dictionary of Music and Musicians. Ed. J. A. Fuller-Maitland. London: Macmillan, 1904–10.

The Grove Dictionary of Musical Instruments. 2nd ed. Ed. Laurence Libin. 5 vols. London: Macmillan, 2015.

Gudmestad, Robert. *Steamboats and the Rise of the Cotton Kingdom.* Baton Rouge: Louisiana State University Press, 2011.

Gunn Historical Museum. gunnhistoricalmuseum.pastperfectonline.com.

Hall, Edward Hagaman. "A Brief History of City Hall Park, New York." *Fifteenth Annual Report of the American Scenic and Historic Preservation Society.* Albany: J. B. Lyon Co., 1910.

Hamlin, Talbot. *Benjamin Henry Latrobe.* New York: Oxford University Press, 1955.

Hancock, James E. *Fort McHenry.* Baltimore: Maryland Trust Co., 1928.

Harrison, Lowell Hayes, and James C. Klotter. *A New History of Kentucky.* Lexington: University Press of Kentucky, 1997.

Hawes, George W. *Commercial Gazetteer and Business Directory of the Ohio River.* Indianapolis: G. W. Hawes, 1861.

Hayden, Ralston. *The Senate and Treaties, 1789–1817: The Development of the Treaty-making Functions of the United States Senate During Their Formative Period.* New York: Macmillan, 1920.

Hellmann, Paul T. *Historical Gazetteer of the United States.* New York: Routledge, 2005.

Hench, Vivian. *History of St. Paul's Methodist Church.* State College, PA, 1962.

Hereford, Robert A. *Old Man River: The Memories of Captain Louis Rosché, Pioneer Steamboatman.* Caldwell, ID: Caxton, 1942.

Hesse-Wartegg, Ernst von. *Travels on the Lower Mississippi, 1879–1880: A Memoir.* Ed and trans. Frederic Trautmann. Columbia: University of Missouri Press, 1990.

Hetherington, James. *Indianapolis Union Station: Trains, Travelers, and Changing Times.* Carmel: Guild Press of Indiana, 2000.

History and Families, McCracken County, Kentucky, 1824–1989. Paducah, KY: Turner Publishing Co., 1989.

"A History of John Hopkinson, Piano Manufacturer." www.piano-tuners.org/history/hopkinson/ (accessed 30 August 2016).

Hopkins, Charles H. *History of the Y.M.C.A. in North America.* New York: Association Press, 1951.

Howard, A. C. *A. C. Howard's Directory for the City of Indianapolis: Containing a Correct List of Citizens' Names, their Residence and Place Of Business, With a*

Historical Sketch of Indianapolis from its Earliest History to the Present Day. Indianapolis: A. C. Howard, 1857.

Huber, Leonard V. *The Battle for New Orleans and Its Monument.* New Orleans: Louisiana Landmarks Society, ca. 1983.

———. *New Orleans: A Pictorial History.* Gretna, LA: Pelican Publishing, 1971.

———. *New Orleans Architecture.* Vol. III: *The Cemeteries.* Gretna, LA: Pelican Publication Co., 1974.

Huneker, James G. *The Philharmonic Society of New York, and Its Seventy-fifth Anniversary.* New York, [1917].

Hunt, Freeman. *Merchants' Magazine and Commercial Review,* 24 (January–June 1851), 764–65.

Hunter, Louis C. *Steamboats on the Western Rivers: An Economic and Technological History.* Cambridge, MA: Harvard University Press, 1948.

Inflation Calculator. www.westegg.com/inflation (accessed 20 July 2020).

Isles, George. *Leading American Inventors.* New York: H. Holt and Co, 1928.

"Jackson's Monument at Memphis: And, Hoisting the National Flag Over the Post-Office at Memphis." *Harper's Weekly,* 5 July 1862.

Johnson, Abby A., and Ronald M. Johnson. *In the Shadow of the United States Capitol: Congressional Cemetery and the Memory of the Nation.* Washington, DC: New Academia Publishing, 2012.

Johnson, Walter. *Soul by Soul: Life inside the Antebellum Slave Market.* Cambridge, MA: Harvard University Press, 2001.

Johnston, Josiah Stoddard. *Memorial History of Louisville from Its First Settlement to the Year 1896.* 2 vols. Louisville, KY: American Biographical Publishing Co., 1896.

Journal of the Common Council, of the City of Philadelphia. Philadelphia: J. Van Court, 1856.

Kapsch, Robert J. *Canals.* New York: Norton and Co., 2004.

Kennedy, Roger G. *Architecture, Men, Women and Money in America, 1600–1860.* New York: Random House, 1985.

Kenny, Daniel J. *Illustrated Cincinnati: A Pictorial Hand-book of the Queen City.* Cincinnati: Robert Clark and Co., 1875.

Kimball, Fiske. *The Capitol of Virginia: A Landmark of American Architecture.* Richmond: Virginia State Library and Archives, 1989.

Kimball, Greg D. *American City, Southern Place: A Cultural History of Antebellum Richmond.* Athens: University of Georgia Press, 2000.

Kleber, John E. ed., *The Encyclopedia of Louisville.* Lexington: University Press of Kentucky, 2001.

———. *The Kentucky Encyclopedia.* Lexington: University Press of Kentucky, 1992.

Klunder, Willard Carl. *Lewis Cass and the Politics of Moderation.* Kent, OH: Kent State University Press, 1996.

Koon, Thomas J., and Oce Smith. *Marion County, West Virginia: A Pictorial History.* Virginia Beach, VA: Donning Co., 1995.

Kotar, S. L., and J. E. Gessler. *The Steamboat Era: A History of Fulton's Folly on American Rivers, 1807–1860.* Jefferson, NC: MacFarlane and Co., 2009.

Krohn, Ernst. *Music Publishing in St. Louis: Bibliographies in American Music XI.* Completed by J. Bunker Clark. Warren, MI: Harmonie Park Press, 1988.

Lacy, M. Rophino, adapter. *Cinderella; or, The Fairy and Little Glass Slipper, an Opera, as Performed by the Pyne & Harrison Opera Troupe.* New York: S. French, 1855.

Lakwete, Angela. *Inventing the Cotton Gin: Machine and Myth in Antebellum America.* Baltimore: Johns Hopkins University Press, 2003.

Lane, Mills. *Architecture of the Old South: Louisiana.* New York: Abbeville Press, 1990.

———. *Architecture of the Old South: Maryland.* New York: Abbeville Press, 1991.

Lawrence, Vera Brodsky. *Strong on Music II: Reverberations, 1850–1856.* Chicago: University of Chicago Press, 1995.

Lee, Dan. *Kentuckian in Blue: A Biography of Major General Lovell Harrison Rousseau.* Jefferson, NC: McFarland, 2010.

Leffel, John C. *History of Posey County, Indiana.* Chicago: Standard Publishing Co., 1913.

Lewis, Gene D. *Charles Ellet, Jr.: The Engineer as Individualist, 1810–1862.* Urbana: University of Illinois Press, 1968.

Lewis, Henry. *The Valley of the Mississippi Illustrated.* Trans. A. Hermina Poatgieter. St. Paul: Minnesota Historical Society, 1967.

Libin, Laurence. "Nuns & Clark." In H. Wiley Hitchcock and Stanley Sadie, eds., *The New Grove Dictionary of American Music.* 4 vols. London: Macmillan, 1986.

Lindow, Blanche, and Zane L. Miller. "Queen City History: The Burnet House Hotel and Central Business District." *Cincinnati Magazine,* May 1976, 16–17.

Lloyd, James T. *Lloyd's Steamboat Directory and Disasters on the Western Waters.* Cincinnati: James T. Lloyd and Co., 1856.

Logan, Olive. *Before the Footlights and Behind the Scenes: A Book about "the Show Business."* Philadelphia: Parmelee, 1870.

Love, Harold. *The Australian Stage: A Documentary History.* Kensington: University of New South Wales, 1984.

———. *The Golden Age of Australian Opera: W. S. Lyster and His Companies, 1861–1880.* Sydney: Currency Press, 1981.

Lyell, Charles. *A Second Visit to the United States of North America.* 2 vols. London: John Murray, 1849.

Lynott, Mark. *Hopewell Ceremonial Landscapes of Ohio: More Than Mounds and Geometric Earthworks.* Oxford, UK: Oxbow Books, 2016.

Lytle, William M., and Forrest R. Holdcamper. *Merchant Steam Vessels of the United*

States, 1790–1868. Rev. and ed. C. Bradford Mitchell. Staten Island, NY: Steamship Historical Society of America, 1975.

Mackintosh, Will B. *Selling the Sights: The Invention of the Tourist in American Culture*. New York: New York University Press, 2019.

Magill, John. "French Market Celebrates 200th Anniversary." *Preservation in Print*, vol. 18, no. 4 (1999), 7–10.

Manca, Joseph. *George Washington's Eye: Landscape, Architecture, and Design at Mount Vernon*. Baltimore: Johns Hopkins University Press, 2012.

Marshall, James W. *The Presbyterian Church in Alabama*. Montgomery, AL: Presbyterian Historical Society of Alabama, 1977.

Mason, Randall F. *Building Memory in New York*. Minneapolis: University of Minnesota Press, 2016.

Maxwell, Hu. *The History of Barbour County, From Its Earliest Exploration and Settlement to the Present Time*. Morgantown, WV: Acme Publishing Co., 1899.

McClure, Daniel E., Jr. *Two Centuries in Elizabethtown & Hardin County Kentucky*. Elizabethtown: Hardin County Historical Society, 1979.

McCormick, Mike. *Terre Haute: Queen City of the Wabash*. Charleston, SC: Arcadia Publishing, 2005.

McCracken County Genealogical-Historical Society. *History and Families, McCracken County, Kentucky, 1824–1989*. Paducah, KY: Turner Publishing Co., 1989.

McCullough, Jack W. *Living Pictures on the New York Stage*. Ann Arbor, MI: UMI Research Press, 1983.

McDermott, John Francis. *The Lost Panoramas of the Mississippi*. Chicago: University of Chicago Press, 1958.

Measuring Worth. www.measuringworth.com.

Mehrländer, Andrea. *The Germans of Charleston, Richmond and New Orleans during the Civil War Period, 1850–1870: A Study and Research Compendium*. Berlin: Walter de Gruyter, 2011.

Melebeck, Claude Bernard, Jr. "A History of the First and Second Varieties Theatres of New Orleans, Louisiana, 1849 to 1870." 2 vols. PhD diss., Louisiana State University, 1973.

Merrick, George Byron. *Old Times on the Upper Mississippi: The Recollections of a Steamboat Pilot from 1854 to 1864*. Cleveland: Arthur H. Clark, 1909.

Miller, Thomas Condit, and Hu Maxwell. *West Virginia and Its People*. 3 vols. New York: Lewis Historical Publishing Co., 1913.

Milward, Burton. *A History of the Lexington Cemetery*. Lexington, KY: Lexington Cemetery Association, 1989.

Mitchell, C. Bradford. *Supplement* to Lytle and Holdcamper, *Merchant Steam Vessels of the United States, 1790–1868*. Staten Island, NY: Steamship Historical Society of America, Inc., 1978.

Mitchell, Reid. *All on a Mardi Gras Day: Episodes in the History of the New Orleans Carnival.* Cambridge, MA: Harvard University Press, 1995.

Moscow, Henry. *The Street Book: An Encyclopedia of Manhattan's Street Names and Their Origins.* New York: Hagstrom, 1978.

Munro, John. *The New York Tombs: Inside and Out.* New York: Big Byte Books, 2016.

National Register of Historic Places. https://www.nps.gov/subjects/nationalregister/index.htm (accessed 20 July 2020).

The Navigator, Containing Directions for Navigating the Ohio and Mississippi Rivers. Pittsburgh, 1824.

Nelligan, Murray H. *Custis-Lee Mansion: The Robert E. Lee Memorial, Virginia.* Washington, DC: National Park Service, 1962.

Nelson, Colonel Soren, and Mrs. Soren Nelson. *A History of Church Street Graveyard, Mobile, Alabama.* Mobile: Historic Mobile Preservation Society, 1963.

The New Grove Dictionary of Music and Musicians. 2nd ed. Ed. Stanley Sadie. 29 vols. London: MacMillan, 2001.

The New Grove Dictionary of Opera. Ed. Stanley Sadie. 4 vols. London: Macmillan, 1992.

Nichols, Thomas L. *Forty Years of American Life.* London: John Maxwell and Co., 1844.

Norman, B. M. *Norman's New Orleans and Environs.* New Orleans: B. M. Norman, 1845.

Olitzky, Kerry M., and Marc Lee Raphael. *The American Synagogue: A Historical Dictionary and Sourcebook.* Westport, CT: Greenwood Publishing Group, 1996.

Olmsted, Frederick Law. *A Journey in the Seaboard Slave States.* New York: Dix and Edwards, 1856.

Oxford Dictionary of National Biography. Ed. H. C. G. Matthew, Brian Harrison, and Lawrence Goldman. 60 vols. Oxford, UK: Oxford University Press, 2004.

Oxford English Dictionary. 2nd ed. Prepared by J. A. Simpson and E. S. C. Weiner. 20 vols. Oxford, UK: Clarendon Press, 1989.

Palmer, Beverley Wilson. *The Selected Letters of Charles Sumner.* 2 vols. Boston: Northeastern University Press, 1990.

Palmquist, Peter E., and Thomas R. Kailbourn. *Pioneer Photographers from the Mississippi to the Continental Divide: A Biographical Dictionary, 1839–1865.* Stanford, CA: Stanford University Press, 2005.

Paskoff, Paul F. *Troubled Waters: Steamboat Disasters, River Improvements, and American Public Policy, 1821–1860.* Baton Rouge: Louisiana State University Press, 2007.

Petersen, William J. *Steamboating on the Upper Mississippi.* Des Moines: State Historical Society of Iowa, 1968.

Pierce, Edward L. *Memoirs and Letters of Charles Sumner.* 4 vols. Boston: Roberts Brothers, 1898.

Pillar, James J. *The Catholic Church in Mississippi, 1837–65.* New Orleans: Hauser Press, 1964.

Poesch, Jessie, and Barbara SoRelle Bacot, eds. *Louisiana Buildings, 1720–1940: The Historic American Buildings Survey.* Baton Rouge: Louisiana State University Press, 1997.

Poor, H. V., and H. W. Poor. *Poor's Manual of Railroads.* New York: H. V. and H. W. Poor, 1885.

Poulet, Anne L. *Jean-Antoine Houdon, Sculptor of the Enlightenment.* Washington, DC: National Gallery of Art, 2003.

Preston, Kathryn K. "Between the Cracks: The Performance of English-Language Opera in Late Nineteenth-Century America," *American Music,* vol. 21, no. 3 (Autumn 2003), 349–74.

———. "Notes from (the Road to) the Stage." *Opera Quarterly,* vol. 23, no. 1 (2007), 103–19.

———. *Opera for the People: English-Language Opera and Women Managers in Late 19th-Century America.* New York: Oxford University Press, 2017.

———. *Opera on the Road: Traveling Opera Troupes in the United States, 1825–1860.* Urbana: University of Illinois Press, 2001.

Pulszky, Francis, and Theresa Pulszky. *White, Red, Black: Sketches of American Society in the United States.* New York: Redfield, 1853.

Rabb, James W. *Confederate General Lloyd Tilghman: A Biography.* Jefferson, NC: McFarland, 2006.

Redway, Virginia Larkin. *Music Directory of Early New York City.* New York: New York Public Library, 2017.

Reed, Merl E. *New Orleans and the Railroads: The Struggle for Commercial Empire, 1830–1860.* Baton Rouge: Louisiana State University Press, 1966.

Reiff, Daniel D. *Washington Architecture, 1791–1861.* Washington, DC: US Commission of Fine Arts, 1971.

Reinders, Robert C. *End of an Era: New Orleans, 1850–1860.* Gretna, LA: Pelican Publishing, 1989.

———. "Militia in New Orleans, 1853–1861." *Louisiana History,* vol. 3, no. 1 (1962).

Remini, Robert V. *The Battle of New Orleans.* New York: Penguin Books, 1999.

Rennick, Robert. *Kentucky Place Names.* Lexington: University Press of Kentucky, 1984.

Report of the Committee on the James River Improvements. Richmond, VA: H. K. Ellyson, 1855.

Robertson, John E. L. *Paducah, Kentucky: A History.* Paducah, KY: History Press, 2014.

Robinson, Joseph W. *Railroad and Steamboat Sketches between New York and Kansas.* Philadelphia, 1858(?).

Roud Folk Song Index. Vaughan Williams Memorial Library. www.vwml.org.

Ryan, Paul E. *History of the Diocese of Covington, Kentucky, on the Occasion of the Centenary of the Diocese, 1853–1953*. Covington: The Diocese, 1954.

Sala, George Augustus. *America Revisited: From the Bay of New York to the Gulf of Mexico, and from Lake Michigan to the Pacific*. London: Vitelly & Co., 1883.

Salmon, John S. *The Official Virginia Civil War Battlefield Guide*. Mechanicsburg, PA: Stackpole Books, 2001.

Scharf, John Thomas. *History of Saint Louis City and County: From the Earliest Periods to the Present Day*. 2 vols. Philadelphia: Louis H. Everts, 1883.

Scharf, John Thomas, and Thompson Westcott. *The History of Philadelphia, 1609–1884*. 3 vols. Philadelphia: L. H. Everts, 1884.

Scherrer, Anton. "Francis Costigan, Architect, 1810–1865." *Journal of the Society of Architectural Historians*, vol. 17, no. 1 (1958), 30–33.

Scott, Walter. *Guy Mannering; or, The Astrologer*. Edinburgh: Constable, 1815.

Scott, Winfield. *Memoirs of Lieut.-General Scott, LL.D.* New York: Sheldon & Co., 1864.

Seymour, William H. *The Story of Algiers, 1718–1896*. Gretna, LA: Pelican Publishing, 1971.

Shockley, Martin Staples. *The Richmond Stage, 1784–1812*. Charlottesville: University Press of Virginia, 1977.

Sledge, John Sturdivant. *Cities of Silence: A Guide to Mobile's Historic Cemeteries*. Tuscaloosa: University of Alabama Press, 2002.

———. *The Pillared City; Greek Revival Mobile*. Athens: University of Georgia Press, 2009.

Slout, William L., ed. *Burnt Cork and Tambourines: A Source Book of Negro Minstrelsy*. San Bernardino, CA: Borgo Press, 2007.

Smith, Donald L. *Lefevre James Cranstone: His Life and Art*. Richmond, VA: Brandylane, 2004.

Smith, Samuel S. *The Battle of Trenton/The Battle of Princeton: Two Studies*. Yardly, PA: Westholme, 2009.

Smith, Thomas Ruys. *River of Dreams: Imagining the Mississippi before Mark Twain*. Baton Rouge: Louisiana State University Press, 2007.

Smith, William Prescott. *The Book of the Great Railway Celebrations*. New York: D. Appleton & Co., 1858.

Spence, W. Jerome D., and David L. Spence. *A History of Hickman County, Tennessee*. Nashville: Gospel Advocate Publishing Co., 1900.

Stanton, Phoebe B. *The Gothic Revival and American Church Architecture: An Episode in Taste, 1840–1856*. Baltimore: Johns Hopkins University Press, 1968.

Starling, Edmund Lyne. *History of Henderson County, Kentucky*. Henderson, KY, 1887.

Stimson, Alexander L. *History of the Express Companies: And the Origin of American Railroads*. New York: Baker and Godwin, 1881.

Stockett, Letitia. *Baltimore: A Not Too Serious History.* Baltimore: Norman, Remington Co., 1928.

Stoddard, Christine, and Misty Thomas. *Richmond Cemeteries.* Charleston, SC: Arcadia Publishing, 2014.

Stover, John F. *The History of the Baltimore and Ohio Railroad.* West Lafayette, IN: Purdue University Press, 1987.

————. *The History of the Illinois Central Railroad.* New York: Macmillan, 1975.

Stowe, Harriet Beecher. *Uncle Tom's Cabin.* London, J. Cassell, 1852.

Sulzer, Elmer G. *Ghost Railroads of Indiana.* Indianapolis: Vane A. Jones, 1970.

Summers, Thomas J. *History of Marietta.* Marietta, OH: Leader Publishing Co, 1903.

Sutton, Charles. *The New York Tombs: Its Secrets and Its Mysteries.* San Francisco: A. Roman & Co., 1874.

Terry, Daniel. *Guy Mannering; or the Gipsy's prophecy, a musical play.* London: John Miller, 1816.

Thorpe, Thomas B. "General Taylor's Residence in Baton Rouge." *Harper's New Monthly Magazine,* vol. 9 (1854), 765.

————. "Remembrances of the Mississippi." *Harper's New Monthly Magazine,* vol. 12 (December 1855–May 1856), 27.

Todd, Nancy L. *New York's Historic Armories: An Illustrated History.* New York: State University of New York Press, 2006.

Treese, Lorett. *Railroads of New Jersey: Fragments of the Past in the Garden State Landscape.* Mechanicsburg, PA: Stackpole Books, 2006.

Trowbridge, John T. *The Desolate South, 1865–1866.* Ed. Gordon Carroll. New York, 1956.

Twain, Mark. *Life on the Mississippi.* London: Chatto & Windus, 1883.

Tyler-McGraw, Marie. *At the Falls: Richmond, Virginia and Its People.* Chapel Hill: University of North Carolina Press, 1994.

Van Cott, Margaret. "Thomas Burling of New York City, Exponent of the New Republic Style." *Furniture History,* vol. 37 (2001), 32–50.

Van Horne, John C., ed. *The Correspondence and Miscellaneous Papers of Benjamin Henry Latrobe.* 3 vols. New Haven, CT: Yale University Press, 1988.

Vessey, John Henry. *Mr. Vessey of England, Being the Incidents and Reminiscences of Travel in a Twelve Weeks' Tour Through the United States and Canada in the Year 1859.* Ed. Brian Waters. New York: G. P. Putnam's Sons, 1956.

Wallace, Edward S. *General William Jenkins Worth: Monterey's Forgotten Hero.* Dallas: Southern Methodist University Press, 1953.

Ward, George Washington. *The Early Development of the Chesapeake and Ohio Canal Project.* Baltimore: Johns Hopkins University Press, 1899.

Weber, Gustavus A. *The Naval Observatory: Its History, Activities and Organization.* Baltimore: Johns Hopkins Press, 1926.

Weddell, Alexander Wilbourne, and John Lee McElroy. *Richmond, Virginia, in Old Prints, 1737–1887.* Atlanta: Johnson Publishing Co., 1932.

Weisert, John, Jacob, *Mozart Hall, 1851 to 1866: A Checklist of Attractions at a Minor Theatre of Louisville, Kentucky, Known Variously as Mozart Hall, Wood's Theatre, The Academy of Music.* Louisville, KY, 1962.

Weisiger, Benjamin B. *Old Manchester & Its Environs, 1769–1910.* Richmond, VA: B. B. Weisiger, 1993.

Wharton, Thomas K. *Queen of the South: New Orleans, 1853–1862. The Journal of Thomas K. Wharton.* Ed. Samuel Wilson, Patricia Brady, and Lynn D. Adams. New Orleans: Historic New Orleans Collection, 1999.

Whitcomb, Royden Page. *First History of Bayonne, New Jersey.* Bayonne: R. P. Whitcombe, 1904.

White, Charles. "Negro Minstrelsy: Its starting place traced back over sixty years arranged and compiled from the best authorities." *New York Clipper,* 28 April 1860.

Williams, Paul K. *Southwest Washington.* Charleston, SC: Arcadia Publishing, 2005.

Williams, Peter. "Longman." In Stanley Sadie, ed., *Grove Dictionary of Musical Instruments.* 3 vols. London: Macmillan, 1984.

Williams' Paducah City Directory. Paducah, 1859.

Wilmeth, Don B., and Christopher Bigsby, eds. *The Cambridge History of American Theatre.* 3 vols. Cambridge, UK: Cambridge University Press, 1998.

Wilson, H., comp. *Trow's New York City Directory for the Year Ending May 1, 1856.* New York: J. Trow, 1855.

Wilson, John Lyde. *The Code of Honour.* Charleston, SC: Thomas J. Eccles, 1838.

Wilson, Samuel. *Plantation Houses on the Battlefield of New Orleans.* New Orleans: Battle of New Orleans, 150th Anniversary Committee of Louisiana, 1965.

Winders, Richard Bruce. *Mr. Polk's Army: The American Military Experience in the Mexican War.* College Station: Texas A&M University Press, 1997.

Wolfford, George. *A History of Ashland, Kentucky, 1854–2004.* Ashland: Sesquicentennial Committee. 2004.

Woods, John W. *Woods' Baltimore Directory for 1856–57.* Baltimore: John W. Woods, [1857?].

Woods, Terry K. *The Ohio & Erie Canal: A Glossary of Terms.* Kent, OH: Kent State University Press, 1995.

Worrall, David. *Celebrity, Performance, Reception: British Georgian Theatre as Social Assemblage.* Cambridge, UK: Cambridge University Press, 2013.

Wright, Nathalia. *Horatio Greenough, the First American Sculptor.* Philadelphia: University of Pennsylvania Press, 1963.

———, ed. *Letters of Horatio Greenough, American Sculptor.* Madison: University of Wisconsin Press, 1972.

Newspapers and Journals

Daily Missouri Democrat (St. Louis).
Daily Orleanian (New Orleans).
Daily Pilot (St. Louis).
Dwight's Journal of Music (Boston).
Harper's New Monthly Magazine (New York).
Harper's Weekly A Journal of Civilization (New York).
Illustrated London News.
Liberator (Boston).
Louisville Journal.
Louisville Morning Courier.
Mobile Daily Advertiser.
Mobile Register.
Morning Herald (St. Louis).
New York Clipper.
New York Herald.
New York Herald Tribune.
New York Times.
L'Orléanais (New Orleans).
L'Orleanian (New Orleans).
Paducah American.
Paducah Herald.
Paducah Journal.
Picayune (New Orleans).
Richmond Times-Dispatch (VA).
St. Louis Leader.
Wheeling News Register (WV).

Index

www.ingramcontent.com/pod-product-compliance
Lightning Source LLC
Chambersburg PA
CBHW030305100426
42812CB00002B/578